PERSONS ENTITLED TO VOTE AT MUNICIPAL ELECTIONS.

No.	No on Roll	NAME.	OCCUPATION.	LOT			RES. OR N R
46	91	Edgar, W. C.	Tailor	Lot			R
47	12	Farrer, George	Merchant	Lot			R
48	108	Finkleston, T.	Merchant	Lot			N R
49	110	Fathergill, John	Carpenter	Lot 15 Block			R
50	111	Falconer, E. A.	Lady	Lot 15 Block 6	T		R
		Fortune, Jos.		19 " 9			
51	122	Galt, G. F.	Merchant	Lot 1 Block 21	O	Winnipeg	N R
52	122	Galt, I.	Merchant	Lot 1 Block 21	O		N R
53	74	Gable, Sam	Miller	Lots 13, 14, 15, Blk 1	O	Dauphin	R
54	125	Graham, M	V. S.	Lot 4 Block 23	O		R
55	126	Gibson, R. D.	Farmer	Lot 11 Block 23	O		N R
56	221	Gill, Thomas	Grain buyer	Lot 2 Block	T		
57	128	Griffin, A. J	Mason	Lot 6 Block	O		R
58	123	Gale, Alexander	Laborer	Lot 20 Block 24	T		R
59		Gunne, J. R	Druggist	Lot 12 Block 10	O		R
60	118	Griffin, Nelson	Blacksmith	Lot 3 Block 21	T		
		Green, Robt		2 " 11			
61	110	Hall, William	Carpenter	Lot 10 Block A	O	Dauphin	R
62	141	Halstead, Rev. W	Clergyman	Lt 18, 19, 20, Block 21	O	Portage la Pre	N R
63	144	Harvey, Jos. G.	Solicitor	Lot 4 Block 9	O	Dauphin	
64	146	Hedderly, J. E	Agent	Lot 5, 6, Block F	O		R
65	147	Hearty, Benjamin	Carpenter	Lot 18 Block 23	O		R
66	158	Hearty, Caroline	Lady	Lot 7 Block 9	O		R
67	148	Hoy, Charles	Baker	Lot 18 Block 22	O		R
68	152	Herchmer, F. K	Land agent	Lot 8 Block 10	T		R
69	149	Hogarth, George	Clerk	Lot 14 Block A	O		R
70	151	Hunt, Robert	Agent	Lot 9, 10, Block 8	O		R
71	119	Hart, ———	Foreman	Lot 20 Block 21	T		R
72	178	Iredale, Thos. sr	Postmaster	Lot 16 Block 9	O	Dauphin	R
73	174	Irwin, Fred	Laborer	Lot 13 Block 6	O		R
74	165	Jackson, M. G.	Conveyancer	Lot 6 Block 10	O	Dauphin	R
75	163	Johnstone, J. E	Drayman	Lots 12, 13, Block C	O		
76	122	Johnstone, J. W	Grain buyer	Lot 20 Block 24	T		R
77	178	Johnstone, Robert		7 " 16			
		Kennee, John S.	Carpenter	Lot 6 Block 13	O	Dauphin	R
78	188	Lee, Wing		11 " 6			
		King, George					
79	189	Lilly, William	Laundry mn	Lot N½, 13, Block 10	O	Dauphin	R
80	56	Law, Joshua	Merchant	Lot 13 Block 8	O		R
		Malcolm, B. S.	Painter	Lot 14 Block A	T		
				12 " 10			
82	200	Manly, Chas.	Farmer	Lot 5 Block 27	O	Dauphin	R
83	201	Manly, Levy	H. maker	Lot 44 Block 22	O		R
		Manly, J. J	Merchant	Lot S½ 13 Block 10	O		R
84	202	Maughan, Joseph A	Solicitor	Lot 2 Block 11	O		R
85	204	Moore, A. A	Lady	Lot W½ 17, 1, 2, bl 9	O		R
86	205	Moore, David	Agent	Lot W½ 17, 1, 2, bl. 9	Oc		R
87	206	Murray, William	Clerk	Lot 20 Block 5	O		R
88	258	Mann, D	Contractor	Lots 9, 11, 12, blk. E	O	Toronto	N R
89	207	Murray, E. J	Lady	Lot 19 Block 5	O	Dauphin	R
90	130	Malcolm, Thos	Druggist	Lot 12 Block 10	O		R
91	28	Morton, T L	Grain buyer	Right of way	O	Gladstone	N R
92	220	Mouat, J. N	Im. agent	Lot 20 Block 24	T	Dauphin	R
93	225	McDonald, Wm	Carpenter	Lot 17 Block 23			R
94	24	McGregor, Joseph	Barber	Lot	T		R
95	228	McDonald, John	Sawyer	Lot 17 Block 5	O		R
96	79	McKinnon, Jean	Merchant	Lot 8 block 8	T		O
97	227	McIntosh, H. G. R	Lady	Lot 20 Block 9	O		R
98	228	McIntosh, David	Agent	Lot 11 Block 11	O		R
99		McIntosh, W. T. S	Merchant	Lot 19 Block 9	O		R
100	230	McNeill, Henry	Farmer	Lot 5 Block 21	O	Swan River	N R
101	237	McKenzie Duncan	Merchant	Lot 19 Block 22	O		N R
102	287	McKenzie, Alex	Merchant	Lot 19 Block 22	O	Dauphin	

DOGTOWN TO DAUPHIN

ADAM S. LITTLE

*This Copy Was Graciously Donated
By Marilyn Gray, The Book Nook
Dauphin, Manitoba – May, 1996*

© 1988 Dr. ADAM S. LITTLE

All rights reserved

No part of this book may be reproduced
in any form without permission from the
Publishers, except for a reviewer who
may quote brief passages.

Canadian Cataloguing in Publication Data

Little, Adam S.

   Dogtown to Dauphin

   Bibliography: p
   Includes index.
   ISBN 0-920486-28-2

1. Dauphin (Man.) — History. 2. Dauphin (Man.) —
Biography   I. Title.

FC3399.D38L5   1988   971.27'2   C88-098113-X
F1064.5D38L5   1988.

Watson & Dwyer Publishing
232 Academy Road
Winnipeg, Manitoba R3M 0E7

CONTENTS

Preface 1
Beginnings 5
Early Settlers 23
Search for Liberty 51
From Village To Town 63
The Foundation 87
The Great War 121
The Sporting Twenties 145
Depression Years 185
Second World War 209
The Reconstruction 225
Postscript 240

Dr. Adam S. Little

Dr. Adam Little was born in 1919 in Dauphin, where he grew up in a family of ten, attending Dauphin's public schools and Collegiate Institute.

His father, Thomas Little (1885-1959) emigrated from Scotland in 1906. He came to Dauphin when the Northern Judicial District was opened in 1917. He studied law at home, was admitted to the Manitoba Bar and appointed Police Magistrate in 1934. In 1927 he founded Little's Business College.

His mother, Eliza Little, emigrated from Belfast in 1905. She raised her family in Dauphin and developed her ulcer after her children left home.

Adam Little graduated in medicine from the University of Manitoba in 1942 and returned to Dauphin to establish a family practice in 1951. In 1953 he took post graduate studies at the New York-Bellevue Medical Centre. On his return he had a consulting practice, internal medicine, in Alberta until his retirement in 1974.

He is a Fellow of the Royal College of Physicians of Canada, and a Fellow of the American College of Physicians. He is a past president of the American Academy of Medicine and was Osler Orator, Vancouver Medical Society, 1982.

To Helen,

who came to Dauphin with me,

and to

Cameron, Jeanne and Charlotte,

who were born to us there,

and to the memory of their grandparents,

Eliza and Thomas Little,

who came to Dauphin in 1917.

PREFACE

In writing a history one encounters many unforeseen and unexpected situations. It seems that one should be able to give lucid expression to the facts and occurrences of the past. One should, if you like, be able to recount what has happened. That, after all, is what constitutes history.

Since one cannot have lived through or experienced all of the events which make up a particular history, there develops a dependence on recorded material or on the memory of those who did experience the event or, more commonly, who have been told a story about the event by someone who experienced it. Often the event is several generations removed from the telling of it and in that period the details of time, place and characters may have dimmed or have been altered to such a degree as to be barely recognizable. The pleasure of the events is often magnified, the distastefulness is frequently forgotten or minimized while the roles and the personalities of the characters are frequently distorted. Also, those who experienced the event often have different interpretations of what occurred.

Politicians and newspaper editors may present a view of events to fit their own particular need and political outlook. Historians may disagree about the relative importance of the events, depending on their own knowledge, experience and biases. Their recording of the events will certainly be influenced by the depth of their research and their ability to sift the true facts from the tales that grow up around those facts. All of these influences acted to colour the history of the Dauphin country and had to be checked and cross-checked constantly. The more remote the event, the more difficulty there was in arriving at an entirely accurate portrayal of the early life of the community. Perhaps this is why Henry Ford once stated, during a libel trial, that "history is bunk". An eminent British statesman referred to "the dust heap called history".

Carlyle and Emerson both suggested that the essence of history is in the biography of its great men. Carlyle expressed it best, in our opinion, when he said, "History is the essence of innumerable biographies". We have the feeling that both Carlyle and Emerson had in mind world or national history and were referring to such as the statesmen, scientists, artists, clerics and philosophers whose works or thoughts influenced the direction of history.

There is, however, a history of smaller and humbler events which affects the personal, daily lives of all of us, perhaps to a greater extent than the less frequent, although more momentous, events acting over a prolonged time period. This humbler history is, in our opinion, the mortar which cements and holds together the fibres of the larger history. It more nearly reflects the type of people we are.

The history of Dauphin falls into the category of the latter type of history. It is certainly a distillation of the lives of the men and women, all of them, who came and went, who stayed and toiled, and who, in various and distinctive ways, left their stamp on the town and its surrounding valley. It is a story about common people who came to an isolated area and founded a community in what, until 1883, had been a relative wilderness. In the course of their efforts they discovered courage, a willingness to labour diligently, a generosity towards their neighbors and a desire to cultivate, within their community, the institutions which are the heart of a civilized society. That they succeeded, to a large extent, in their ambitions, is to be seen not solely in the growth and commerce of the community but in the exploits of their children and grandchildren who, armed with the principles and education of the community, have excelled in many fields, have proven to be heroic in the defense of their country and have, in the main, looked back with love to their days in Dauphin or on the farms surrounding Dauphin.

Since history has such a personal aspect to it, one must acknowledge that the picture of Dauphin presented here is one person's notions about what happened. Others may remember it differently. Some may find errors in the dates and personages. We were often confronted by different dates for an event, even in the same publication. We have seen official photographs bearing the same titles but showing different persons. We have tried to apply our own knowledge, sometimes with the help of others, to present an accurate account. The author takes full responsibility for the outcome.

We have been helped in our endeavours by many who contributed photographs or accounts of early Dauphin. We acknowledge the great assistance of the Legislative Library of Manitoba, the Public Archives of Manitoba, Natural Resources Manitoba, Public Archives of Canada, the library of the University of Saskatchewan, the Hudson's Bay Company Archives, the library of the University of Victoria and the Greater Victoria Public Library. They have all been considerate and unsparing in their efforts to assist in supplying information, manuscripts and photographs. We would also like to acknowledge those who put together the volume, *Dauphin Valley Spans The Years,* a volume which supplied a great deal of information about Dauphin.

Among the individuals to whom we owe thanks are Marion Campell, Bob Gardner, Sr., Ron Mulligan, Alf Buchwold, Rex and Irene Boughen, Nina Kindyfore, Mrs. Gar Leech, Ruth Judson, Bernice Reid, Ruth Brekke, Helen Waters, Harry Poole, Vina Porterfield, Jean Nicholson, Elgin Kells, the late Gerald Harrington, Jean Tucker and Ernie Bennett. A special word of thanks should go to Jordan Zinovich of New York who led me into a more accurate account of the Nagle brothers and their life on the shores of Lake Dauphin. His book, *The Fur Trader — Edmund Barry Nagle*, which is now in progress, deals in much greater detail with the life of Edmund Nagle. We would also acknowledge the very great co-operation of Frances Kimpton, Edmund Nagle's granddaughter, who allowed us access to documents and letters of the Nagle brothers which pertained to their life in the Dauphin Lake area.

Finally, my gratitude to Helen poorly expresses my thanks for her patience during the weeks and months when I secreted myself, to delve into the history of a town in which I spent many happy years.

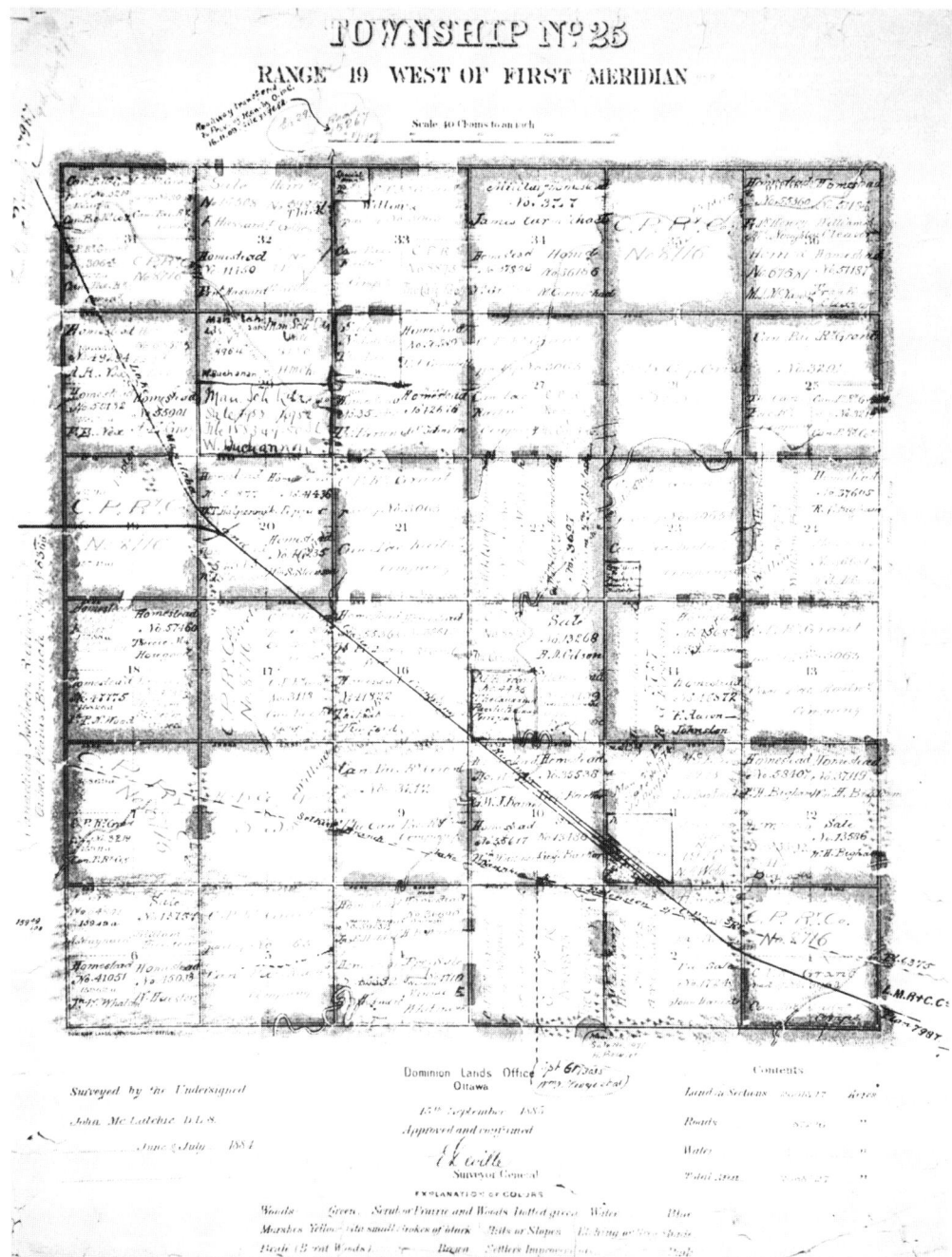

Plan of Township 25 19W showing original homesteads of some Dauphin pioneer families, 1885.

1

THE BEGINNINGS

The land was still. Only the rustle of the aspen leaves in the summer's breeze, the slap of the beaver's tail in the nearby pond or the noisy chit-chat of the red squirrel broke the silence.

Occasionally, the footfall of the native trapper could be heard as he searched the forest for food or for furs. Such sound as there was, was lost in the immensity of the land so that the hush of nature was the constant companion of its few inhabitants, at least in the warm days of summer and fall.

In winter the land was even more tranquil. The covering insulation of snow muffled the sound of the white-tailed deer and elk and provided a protective shield for the many small creatures who bustled about under the white covering, safe from the eye of eagle and hawk, the owl and the fox. The black and cinnamon bears were in their winter sleep. Only the sound of the north wind in winter or the fury of a summer storm after a hot day, punctuated the peace which permeated the great boreal forests and woodlands which constituted the face of what would become the Dauphin country.

Millions of years before, the land had been in great turmoil as the earth's crust trembled under the enormous inner forces of molten rock which caused continents to shift and bump, to crash and break or to rise and fall. Out of this cataclysm came a country, bound on each coast by mountain ranges, with a central core of gently undulating or relatively flat lands which, then, was altered over many years by the comings and goings of glaciers. The result was a land of lakes and rivers, mountains and prairies, and an abundance of wild animals and plant life.

All of the land was uninhabited until the ice receded sufficiently to allow the Asiatic hunters to move across a land bridge from Asia to North America in the Bering Sea area. The early Asiatics followed the migration routes of animals crossing the Bering land bridge, the animals providing their source of food. Our first inhabitants, the ancestors of our native tribes, came to North America from northern Asia. Here, they remained in a land teeming with wild game, fish, abundant plant and tree fruit, wildfowl and other birds. There is some evidence that at an early date there was some migration from the south. The "mound builders", who came as far north as southern Manitoba, were probably of Mexican or Central American Indian origin. Their civilization, however, seems to have disappeared completely from this area.

As the ice receded after the last ice age, it left large troughs and depressions which, as the ice melted, became the lakes and rivers of the new continent. In Manitoba a large lake was formed covering the largest part of the central portion of the province and extending into much of what is now the Dakotas and Minnesota in the United States of America. Rock laid down or pushed aside by the receding ice formed the boundaries of Lake Agassiz. As time went by the water receded even further but the remnants of the great lake are still present as the large interior lakes of Manitoba — Lake Winnipeg, Lake Manitoba and Lake Winnipegosis — and in thousands of smaller lakes throughout Manitoba, including Lake Dauphin.

The limits of Lake Agassiz are marked by a chain of hills and low mountains, running from southeast to northwest, along the western part of central Manitoba. Along the east side of Manitoba the boundaries are marked by the rise of the Canadian shield. As a result of the sedimentary silt deposited in the old lake bed, a large part of the area has shown rich forest and grass growth and, in more recent times, some of the best farming land for cereal and vegetable crops.

The lakes and streams of Manitoba, particularly in the north, made a highway system which permitted the exploration of the country on a grander and easier scale than would have been possible without them. They have also, from prehistoric times, provided the flightways of the great waterfowl migrations of the continent. Early man must have thrilled, as we do today, to hear the deep honk-honk of the Canada goose or to watch the majestic flight of Trumpeter and Whistling swans as they flew to their northern breeding range in spring and south again in the autumn. The great flocks of mallards, teal, canvasback and pintail ducks that frequent these highways each spring and fall is one of the awe-inspiring sights of nature.

The Indian tribes who journeyed on these waterways and fished and hunted for food belonged, almost entirely, to one of three races: the Crees, the Ojibways or the Assiniboines. In the Dauphin country were representatives of each race, since the area was at the borderline of the territory of several groups. The majority were Crees. There are estimated to have been some four thousand Crees in Manitoba in 1725.

The Crees were part of the Algonquin nation and were divided into three tribes occupying distinct but adjoining districts. The Plains Crees occupied the territory between the Assiniboine and Saskatchewan rivers. The Woods Crees lived north of the Saskatchewan and the Swampy Crees had their domain in the region of the woods, lakes and rivers and swamps which extend from the low eastern prairie plain to Hudson Bay. The Ojibways, another part of the Algonquin nation, lived in the area between the Great Lakes and the prairies. They, like the Swampy Crees, lived in similar terrain and were said to be like the Swampies in nature. The Assiniboines were part of the Sioux nation who lived south of the Assiniboine river, although they frequently strayed from their own territory and moved further north. They also were friendly with the Crees, as intermarriages and mutual treaties were common between them.

The Indians must have fared reasonably well in the Dauphin country. They were nomadic in custom and moved from one area to another in different seasons and for varying reasons. The presence of game, fish and buffalo might cause them to move. Inter-tribal wars would produce a shifting of an entire tribe. However, the existence of game, fish and waterfowl, the presence of forest protection and the abundance of both birch and spruce trees were essential for the needs of the tribe. The Dauphin country was a generous land with a relatively small population, who did not exploit the land severely.

It was a land teeming with fur-bearing animals of many kinds. The beaver was then, and for many years, an ever-present animal along the rivers and streams of the Riding and Duck mountains. Aspen flourished in the Dauphin country and as that tree flourished so did the beaver. In the same area and further north the forests contained adequate spruce and pine trees to provide the fur trader and trapper with gum for sealing the seams of his birchbark canoe, a watercraft which could easily be provided on the spot because of the stands of white birch present throughout the area. Hind reported that, on a trip to the Riding mountain in 1858, he found white spruce trees of six-foot to seven-foot circumference, white birch measuring three to three and a half feet in circumference, aspen up to five feet in circumference and poplar almost five feet in circumference.

John Macoun, Canada's early pre-eminent botanist, reports, in 1882, on the large populations of wolves, marten and fisher, mink, otter, muskrat, weasel and ermine, cross and silver fox, wolverines and other fur-bearing animals seen throughout the forests and prairies of the northwest. In addition, aside from buffalo, which by this time were decreasing rapidly in number — there were great numbers of black bears, elk, moose, mule deer and white-tailed deer as well as skunks, porcupines and squirrels.

It is no wonder then, that as the fur trade came to Canada, the western and northern regions of the country should be seen as lucrative areas and that exploring parties should be sent along its rivers and lakes, not only to search for the western sea but, as importantly, to contact and make friends with the Indian tribes and to encourage these tribes to trade with the fur companies in the riches of the land.

The first of these trader-explorers to reach the Dauphin area came under the French flag in the person of Pierre Gaultier de Varennes, Sieur de la Verendrye, who, in 1730, was appointed by the Governor of New France to the command of the northern French fur trading posts. LaVerendrye was a native Canadian, born in Trois Rivières, Quebec, on November 17, 1685. His life in this Quebec community provided him with a knowledge of the country and its native people and of the fur trade, which had been carried on between the French and the Indians. It had also given him the opportunity to serve in the armed services of the French king where he gained experience for command which was to stand him in good stead during his days in the Northwest.

LaVerendrye was the father of four sons, all of whom played a part in the voyages which the father took in the interests of the French fur trade in the west. Indeed, LaVerendrye himself did not make the trip into the Dauphin country. The travels into this area were made by his sons and it was under their supervision that Fort Dauphin was built.

It was the western sea that chiefly interested LaVerendrye. Years earlier he had heard from an Indian named Ochagach of a western lake from which flowed a river leading further westward until it reached a tidal flow. He believed that such a river would open the route to the Orient.

This belief was the basis of his determination to pursue a life of exploration in the hope of discovering the northwest passage by a land route. He approached the Marquis de Beauharnois, the Governor, with plans for exploration. Although the Governor would give no money, he did give LaVerendrye a monopoly on the fur trade in the regions he would epxlore. With this monopoly he persuaded several business leaders in Quebec to invest with him in forming a company to trade for furs and to allow him to further his explorations in the west. The story of his first few years is a story of hardship and disappointment. LaVerendrye had a relative lack of support from his partners in Quebec. They underwent periods of starvation and bitter cold. Some of the party met death by drowning; others, at the hands of Indians.

Eventually, however, his travels took him, with his sons François and Louis, to Lake Winnipeg and to the mouth of the Red River and up that river to its junction with the Assiniboine River on September 26, 1738. After making friends with the Indians, LaVerendrye continued up the Assiniboine to build a fort where he intended to spend the winter. He built this fort near the present site of Portage la Prairie and called it Fort la Reine in honour of the French Queen. While Fort la Reine was being built LaVerendrye sent men back to the Red River to build a second fort at the junction of the Red and the Assiniboine which he named Fort Rouge, a name still prominent in Winnipeg.

During the rest of that year and much of 1739 LaVerendrye made expeditions into the Mandan country, south and west of Fort la Reine. There were deputations from Indian bands from northern areas around Lake Manitoba imploring him to establish posts in their areas so that they might join in the trade of furs with him without having to travel so far as had been necessary prior to his coming, when they travelled the long route to the Hudson's Bay Company's post at Fort York. The state of his supplies, however, prevented him from taking advantage of such invitations at the time. He returned to Montreal to replenish his supplies and muster further financial support for his ventures. After considerable difficulties in that city he returned with the supplies which allowed him to undertake further explorations into a country which, until that time, had been known only to the native peoples. In 1741 he sent his two sons to build forts in the more northern parts of the territory. They built Fort Dauphin in the lake area north and east of the present town of Dauphin and named it for the Dauphin of France. They built Fort Bourbon on Cedar Lake. Both forts were to serve as action trading posts for a number of years.

It was from the name of the fort that the Dauphin country took its name. It encompassed most of the land lying in the angle formed by the Riding mountains and the Duck mountains. It was traversed by several streams coming down from the watershed of these mountains, principally the Valley, the Wilson, the Vermilion, the Ochre and the Turtle rivers, all of which empty into Lake Dauphin. The outflow of the lake consists only of the Mossey (originally Mossy) River which carries the water of Lake Dauphin into Lake Winnipegosis. Henry Youle Hind referred to this river as the Moss River in his report on the Assiniboine and Saskatchewan exploration of 1857-58. Lake Winnipegosis, in turn, empties into Lake Manitoba by way of the Waterhen system and Lake Manitoba into Lake Winnipeg via the Dauphin River. Lake Dauphin is twenty-one miles long and twelve miles wide at its widest point. It covers an area of one hundred and seventy square miles. When the first settlers reached the Dauphin country this lake and its feeding streams were bountiful sources of fish of several species.

Most of the area of the Dauphin country is described as being aspen grove boreal forest with rich grey-brown sedimentary soils and with a prairie climate having hot summers and cold winters. The growing period extends from mid-May to early September. There is about twenty inches of precipitation annually. It is considered part of the central lowlands of Canada although it abuts the second Devonian rise of the prairies. It has become part of the major wheat growing areas of Canada and is an excellent area for mixed farming. The western part of the region, earlier known as Gilbert's plains was principally grassland. The name was given to the area because of a Métis resident named Gilbert Ross who, for a time, with his wife, was the only resident of these grassy plains. It was not until Glenlyon Campbell, a son of Robert Campbell, the Yukon explorer, rode across the Riding mountain and bought Ross's land that the western part of the Dauphin country was opened.

The precise location of LaVerendrye's Fort Dauphin remains obscure and is still debated. LaVerendrye's description of its site places it on the northwest extremity of the "Lac des Prairies" at a point on the upper part of a river which "enters the lake and which comes from the great prairies". Morton deduces that it must then have been "near the mouth of the Waterhen River" since this river does flow into Lake Manitoba at its northwest extremity. It does not, however, come from the great prairies, nor have any remains been found at this location.

Others have reminded us that in LaVerendrye's time "Lac des Prairies" included both Lake Manitoba and Lake Winnipegosis. Using this information and the fact that LaVerendrye had never, himself, seen Fort Dauphin, they believe that Fort Dauphin was "on a grassy clearing between the river and the woods" near the mouth of the Mossey River. The remains of several forts have been found in this location and Tyrrell reports seeing the remains of a fort on the east bank of the Mossey about three-quarters of a mile from the mouth of the river. There are other reports of Indians and traders meeting at such a place.

Still others place LaVerendrye's fort on Lake Dauphin near the place where the Valley River enters the lake from the west. This site is, indeed, near the northwest extremity of Lake Dauphin but not at all on "Lac des Prairies", including Lake Manitoba and Lake Winnipegosis. Remains of a fort have been found in this

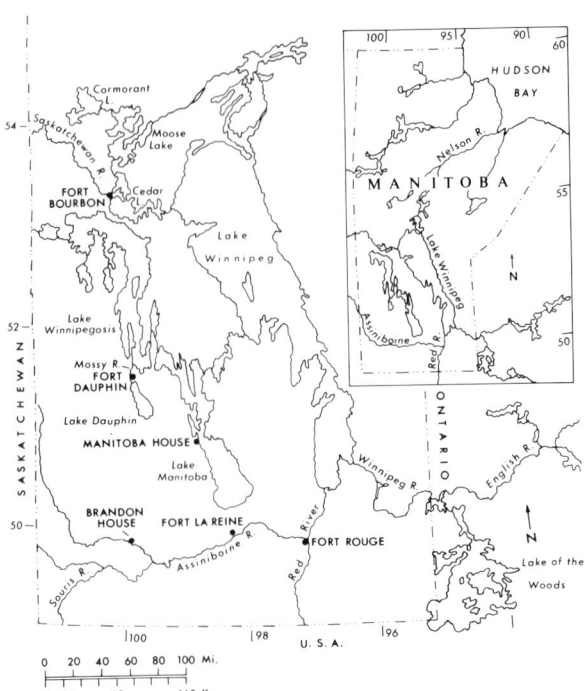

Fort Dauphin on the Mossy River; and Lake Dauphin.

Fort Dauphin Cairn and plaque commemorating the early fur trade post, Winnipegosis, Manitoba

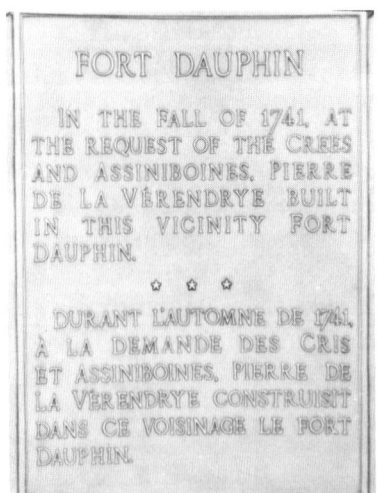

PROVINCIAL ARCHIVES OF MANITOBA

location. Indeed, a ceremonial chair, owned by the LaVerendrye chapter of the I.O.D.E. in Dauphin, was made from timbers found at this location.

The debate arises over the fact that Peter Pond is known to have had a fort in the same or closely situated area. David Thompson's map of 1797 shows Fort Dauphin as being on "the left bank of a stream flowing into Lake Dauphin from the south". Thompson's map, however, shows Lake Dauphin rotated in a counter-clockwise direction in such a way as to put the mouth of the Valley River on its south shore. E. Voorhis refers to Peter Pond's fort at the Valley River as "Dauphin Lake House" and LaVerendrye's fort on the Mossey River as "Fort Dauphin".

A very good summation of the arguments was presented by James Parker in 1974, in the *Dauphin Herald*. His conclusion was that the evidence favours the mouth of the Valley River as the site of LaVerendrye's Fort Dauphin. The debate still continues, however, with the Mossey River site as a definite possibility. Parker, himself, refers to a Jesuit document as being an important one: "It indicates definitely that Fort Dauphin was at the mouth of the Mossey River in 1760". Prud'homme and Bryce seemed to have concluded that LaVerendrye's Fort Dauphin was near the mouth of the Valley River as it empties into Lake Dauphin but neither Bryce nor Prud'homme cite an authority for their conclusions. All we can say with assurance is that the site is uncertain.

Part of the confusion about the site of Fort Dauphin results from the fact that, in addition to LaVerendrye's Fort Dauphin, there were Hudson's Bay Company forts with the name of Fort Dauphin. Often these forts were close to one another on opposite banks of a river. In 1795 and 1796 the H.B.C. had a house on the Dauphin River near its outlet into Lake Winnipegosis. Here, John Best carried on some trade for the company. In 1817 they established a new post on the Dauphin River "half a mile below where the river falls out of the lake". By 1819 they moved the fort again to a site on Lake Dauphin within sixty yards of the Northwest Company's post in order to "compete more easily" with the Northwest Company. Was this the Valley River site? Very likely it was.

Following the LaVerendryes' expeditions into the Dauphin country, Fort Dauphin continued as a trading post for the French, but only in a minor way and for a short period of time. Fort Dauphin was not one of the busier trading posts and within a short time fell into disuse. It was abandoned in 1742 for lack of provisions but the French re-occupied it and strengthened it in 1748. The traffic across the Dauphin country subsided and except for lone trappers or the annual movement of Indians from summer to winter habitats, the area saw few people in any one year. During the time that Fort Dauphin was active, some of its tenants may have done a small amount of gardening or farming.

During these years the water routes to and from the Dauphin country and the fort itself, saw many passers-by and housed or wintered some of them. In the 1760s Maurice Blondeau was a frequent visitor and fur trader in and around the Manitoba lakes and Fort Dauphin. In 1767, Francois le Blanc is said to have wintered at Fort Dauphin. In the winter of 1769-70, William Tomison came south from Fort Severn on Hudson Bay, across Lake Winnipeg and over to Lake Manitoba by the Dauphin River. He went down the west side of Lake Manitoba to the prairies along the Assiniboine River and up the valley of the Assiniboine as far as Birdtail Creek, north of Birtle. At that point he turned north and east across the Riding mountain and then down the valley of the Ochre River to Lake Dauphin where they made new canoes for the return to Fort Severn. In 1773 and 1774 Joseph Fulton, a pedlar and a partner of Peter Pangman, was at Fort Dauphin. Peter Pond wintered at his own post in the season of 1775-76. Alexander Henry, the younger, wintered at Fort Dauphin in 1779-80 and in 1803, when McMurray was commandant at Fort Dauphin, Thomas de Boucherville met Mr. Nolin of the Northwest Company there. In 1858 Professor Henry Youle Hind made his historic trip through a great part of the northern territory of western Canada, including much of the area around Dauphin and the lake country.

In 1781 a smallpox epidemic struck with vengeance in Western Canada. The disease had been brought back from the Mandan country by a group of Assiniboines who had gone to purchase horses. It prevailed for two years; at the end of this time much of the Indian population was dead and the fur trade was almost brought to a halt. Many of the traders had left the country.

When the fur trade resumed it followed a different pattern.

THE BEGINNINGS   15

Fur trading companies were organized in competition with the Hudson's Bay Company and with each other. There was a keen and often violent competition between the companies for the furs. During this time we know that a Mr. McMurray was commandant at an active Fort Dauphin.

After the union of the two fur trading companies in 1821, only one post operated in the Dauphin Lake area. There had, however, been such a decimation in the population of fur-bearing animals that the post closed in 1824 to allow for the recovery of the animal population. Although it opened again in 1827, it was kept small and operated in the winter only.

In 1831, after the union of the fur trading companies, Fort Dauphin disappeared from the lists of posts in the west. The relative isolation of the area continued unabated while settlement occurred in the south and west of Manitoba.

The settlement at the junction of the Red and Assiniboine rivers continued to serve as the focus of the waterways of the Assiniboine and the Saskatchewan river valleys. Its nature changed remarkably, however, after the acquisition by Lord Selkirk in 1811, of a tract of land from the Hudson's Bay Company of one hundred and sixteen thousand square miles along the Red River, and its settlement in 1812 by the new governor, Miles Macdonell, and thirty-six Irish and Scottish labourers. Until then the land had been the domain of the fur trader and the explorer. Now it was to have an agricultural and settlement aspect. For many years the history of the country centred, in the main, on the history of the Red River settlement, although Lord Selkirk's land holdings, named Assiniboia, were much more extensive than the outer limits of the settlement itself.

Assiniboia was a massive area which covered a large part of present-day Manitoba, including the Dauphin country, a strip of the eastern part of Saskatchewan, a large area of the Dakotas and Minnesota and the drainage area of the Rainy River water system through the Lake of the Woods and the Winnipeg River in Ontario back to Lake Winnipeg.

From the time that Fort Dauphin was closed to fur trading in about 1830 the comings and goings in the area consisted almost entirely of Indian and Métis trappers and hunters who brought their

The Henry Youle Hind Exploration Party reached Lake Dauphin in October 1858. They reported incorrectly, that agricultural possibilities in the area were poor.

In 1895, when this photograph was taken, Dauphin's pioneer farmers had yields of 40 to 45 bushels of wheat to the acre.

THE BEGINNINGS   17

furs to be traded at Manitobah House near Ebb and Flow Lake, to Riding Mountain House or across the Riding mountain to Brandon House. The trails used by these traders and by the Indians in their annual migrations from summer to winter lodgings, became the trails used many years later by early settlers looking for farmlands in the new areas of Manitoba.

In the meantime, settlements were springing up outside the Red River valley and the Saskatchewan Trail towards Portage la Prairie. Settlers moved along the Portage Trail and continued westward, south of the Riding mountain, towards the present towns of Birtle, Russell, Souris and Shoal Lake in the years from 1873 to 1879, or northward from Portage la Prairie towards the Whitemud River and Gladstone between 1875 and 1880.

The major study of the Dauphin country and its potential as an agricultural area was made by Henry Youle Hind and S.J. Dawson. The report of their journey of 1858 reveals that after travelling from the Red River settlement down the Red River to Lake Winnipeg, they crossed by way of the Dauphin River to Lake Manitoba, which they entered on September 30, 1858. They travelled on towards the Waterhen River, a journey which impressed them by the presence "of clear water with many fish, bald eagles, swans and pelicans". They reached Lake Winnipegosis by noon of October 3, 1858 and on October 4 they were shown the salt works at Lake Winnipegosis which were composed of about twenty-five salt springs, located four hundred yards from the lakeshore and which had been worked for forty years by James Monkman. He had huts and evaporating furnaces with which he could extract a bushel of salt from thirty gallons of brine.

They left Lake Winnipegosis by way of the Mossey River and entered Lake Dauphin at four p.m. on October 7, 1858. They "came in sight of the Riding Mountains in front and the Duck Mountains on our right". In the evening they "passed the mouth of the Valley River and camped on a beautiful beach, beneath some fine oaks growing upon a ridge close to the water's edge". On the morning of October 8, they started for a part of the lakeshore nearest to the Riding Mountain and landed opposite to what seemed to be the highest part of the mountain. This must, surely, have been close to the lakeshore between the outlet of the Vermilion

River and the outlet of the Ochre River. Here, they caught five pike weighing fifteen pounds each.

From October 9 to October 12 inclusive, they completed a journey on foot to the height of land in the Riding Mountain and back to Lake Dauphin. Hind describes the view from the mountain over the plain as "superb, enabling the eye to take in the whole of Dauphin Lake and the intervening country, together with part of Winnipegosis Lake. The outline of the Duck Mountains rose clear and blue in the northeast [sic] and . . . Riding and Duck mountains appeared continuous, and preserved a uniform, bold, precipitous outline, rising abruptly from a level country lying from eight hundred to a thousand feet below them. The swamps . . . were mapped in narrow strips far below; they showed by their condition with the ridges, and their parallelism to Lake Dauphin, that they had been formed by its receding waters". Morton comments that "Hind was gazing out over the ancient basin of Lake Agassiz, its vanished waters transformed into an Agassiz of blue distance stretching out of sight over the Manitoba lowlands. The lofty shoulder from which he surveyed the lowlands was exceeded in height only by Mount Baldy on the Duck Mountains to the northwest. Hind's penetration of the northwest highlands by the old fur trade route, produced the first recorded description of that one-time fur region and future rich farming district, the Dauphin country."

The expedition members made observations on the size of the trees on the mountain. On October 11, they came upon a lake in the mountain which may have been Moon Lake. The next day, as they made their way back towards Lake Dauphin, they did so in six inches of snow which had fallen during the previous night as they camped under a large spruce tree. On the first night they had seen a comet and a brilliant display of northern lights. Little did they suspect that they were viewing a comet which had only been discovered on June 2 of that year by the Italian astronomer Giovanni Donati. It was one of the most brilliant comets seen in the nineteenth century and was described as being most spectacular on October 10, when nearest the earth. This was the very night that Hind and his group slept in the open in the Dauphin country. Donati's comet will come again only after about two thousand years. They came across many moose tracks and "shot a bear in good condition."

After their return to Lake Dauphin they followed the south shore of the lake to the Turtle River, crossed it and continued on to Ebb and Flow Lake and subsequently to Manitobah House, which was on the west shore of Lake Manitoba.

Hind's report to the Canadian government spoke poorly of the agricultural possibilities in the Daupin area. Hind doubted that it was a desirable area for settlement. Its time, therefore, had to await a more accurate appraisal of its potentials and a greater demand for land than was present while empty land still existed in the more populous and settled areas of southern Manitoba.

Southern Manitoba had no inclination, in those years, to give attention to a remote and little known area. It had, after all, enough trouble on its own doorstep. Even after the bitter rivalries between fur trading companies and individuals, Manitoba began to experience troubles with its Indian and Métis peoples and with obtaining status as a province in the newly formed Dominion of Canada. In 1869 the Hudson's Bay Company transferred the lands deeded to it by charter. In 1870 Manitoba became the seventh province to join the confederation. A year before that, however, it had the first of the Riel Rebellions which ended in the exile of Louis Riel from Canada. It was Riel's suggestion that the new province be named Manitoba, a name taken from the Ojibway word for "the strait of the spirit" and used by the Ojibway who thought the sound of the water rushing through its narrows was made by spirits residing in the waters.

After the suppression of the Riel uprising in 1869 and five years after the new province was formed, parties were sent out by the federal government, in 1875, to survey the uninhabited territory, north of the Riding Mountains. One of these parties, headed by William Ogilvie, Dominion Land Surveyor, had as a member a young man named Theodore Burrows. He stayed in the area until late 1876 when he returned to Winnipeg to further his education. During his time in the area he became very familiar with the district and its resources. He returned later to contribute materially to the development of the Dauphin valley and to the political life of Canada.

Two other people to be found in the Dauphin Lake area were

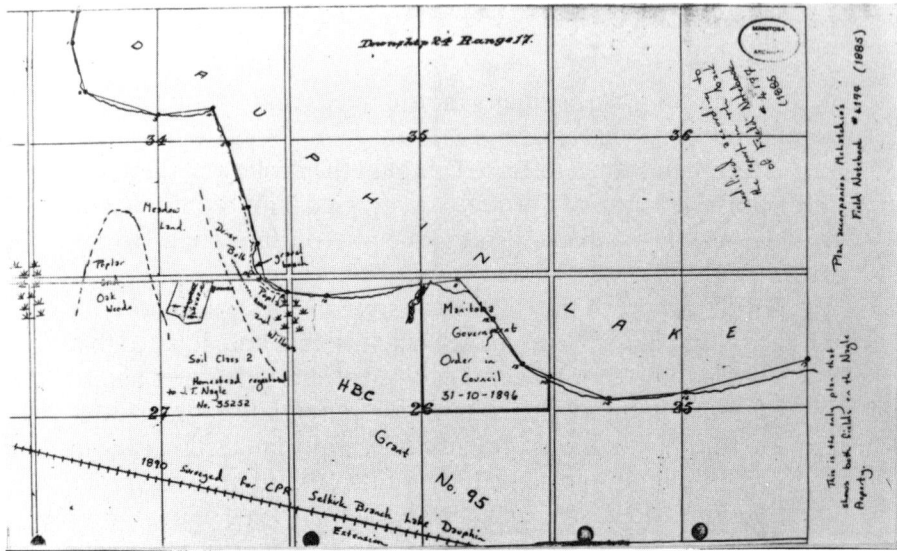

The location of the Nagle homestead on Lake Dauphin. From a field notebook dated 1885.

Homestead Certificate #35252 of August 18, 1886.

THE BEGINNINGS 21

the Nagle brothers. The prevalent and familiar story about them is that they were two Métis brothers who stopped at the Whitmore homestead in Gladstone on their way out of the Dauphin country. Their description of the land surrounding Lake Dauphin lay behind the first visit of Tom Whitmore and his party to the Dauphin area.

There was a great deal more to the Nagle story than has been passed from generation to generation.

There were three Nagle brothers, all of whom spent some time in the Dauphin Lake area. Edmund Nagle and his brother, Garrett, came to Manitoba in 1874 from St. Hyacinth, Quebec. Garrett, unhappy with his life in Winnipeg, returned to his home in Quebec. By 1876 another brother, John Thomas, arrived to take Garrett's place. In July, 1877, Ed and Jack homesteaded on two adjoining, unsurveyed quarter sections of land near present-day Ochre River.

The Nagles lived on their land from 1877 to 1881 or thereabouts. In 1877 Ed broke eleven acres of land and in 1878 bought three oxen and a horse. The following year he added some pigs, a cow and some poultry, and continued to break land. By 1881 he and his brother had a 26'x26' log house on the homestead. It appears to have straddled the boundary between the northeast and northwest quarters of the section. The northeast quarter, which was registered to J.T. Nagle on April 19, 1886 as homestead #35252 was the N.E. ¼ of 27-24-17W. This quarter is presently farmed by James Leslie of the Rural Municipality of Ochre River. A corner of this land faced on Lake Dauphin about three-quarters of a mile west of the entry of the Ochre River into the lake. The cabin was situated along the northern border of this quarter. Ed Nagle, at this time, did not register his land because no survey had been done. He later attempted to have his claim recognized, but nothing seems to have come of his pleas. During some of these years the brothers spent considerable time on the Métis buffalo hunts in southern Manitoba and the Dakotas. It is probably for this reason, and their fluency in the French language, that they were frequently mistaken for Métis.

In a notebook left by Ed Nagle, which begins in January, 1879, there is an entry mentioning that he camped "at the Whitfords" for two nights. No dates are given but it is known that Ed was a member of a survey party in the Northwest Territories from August 24 to December 1, 1882 and was in Edmonton in January of 1883. It seems likely that the Nagle brothers left the Dauphin Lake area in the late summer or fall of 1882, stopping at the Whitmores on the way.

It seems likely, also, that the Nagle brothers, mentioned by the Whitmores as Métis, were the Nagle brothers of the Dauphin Lake area, originally form St. Hyacinth, Quebec. It was they who regaled the Whitmores with their impressions of the Dauphin Lake country. The result of that conversation was more than anyone could have anticipated.

Notes to Chapter I

Books and Reports:

Burpee, L.J., ed. *Journals and Letters of La Vérendrye.* Toronto: The Champlain Society, 1927.

Crouse, Nellis, M. *La Vérendrye, Fur Trader and Explorer.* Toronto: Ryerson Press, 1956.

Hind, H.Y. and John Lovell. *Report on the Assiniboine and Saskatchewan Exploring Expedition.* Toronto: 1859.

Innis, Harold A. *The Fur Trade in Canada.* Toronto: University of Toronto Press, 1956.

Kronk, G.W. *Comets: A Descriptive Catalogue.* p. 48 re Donati's comet.

Macoun, John. *Manitoba and the Great Northwest. Guelph: World Publishing Company, 1882.*

Robertson, Heather, ed. *I Fought Riel: Major Charles A. Boulton,* Toronto: James Lorimer & Company, 1985.

Van Kirk, Sylvia. *'Many Tender Ties'.* Winnipeg: Watson & Dwyer Ltd., 1980.

Voorhis, E. *Historic Forts and Trading Posts of the French Regime.* Ottawa: Department of the Interior.

Newspapers:

Parker, James. "The Fort Dauphin Story," *The Dauphin Herald,* April-May 1974.

Letters:

Kimpton, Frances, re the Nagle Brothers, 1987. Collection of A. Little.

2
EARLY SETTLERS

Tom and Harry Whitmore were attracted to Canada by the intensive advertising of the Department of the Interior, extolling the opportunities for settlement in Canada's northwest regions. Their experience in the building trades, taught to them by their father, Thomas, a master builder of Gazeley in Suffolk, England, would surely stand them in good stead in a country where one had to cut his own lumber from the timbered land and erect his own home. The brothers, then thirty and twenty-eight years of age, crossed the Atlantic in 1878, landing in Montreal. They travelled to Duluth by rail, and then by wagon and ox-team to Gladstone in the new province of Manitoba, a distance of approximately five hundred miles, as the crow flies. There they selected their homesteads, stretches of timber and brushland on a wild and lonely prairie. Tom's closest neighbour lived six miles from him. By hard work, through long days, they improved their lands so that, by 1883, they could look back on the completion of five year's work with considerable satisfaction. Harry's satisfaction included that of seeing his work as a builder, a wheelwright and a coachmaker flourish. In addition, he had, in 1880, married Bessie Lofts, a woman who was to contribute a great deal in their future pioneer life.

Still, the Whitmores were interested in more productive land. They knew that the land south and west of the Riding Mountain had been selling quickly and that much of the best of the land had already been taken by homesteaders or by land speculators who hoped for large profits. They knew, also, that much of the land was subject to severe drought. No one knew what lay north of the

Riding Mountain escarpment. So the information brought by the Nagle brothers was of great interest to them, particularly the information that there was ample rainfall for good crops.

They listened intently as their guests described a land rich in timber, interspaced by clear streams flowing from the higher lands of the escarpment into Lake Dauphin. They spoke of the abundant fish in these streams and in the lake. They described the soil as generally deep and dark brown and able to sustain profuse crops of wild raspberries, cranberries, service berries (saskatoons) and other wild fruit. They told of fields red with lilies in the spring and profuse with edible mushrooms in mid-summer. In truth, they also described the summer mosquitoes, but, since these pests were indigenous to Gladstone as well, the Whitmores were not too sensitive to this news.

Generally, the description of the Dauphin country encouraged Tom Whitmore to seek first-hand knowledge of the area. Others, he thought, would be interested as well. So he organized a group to make a trip to gain personal knowledge and to corroborate the information given to him by the Nagles.

In this group, in addition to Tom Whitmore, were John McLaren (a surveyor and a man who would be invaluable as a guide in unknown country), Frank Blackmore, George McRae, S.T. Wilson, John Dickie and John Edwards. They set out on June 5, 1883 with food and tents, a few implements, two teams of horses and two yoke of oxen. There were no roads, so they had to be guided by John McLaren's observations about bearing and distance. They passed, in a northwesterly direction through the area between Lake Manitoba on the east and the Riding Mountain on the west. They reached Lake Dauphin west of the mouth of the Turtle River and followed the lakeshore along its southern edge until they crossed the mouth of the Ochre River. Soon afterwards they reached another creek. The lands around the banks of this creek so attracted John Edwards that he took his small plough and broke enough land to plant a plot of potatoes. The creek became Edwards Creek and John Edwards became the first man to plant a crop in the Dauphin area. This planting and his subsequent homestead were on the north half of 20-25-18W.

The rest of the party continued westward until they reached

the Vermilion River, a small stream running down from the north slope of the Riding Mountain. Here, on the river's right bank, at a place later to become the south edge of the town and the site of a future agricultural grounds, George McRae planted potatoes. Frank Blackmore did the same a mile north of McRae's site. Then, after carving their names on trees and setting up landmarks on their claims, the party returned to Gladstone on June 18, 1883. They had been away fourteen days. That fall John Edwards returned with his family and remained in the area as the first settler in the Dauphin country.

Within a few weeks of the return of the Whitmore group to Gladstone, another party of four — Neill McDonald and his sons Duncan, Charlie and Jack — set out from Woodside, eight miles east of Gladstone, in search of homesteads for themselves. They had been told by government workers that no homesteads were available in the marshy area north of Gladstone which was being drained. It was said that the land was fit only for ducks. Neill McDonald had heard of the Whitmore trip and so, determined to follow the same general direction, he led his sons along the trail, wherever they could find it, and eventually came to Lake Dauphin. From there they followed the south shore for a distance and then, leaving the lakeshore, travelled a few miles west to the spot where they afterwards settled, a few miles south of the present town. They reached their claim in August of 1883, just two months after the arrival of the first party. They also established their landmarks and returned to Woodside.

In the winter of 1883-84 only John Edwards and his family lived in the Dauphin area. They had no neighbours; they had to go up to two hundred miles for the nearest supplies, a journey which often took nine or ten days camping out at night in all kinds of weather. It was a life calling upon every ounce of devotion and endurance.

During the spring of 1884, Neill McDonald and his sons packed up their belongings in Woodside and set out for the Dauphin country over the trail they had trod in the previous autumn. There had been heavy winter snows and early spring rains. They soon found that the marshes and muskegs were so soft and so full of water that passage over them was impossible. The animals foundered in the bogs and they were in danger of losing their belongings, if not their lives. They had knowledge from the Indians of an alternate trail across the Riding Mountain. They set out to use it and became the first settlers to arrive in the Dauphin area by crossing the mountains. In the fall of 1884, when the ground was frozen and covered by snow, the McDonald family moved in by sleigh as far as the Ochre River and then by wagon to their homestead. So now, at the end of 1884, another family had left the company of neighbours and friends to build a future in the untravelled lands between the Riding Mountain and the Duck Mountain escarpments.

Late in the same year (1884) a young man rode his pony across the Riding Mountain from his farm in Elphinstone and came out from the north slope of the Riding Mountain into an enormously rich grassland which was referred to as Gilbert's plains in deference to its only settler, a Métis named Gilbert Ross. The young man on the pony was Glenlyon Campbell, then twenty-one years of age, the son of Robert Campbell of Glenlyon, Scotland, whose name is solidly linked with the early history of the Hudson's Bay Company. Robert Campbell had served the Company for forty years, and is best known for the early exploration of the Yukon Territory, where his exploits were many and his discoveries were major ones. His son, Glenlyon, became the first white settler in the Gilbert Plains area. He was later to serve the Dauphin country as a provincial and a federal representative and to serve Canada gallantly in World War I. He joined Boulton's Scouts as a captain and fought in the Northwest Rebellion of 1885 at Fish Creek and at Batoche. After his return in the fall of 1885, he went back to Gilbert's plains where he traded a pony for Gilbert Ross's log cabin and entered a homestead claim for the land which he later farmed successfully. The district and the post office were subsequently named Glenlyon in his honour.

The Northwest Rebellion of 1885 put a temporary stop to the movement of settlers on the prairies. Those who had already settled remained where they were, while those who wished to settle felt it necessary to await the outcome of the Indian and Métis uprising. None of the fighting in the Northwest Rebellion took place in the Dauphin country although the settlers in the area did note a

EARLY SETTLERS 27

more aggressive and challenging attitude amongst the native people than had been apparent previously. When the uprising had been suppressed after the final battle at Batoche, settlers began again to move into areas and onto land which, until that time, had been empty.

During the early part of 1885, a Dominion government survey party had been sent into the Dauphin country to lay out the range and township lines. One member of the party was Harry B. Whitmore who, with his family and together with his brother Thomas, had returned to the Dauphin area to settle in April, 1884. Tom was still unmarried. He took up his homestead on the land previously marked and claimed, which proved to be at the southern edge of the future town of Dauphin in an area to be known as Gartmore. His brother, Harry, homesteaded on one hundred and twenty acres close by and later added to his farm with adjacent lands. The fall of 1884, then, saw the Edwards, the McDonalds and the two Whitmores in the Dauphin area. That wasn't a great increase in absolute terms, but it was a doubling in families. The Whitmores became solid and enterprising members of a growing community as time passed. Their contributions to early building in the area were appreciable; their constant attention to the upgrading of farming methods; their efforts in the formation and sustenance of the Dauphin Agricultural Society; their interest in the betterment of animal husbandry and breeding and the example set by them as pioneers in the new community served as an inspiration, not only to their numerous children, but to other members of the growing settlement. Together with others yet to come, the Whitmores were to forge a community which was praised by a legion of observers, especially in its first half century.

Who were some of the pioneers who followed the Edwards, the McDonalds and the Whitmores into the land which, according to an Indian legend, was the site of the Garden of Eden? Some were veterans of the Northwest Rebellion but most came over the mountains from southern Manitoba or from Ontario and Quebec.

Initially the homestead claims were concentrated in two localities around which sprang two different communities with their separate social and business activities. Eventually, there were two villages not far apart but quite distinct in their development.

The first area to achieve its own distinction was an area about a mile north of the present town which was known as Dauphin Lake or "Dogtown". The settlement centred around David McIntosh's homestead, where he opened a store and operated the post office in 1886. Because supplies were obtainable here earlier than elsewhere in the district, the Indians, fur traders and trappers often stopped for food and other supplies. Since they frequently travelled by dogteam there were always many dogs in the area — hence the nickname "Dogtown".

In this area, prior to 1895, we find David McIntosh and his brother, Captain William McIntosh. Both were veterans of the 1885 rebellion. As such, they received one quarter section as script land to which they added another quarter by purchase as homestead land. Consequently, David and Will selected section 22-25-19, each taking one-half of the section. This section became the centre of the village of Dauphin Lake, later most often referred to as Old Dauphin, particularly after David opened his store and post office in 1886. James Blackmore, a brother of Frank Blackmore, who had made the Gladstone to Dauphin trip with the Whitmore group in 1883, took up his brother's claim on the S.E. ¼ 15-25-19. in 1886; but he later sold out to R.D. Gibson who had been farming the N.E. quarter of the same section since 1886. Archie Esplen and his cousin, Alex Cameron, came in 1886 to stake their homestead claims. Archie returned in 1887 with his wife Mary. The Esplens and their progeny made a major contribution to the welfare of the community for many, many years. Archie represented Dauphin as an M.L.A. from 1922 to 1927.

Many others who were to form a solid core for the agricultural community arrived in quick succession in the ensuing years. Most came because of the farming prospects, although some were attracted by the possibility of the discovery of oil, a possibility made plausible by the finding of small amounts of oil in land near the foot of the Riding Mountain in 1885. *The Emigrant* in its August 1, 1886 issue, said, "The fact that petroleum has been found in Lake Dauphin district, Manitoba, opens a new and rather surprising source of wealth to the Northwest". This hope vanished quickly, however, and attention was fully turned to agrarian matters.

J.H. Bigham and R. Bigham were well known to early pioneers as capable farmers and woodsmen. They arrived in the area in 1886. J.H. Bigham operated a hardware store later, when the railway came to the district. George Barker, Sr., a blacksmith by trade, came over the Riding Mountain with his family from Minnedosa in 1888 and became a prominent figure in Dauphin Lake and, later, the first mayor of the village of Dauphin. His grandson, Billy, became one of Canada's air aces in World War I. Paul Wood took up a homestead in 1890, having left England with an advanced education. He subsequently became an official interpreter for the immigration department when the Ukrainian immigration began in 1896.

The Buchannons, James and William, arrived in 1890 and 1893 respectively. Robert Gunne came to Dauphin as the land agent for the Dominion government in 1891, initially on a part-time basis in the summer but by 1893 he ran a full-time office. His son, Robert J. Gunne, became Dauphin's first qualified doctor, although Philip J. Beauchamp, who had been in the Gartmore area since 1886, tended many of the sick and injured in the earlier days. He was a trained pharmacist. R.J. Malcolm, who arrived with his parents in 1889, took out a homestead claim east of Dogtown, near the lake. Bob Wishart and his wife, Clementine, with their ten children, left an area in the Touchwood Hills in Saskatchewan, just south of Elfross, which now bears their name. They had suffered drought and prairie fire in their years in that area and were, consequently, looking for farmland with a more ample rainfall. News of the Dauphin area's fine farming climate brought them to the Dauphin Lake area in 1890. A somewhat similar fate befell their Touchwood Hills neighbours, the Gavin Strangs. They also made the decision to move their family to Dauphin. After an eventful trip across eastern Saskatchewan they reached the Yorkton area only to have their horses bolt and return to the Touchwood Hills. The men returned for the horses while the women and children waited. Six weeks after starting their trip the Strangs arrived at Dauphin Lake to rejoin their old neighbours.

Tom Pollon, Tom Parsons, Sam Perry, James Shand, James Carmichael and John Dunfield were other pioneers close to the community around Dauphin Lake, who farmed before the railway arrived. There was also Joseph Clarke who arrived in 1893 to build his Dauphin House, a stopping-off house for those coming to or passing by the area.

During the early years the farmers around Dogtown saw the traffic of new homesteaders increase to the north and west. The Dan McKillop family, Peter and Archie Gillies and Mary Gillies arrived on June 22, 1888, having spent about four years farming near Batoche in Saskatchewan. Earlier Dan McKillop and the Gillies brothers had been caught up in the Northwest Rebellion. Some of the men, hauling supplies for the Canadian government, were taken prisoner by the rebel forces but escaped within a few days. Following the rebellion, for reasons of drought, they decided to move to more hospitable land in Manitoba. Archie Gillies and Dan McKillop went to the Dauphin country, a distance of three hundred miles, to scout the area for homestead land. When they decided to pick up their belongings by the end of April, 1887 and move to the Dauphin area, there was a group of eleven people, three yoke of oxen, sixty head of cattle, a team of ponies and a "prairie schooner". They came by way of the Riding Mountain. John McKillop said the amount of food they consumed was terrific. Twice a week they ate two sacksful of Scotch scones. Peter McKillop shot much of their meat food, including a whooping crane. The trip took seven weeks, three of which were spent in the mountains. Often they would cover only three miles a day. They encountered "mosquitoes by the millions".

On June 22, 1887 they arrived in the Dauphin district where they came first to Neill McDonald's farm. The next day they followed the Vermilion River past the Whitmore farms and George Barker's farm, where the town now stands. They continued on another mile where they crossed the Vermilion River to the settlement of Dauphin Lake, where they camped for a week near David McIntosh's store. The men scouted land north of the Wilson River and at the end of the week they swam themselves, the cattle and their belongings across the Wilson River. Dan McKillop claimed the S.W. ¼ 3-26-19 as his homestead and the rest of the group settled in the same neighbourhood. During the following winter, the men felled a sixty-foot tree which they laid across the banks of the Wilson River to serve as the first bridge over a river in the

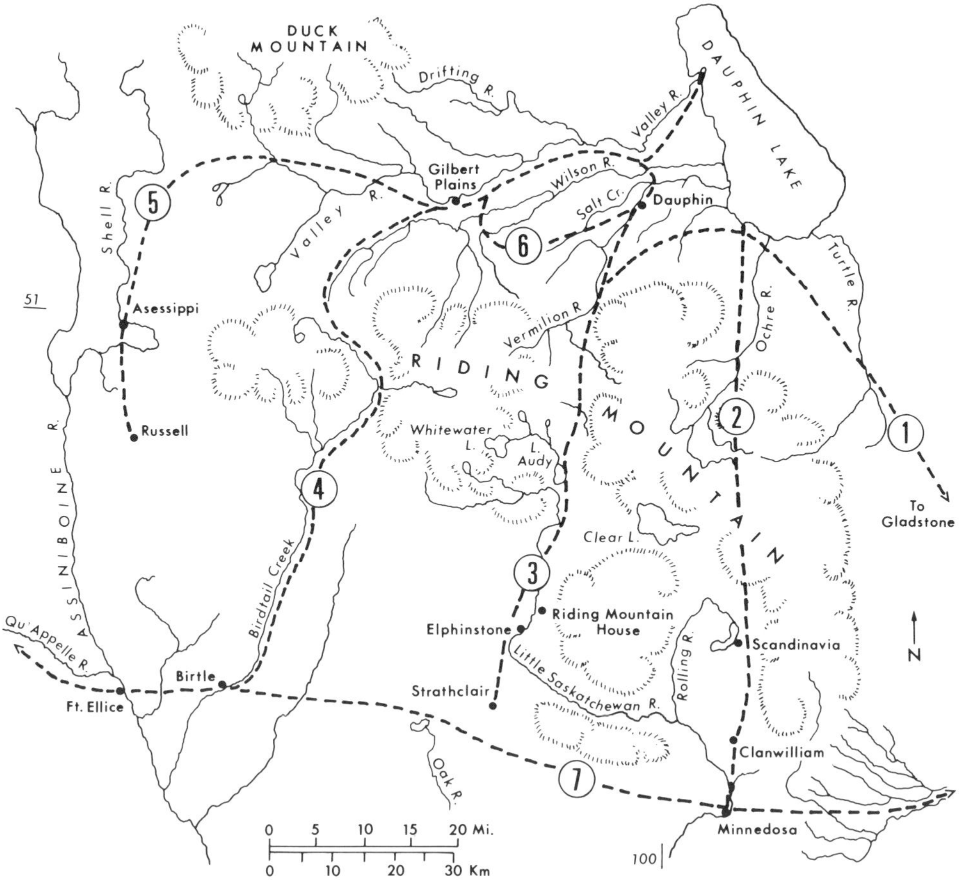

Early trails, from a map by the author.

1. Trail to Gladstone
2. Dauphin Lake Trail
3. Strathclair Trail
4. Birdtail Valley Trail
5. Russell Trail
6. Gilbert Plains Trail
7. North branch of Old Saskatchewan Trail (Qu'Appelle Trail)

In addition to his work on the Canadian Northern Railway, Thomas Gorby and his family farmed section 22-25-18, and possibly traded furs. Here, he carries pelts on the jigger.

PROVINCIAL ARCHIVES OF MANITOBA

Dauphin area.

James A. Campbell, who had travelled in the earlier days from Duluth to Portage la Prairie, farmed just north of Portage in the Prospect area. He left this farm for another near Minnedosa but in 1888 he and his family, suffering the drought as others had, decided to try their luck in the Dauphin Lake area. They came by way of Elphinstone to Lake Audy, then down from the Riding Mountain into the Dauphin area. He homesteaded on the N.E. ¼ 28-25-19. He secured his claim by setting off from camp at midnight to reach the land office at Minnedosa so that he would arrive before others whom, he suspected, might be claiming for the same land. John McKillop recalls his first meeting with Jimmie Campbell who, he says, was "a young man, wearing a ten gallon hat, a claw hammer coat, knickerbocker trousers, white boiled shirt, red leather leggings and a red moustache. This distinguished looking gentleman always won the hearts of the fair sex."

Mrs. Catherine Hassard and her four sons, John, George, James and Frank came in 1888 and with them were three Playfords (Tom, Jim and Chance), Gilbert Jardine and Ed Batty. James Padfield came in the same year. All of them settled between the Vermilion and the Valley rivers. They began to fill the area near the Valley River, first settled by Angus McDonald in 1886 when he homesteaded on 36-25-20.

In steady succession came Donald Macneill with sons John, Peter and Harry in 1888; Hugh Fulton in 1888; the J.R. McCleans with six sons in 1889; the Fred Boughens with four sons and a daughter in 1890, and Herb Chute and his family in 1894. Thomas and James Shaw who arrived in 1890 provided a grist mill and a lumber mill. In the early 1890's Charles McLachlin, the Cleavers, the McNaughtons, the Carmichaels, the Nex brothers, Albert Johnston and Frank Kilty passed through Dogtown on their way to homesteads northeast and northwest of that settlement.

To the east Duncan Dickson came to the district which bears his name in 1889. He and his wife chose the S.W. ¼ 24-25-18. They had a family of ten children who were joined in the same year by Thomas and Mary Jane Gorby with their family of six boys and a girl. The Gorbys had come over from Souris where they first farmed after leaving Renfrew County in Ontario in 1888. They stayed in Souris until the spring of 1891 when they packed up and crossed the Riding Mountain into the Dauphin country. They farmed the whole of section 22-25-18. Thomas Gorby worked on the Canadian Northern railway in addition to working his farm. Together the Gorbys established excellent mixed farms with heavy crops, honeybees and sheep. They smoked their own meat in a small smokehouse, sheared sheep for wool which Mrs. Gorby cleaned, spun and knitted into the necessary garments for warmth. Like all the pioneers, they preserved wild fruit and vegetables, had cool earthen cellars under the house and stored items in the well for cooling. The Gorbys made one other contribution to pioneer life. Having been taught to play the fiddle by their father, the four boys formed a musical group using fiddles and guitars. They were the source of music for many a dance or social evening and for the Quadrille Club, a dance club which was in existence around the turn of the century. Dancers would arrive in evening gowns or Prince Albert coats and dance the evening away to the music of the Gorby Brothers. Some of the popular pieces of the time were "Listen to the Mocking Bird", "Wait Till the Sun Shines, Nellie", "A Bird in a Gilded Cage", "After The Ball" and "On the Banks of the Wabash".

Other pioneers in the Dickson district included William McCrae, Alfred Coombs and the James Allin family.

By 1893 Dogtown had a hardware store and tinsmith shop operated by Bob McLean, Albert Payne's bakeshop, a land office run by Robert Gunne, the Dauphin House run by Joseph Clarke, the Leland House managed by Charles McLean, a drugstore owned by Dr. Gunne and managed by Jack Waite, a pharmacist. Sandy McPherson had opened a blacksmith shop. James McKinnon also did some blacksmithing. Several of R.J. Wishart's daughters operated a boarding house. Jake Cathers had a sawmill and threshing business. All of these ventures centred around the general store and post office operated by David McIntosh. In addition, the settlement had a magistrate (Mr. Smith) and a constable (Mr. Stinson). George Barker was the bailiff. A Presbyterian log church, built in 1889, had Mr. Jarvis as its minister.

The spirit of trust and helpfulness in the community was exemplified in the sale of land by Paul Wood to Bill Buchannon. With no other persons involved to draw or witness the transaction, and with the use of strong tea to substitute for the lack of ink, the following agreement was written:

Lake Dauphin, November 13, 1893

I, undersigned, agree to forfeit all claim whatsoever on the northwest quarter of section 9, township 25, range 19, west, in favour of Mr. W. Buchannon, for which I have received the sum of ninety dollars (cash), also six sacks of flour, same to be paid before this date, 1894. I also agree to pay Mr. Buchannon one spring pig in spring of 1894.

(1s) Paul Wood

Dogtown was the larger of the two settlements between which a moderate rivalry grew up over the years and encompassed such things as crop yields, soccer games, community dances and picnics. The rivalries were friendly and constructive, in the main.

The second community in the Dauphin area was called Gartmore, situated one to two miles south of the present town of Dauphin. Here, centred along the township line between townships 24 and 25, and nestled in a picturesque setting along the banks of the Vermilion River, which meandered towards Lake Dauphin, were some of the earliest homesteads. Harry and Bessie Whitmore, Tom and Minnie Whitmore and the William Whitmores had their homesteads there. Neill, Duncan and Charlie McDonald were just south of the township line while their daughter, Cynthia, who had married Alex Birss, lived just west of the river which ran through their land. Matt Lee and his family homesteaded on the S.W. ¼ of 3-25-19 in 1886. In the same year Gartmore received one of its favourite homesteaders in the person of Philip J. Beauchamp. He was a small, puckish man who made a great contribution to his adopted district. A pharmacist by training, he was also a veteran of the Fenian raids. He had farmed in the Gladstone area for about six years before coming to Dauphin. In both areas his attempts at farming were frustrated by demands for his services in caring for the sick of the district. He provided these services willingly to the settlers. In their minds he provided an essential service and in their speech they always referred to him as "Dr." Beauchamp. After ten years of farming in the Mayflower area, he moved to the new village where he operated a drugstore for a short time.

Picnic of the Dauphin Pioneers c. 1900 (L-R): Robert Machan and Mrs. Machan, Noel Ross, Phoebe Maclean, Mrs. P.J. Beauchamp, Mrs. Mark Cardiff, Miss Cruise, H.C. Ross, Dr. P.J. Beauchamp, Mr. & Mrs. Dan Sinclair. Seated: Unidentified child, Roy Dean, Bob Cruise, Mrs. Bob Cruise, Henry McCorvie, Jack Brinkman, Maggie McPherson, Mrs. Alex McKerchar, Hugh McKerchar and Alex McKerchar.

PROVINCIAL ARCHIVES OF MANITOBA

Central School, c. 1900

Noel and Chester Ross, two English brothers, operated a store in the Gartmore area on Tom Whitmore's land. Nearby, the Hudson's Bay Company operated another store after 1890. Tom Hedderley, Robert Farrell, Alfred Maynard (Dauphin's first major beekeeper), William Whatson, William Hueston and David Bruce were all pioneers in the area, as was Robert Smith who farmed all of 8-25-18.

John Bryce homesteaded in the Gartmore area and operated an inn. Mrs. Bryce had a seamstress shop. A stopping-off house was run by W. Bayliss and his wife. Isaac Spillett and his son, Merritt, both homesteaded initially in the Gartmore area, as did Mr. and Mrs. Dan Sinclair, Mr. and Mrs. William Miller. Sam Chipman drove the mail from Neepawa to Gartmore where he ran the post office.

Other areas, too, were receiving pioneer settlers who looked to Gartmore as their centre. South of Gartmore, toward the Riding Mountain, homesteads began to fill up after 1889 when the Andrew Malcolms from Minnedosa and the John Durstons from Portage la Prairie made their ways across the mountains to an area lovingly referred to as "Skiligalee". This Scottish word meaning "porridge" was given to the area by Bill Fee and was used to characterize the consistency of the soil in the area during heavy rains or spring flood. It has been suggested that it might also have referred to the staple diet of the pioneers.

John Durston and his son, Bill, spent the winter of 1888-89 in the area which came to be known as Mountview. They scouted for suitable land to bring their family to in the following spring. They lived in a virtual dugout during that winter. The next spring they made a difficult trip across the mountains with the family and their belongings. The story of the Malcolms' trip to Dauphin from Minnedosa is best described by James Malcolm in his *I Took To The Road*, a copy of which is held in the Provincial Archives of Manitoba. It is an absorbing story, marred only by the serious injury to Andrew Malcolm, when he suffered frozen feet, resulting in the partial amputation of one foot. It was on this trip that the Malcolms first met John Durston, their first contact being that they came across the frozen bodies of John Durston's oxen on the mountain trail. Apparently the oxen, because of their short legs were unable to cope with the deep snow and were stalled in the spot where they died. The Malcolms also met up with Ben Fawcett on the trail. In fact, Ben Fawcett almost became a target as he approached the Malcolms on the trail in the evening hours. Not recognizing what was approaching, Tom Malcolm had raised his rifle in readiness to shoot. He was restrained by his mother until the being came closer. Only then did they recognize that it was a man. Ben Fawcett was the first resident minister and teacher in the Dauphin district.

Jacob Cather was another pioneer in the Mountview area and was responsible for bringing the first threshing machine into the district in 1893. Duncan Buchannon brought one in further north in 1894. It was Jacob Cather who employed Herb Chute of Sheho, as a thresher; Mr. Chute then made the decision to bring his family to the Dauphin area in 1894. Frank Fee, the Alex McKerchars, Mr. and Mrs. R.C. McLeod, Robert Cardiff and John Seale were other early settlers in Skiligalee.

West of Gartmore was the Burrows area, named at a later date for T.A. Burrows, the Dauphin lumberman. It was first settled by Sandy McPherson who started a sawmill near the mountain. He later moved to town to operate a hardware store. The area, however, soon received Jim Kerr, Jack Sinclair, Jim Audy, Joe Tucker, Stewart Geekie, Ed Hewitt, William Burke and Fred Smith. Jim Audy was the settler after whom Lake Audy was named. He ran pack trains over the mountains for the Hudson's Bay Company. Stewart Geekie became the first reeve of the Rural Municipality of Dauphin.

W.J. Wickes and A.J. Henderson, with their families, were the first to settle in the Spruce Creek area, then known as Cumberland. Both these men had been in the area in 1887 looking for winter hay, as the drought south of the mountains at Strathclair had created a shortage of feed for their cattle. They returned in 1889 to settle. Following close behind was John Nicholson and his wife who reared twelve children in the area. As a family the Nicholsons went on to make a significant mark in the farming and business life of the Dauphin valley. It was John Nicholson who made an eloquent plea to the federal authorities to have compassion for the Ukrainian "squatters" in the Riding Mountain Reserve when they were being harrassed by the forest authorities at the turn of the century.

James and Janet McLaughlin came to the Cumberland area in 1890. Three years later, James McLaughlin lost his life by drowning when he and Janet were returning from Minnedosa with provisions. The Little Saskatchewan river was in torrent at the time. Janet was able to grasp some branches which kept her safe until rescued. She returned, made a homestead claim in her own name, kept body and soul together for herself and her family by farming her homestead, nursing the sick and the expectant in the community, selling home-baked bread to the bachelors of the district and, often, boarding the teachers or the student ministers who came to the Burrows area. Although fortune called on Janet McLaughlin to face these tasks alone, she experienced the generosity of the pioneer neighbours who assisted her in as many ways as possible. The example she set in the pioneer days could be seen in a variety of ways in almost every home in the community where the pioneer wife, although seldom mentioned in the newspapers of the day, managed a great variety of activities requiring intelligence, devotion, hard work and endurance. It was often she who, in addition to working alongside her husband in the farmyard and field, tended the garden, kept the chickens and harvested the eggs, milked and fed the cows, separated the cream, made the butter, preserved the fruit and vegetables, raised the children and supervised their education, sewed and mended the clothes and worked as a volunteer in church, school and other community activities. She had the time for "bees" where quilting, preparing meat, raising barns and killing the winter meat took place. She fed visitors and wayfarers, and often the natives who came by the farm. She rode, she often hunted and she usually was in charge of the shopping expeditions. Last, but certainly important in the pioneer farm, she organized and made the harvest meals, where upwards of two dozen men were fed from morning to night and housed for the duration of the harvest season. This was work requiring the skill of an expert chef. The amounts of food cooked were prodigious and always anticipated eagerly.

Other pioneers in the Cumberland area were the McCorvie brothers, Henry and Archie, the Halls, Jacob Porter, William

EARLY SETTLERS

Miller, Tom Satterthwaite, Ed Porterfield, Dan McLeod, Ed Keats, Fred McPherson and John Whiteman. Cumberland always played a prominent role in sports. In soccer and in baseball they were always contenders for honours. Part of this success may be attributed to the large supply of Nicholsons, Millers, McCorvies and other participants.

Gradually, land further from the two settlements of Dauphin Lake and Gartmore began to fill in. Towards the lake the Chards, the Campbells, the Terrys, the Wrights, the Akers, the Beavens, the Bonds and the Keats filled the land. At about the same time the Winters, Alguires, the Paynter brothers, Charlie Hicks, W.J. Rice, the Rasmussens, Albert Payne, George Leigh and family and others were homesteading the land west of Dauphin, toward the present village of Asheville.

Homestead claims were springing up all around the area. Between 1883 and the end of 1895, there were ninety-five married couples and ninety-nine single men who took up homesteads in the Dauphin country. Almost all of these located in three townships (24, 25 and 26) in each of three ranges (18, 19 and 20 W.). In addition, fifty-three settlers arrived to take up land previously homesteaded by others. All of these names have an honoured place in the history and development of the Dauphin area and all of them constitute the charter list of the Dauphin Pioneer Association.

As the land began to fill, the two small communities of Gartmore and Lake Dauphin became the sites of more and more commercial activity, supplying the needs of an early and increasingly agricultural community and a dwindling fur trading and trapping community. Day-to-day living in the pioneer days, before the railway reached the area, was a mixture of privation and pleasure. The work was back-breaking, lasting from daybreak to dusk. There was land to clear and plough, crops to plant and reap, buildings to erect and furnish, animals to feed and house, and food to be hunted, fished for or grown. There were neighbours to help on arrival or in times of need, for it was surely an interdependent society.

There were dangers as well. Weather extremes, floods, winter blizzards, summer lightning, animal attacks, drownings and other risks with which each settler had to cope, were not infrequent.

Sickness or injury and childbirth in a land where no hospital was to be found and a solitary pharmacist/doctor, maybe miles away, were causes for further concern.

Interspersed with these travails, however, were the warm, pleasant times of summer picnics, sporting events, community bees, wedding parties or just the getting together with friends and neighbours for an evening of music or dancing. Berry-picking parties, Sunday worship and trips to Gartmore or Dogtown brightened the settlers' days. The beauty of their surroundings, with bush and meadow fronting the azure-blue rise of the Riding Mountains, the big sky with the magnificent, fiery reds of sunset or the brilliant amber of the dawn, the great variety of songbirds, the blue shadows of the snowdrifts on a quiet winter's afternoon, all added to the pleasure felt when the pioneers contemplated their good fortune to have found such an abundant land.

There was a growing need for schools as the children of the pioneers reached, or passed, school age. Schooling was not compulsory at that time but to the credit of the pioneers they recognized the value of a sufficient education for their children and were, generally, helpful in pursuing the establishment of proper schools. The first school was established during the winter and spring of 1889-90 in Lake Dauphin, with the Rev. J.B. Fawcett as the first teacher. A few months later Vermilion school, about a mile north and west of the present town, on Salt Creek, was built. It was consolidated in 1902 with the town schools but remained in use as a school until about 1907 when its students began attending the Dauphin schools. After that time it ceased to exist as a school.

Gartmore school was the third school in the area. It was built in 1891, originally on 29-24-19 but later moved a mile north to 32-24-19. It served the district until 1958, a period of sixty-seven years. It was not until 1892 that other schools were built in response to growing school populations. As that population grew, schools sprang up in the north and west, Valley River and Sandringham in 1892, in the southwest at Cumberland in 1892. In the mid-nineties to late nineties other schools were under consideration and any delays there were seemed almost exclusively related to the difficulty of arranging finances.

John Gorby, one of the four sons of Thomas Gorby of the

Dickson district, was the area's first licensed teacher. Some of the schools in which he taught included Old Dauphin where he was the school's third teacher, Gartmore where he was the fourth teacher and Dickson school where he was the first teacher.

Schools filled an important need for the children of the community but what many settlers longed for just as much was a place of worship. For many years this was denied them, principally because of isolation. When an opportunity did arise for worship it usually came by way of student missionaries who came for short intervals, a few months in the summer season, and left again. In 1888 the first religious services were held in the Dauphin area in the homes of George Barker and Thomas Parsons at Dauphin Lake and were conducted by a missionary of the Methodist church. In 1889 a student missionary was appointed by the Presbyterian church and by 1890 a church was built and opened in Dauphin Lake in May of that year. In 1890 the Church of England built a small log church at Gartmore which was the first place of worship at that location. It was called St. Paul's church. By 1893 the Church of England built another church at Dauphin Lake named All Saints' church. When the villages moved to the new townsite of Dauphin, the church building of All Saints' church became the main church and was renamed St. Paul's. The log church from Gartmore became a parish hall. The church was situated at the northeast corner of Burrows Avenue and Vermilion Street while the parish hall was on the southwest corner of the same intersection.

An Agricultural Society was organized and an agricultural fair was held in Gartmore in 1892. It was held annually at Gartmore until 1897 when it was moved to the agricultural grounds at the south end of the town of Dauphin where it remained until after World War II. Agricultural exhibitions were held in conjunction with the fairs in every year except the war years of 1940 and 1944 inclusive. In addition, the Agricultural Society served as a catalyst to farmers interested in the improvement of their stock herds and the encouragement of good breeding stock. On some occasions it supplied funds for projects designed to improve the quality of farming methods or of animal husbandry. In 1926 it sponsored a winter short course for young people interested in farming which became an annual event.

Aside from the need for schools for their children, and churches for their worship, the pioneers had other pressing worries. Although they found themselves, in most cases, on desirable and productive land, they had, usually, to whipsaw their timber to produce lumber and, in the case of their crops, they had only local markets since there were no roads in or out of the area. Eventually, a sawmill was started by Sandy McPherson and another one later on by Jake Cathers; both were built near the foot of the Riding Mountain where desirable timber was close at hand. Later still, the Shaw brothers operated a sawmill in the mountain area, although they had first started at the Valley River area. The Shaw mill was actively operated for many years. It supplied much of the lumber for the district through a planing mill and lumber sheds in the new town.

James and Thomas Shaw, however, started a more important mill for the Dauphin area. This was a grist mill, built on the banks of the Valley River in the summer of 1890. The mill was erected after purchasing the equipment in Birtle, shipping it to Minnedosa and then hauling it, piece by piece, across the Riding Mountain, before any roads had been completed. The grist mill at least assured the pioneers that they could get flour from their crops to supply the local needs for bread.

The hopes of the early farmers and merchants for a road to the outside were realized when the provincial government undertook the construction of a road across the Riding Mountain. The construction of this road in 1889 brought to the Dauphin area a young man of thirty-two years of age whose future was closely linked to the history of Dauphin and the Canadian Northwest. That man was Theodore A. Burrows, the son of well-to-do parents in the Ottawa area. His grandfather had been the first settler in the Ottawa district and had been involved in the building of the Rideau canal. Burrows came west in the 1870s where he first became involved in land survey and, in fact, had been in the Dauphin area at that time as a member of a Dominion survey party. Subsequently, he studied law in Winnipeg and then entered the real-estate business there. Burrows Avenue in Winnipeg bears his name. During that time he became involved in the lumber business and it was in this connection that he became embroiled with his brother-in-law, Sir Clifford Sifton, in the timber scandals of the early 1900s.

Theodore Burrows superintended the building of the road over the Riding Mountain to Minnedosa in 1889. He is credited as being helpful in getting the railroad to Dauphin and he may well have been influential in the political aspects of that endeavour. In 1896 he was appointed land commissioner for the Canadian Northern railway and held this post until 1904, at which time he became the representative of the new federal constituency of Dauphin.

Shortly afterwards a road was also constructed between Neepawa and Dauphin taking advantage, as much as possible, of the sand ridges which followed the contour of the shore of the old Lake Agassiz and which had been used for centuries as a secure trail by the Indians. This road was also superintended by Theodore Burrows in 1890 and for years was known as the Burrows Road. These roads suffered greatly from the heavy frosts, spring rains, and surrounding muskeg; although they were a great improvement over what had previously existed, one did not travel them in all times of year or without tools and survival gear.

In spite of these improvements the people of the Dauphin area knew that nothing of consequence would come to them as a result of their strenuous efforts unless they could ship their produce to markets in eastern Canada and the rest of the world. There would be no benefits from productive land or greater land clearance if grain could not reach the outside in large quantities. And so the idea that a railroad was essential to the community found fertile ground in the minds of the settlers. Southern Manitoba already benefited from the extension of the Canadian Pacific Railway across the prairies and as that railway continued west it allowed for much more rapid settlement along its course. In addition, many smaller branch lines had been granted charters in the provincial session of 1880, over which a major political struggle had taken place.

Parallelling the C.P.R. as far as Portage la Prairie and then swinging slightly north of the C.P.R. was the Grand Trunk Pacific railway which traversed Manitoba south of the Riding Mountain on its way to Saskatoon. The Northern Pacific Railway had branch lines in southern and western Manitoba. The Dauphin area felt the need of a railway line as well. It petitioned the provincial government to allow a railway charter for the construction of a line into the central part of the province north of the Riding Mountain.

The Manitoba and Northwestern line had been built as far as Gladstone, about forty miles northwest of Portage la Prairie. It had been started in 1883 and although it had reached Gladstone, further extension was prevented for lack of funds, as was true for many small railroads in that era. These were frustrating years for Dauphin's pioneers who waited year after year for the coming railroad.

In 1895, however, William Mackenzie and Donald Mann bought up the moribund charter of the Lake Manitoba Railway and Canal Company which had been granted in 1889 but had not proceeded at that time. This charter allowed for large land and cash subsidies when and if the railway was completed. Mackenzie and Mann were able to get a guarantee from the Manitoba legislature of eight thousand dollars per mile. With this guarantee, the construction expertise of Herbert Holt and the superintendency of David Hanna, they began the construction of a railway to the Dauphin country in the spring of 1896. This line was the beginning of the Canadian Northern Railway, later to be extended across the country and eventually to form a large part of the amalgamation of smaller railroads into the Canadian National System.

Meanwhile, the vexing question as to the path the railroad would follow through the Dauphin country created a turmoil in the communities of Lake Dauphin and Gartmore. The sense of rivalry between the two communities was keen and it was, perhaps, reasonable that each argued that it should be the favoured site for the railroad. Dauphin Lake pleaded that it was the larger community and should become the centre of activity. Gartmore, on the other hand, did its best to promote itself as the more desirable location. The railway, however, solved the problem by choosing a course which fell midway between the two communities. The progress of construction was excellent. Each week the steel rails penetrated further and further into the northwest towards Dauphin.

From the announcement in April of 1896 until the rails crossed Gartmore Road in the new townsite, the area was a beehive of activity. Business firms already in the area enlarged their premises or sold out to more ambitious entrepreneurs. New businesses and businessmen flocked to the new town. There was an upsurge in the acquisition of new homesteads. By July, a news item from Toronto told of a shipment of boxcars for the "Lake Dauphin Railway". The boxcars were designed with the new Jenny coupler, a safety device allowing for the locking and unlocking of cars with a lever. Track began to be laid from Gladstone on August 4, 1896 and, since the track-laying machine was the first of its kind in Canada, it was said that it could lay two miles of track per day. Thirty thousand ties were being sent from Rat Portage. As the tracks were laid, business began on the new line as soon as the roadbed was stable. During that building season the engineer for the line was W.A. (Billy) Walker, while the first conductor was "Dad" Risteen. David Hanna pays each of these men a high compliment in his *Trains Of Remembrance* which should be read by anyone interested in railroad history.

Progress on the line continued with some difficulties. On one occasion fifty Italian workers, who had been brought from Toronto, walked off the job when they found they were obliged to buy their room and board from the contractor at four dollars a week, when it was their wish to board themselves. In addition, they found they had to provide their own shovels and wheelbarrows. All this for one and one-half dollars a day in wages. Other workers found that they could often earn more working in the harvest fields than on the railroad. They, too, jumped the jobs.

By mid-September grading had been completed to Elliott siding (McCreary) and by October 28, 1896, Glen Campbell made the first shipment of cattle over the Dauphin railroad by loading them at Ochre River and sending them east. On Saturday, November 5, 1896 the tracks crossed the main street of the new town. The first railway freight received in Dauphin was brought in by J.B. Nicholson on November 5, 1896. The first telegraphic despatch was sent by H.W.D. Armstrong on Monday, November 9, 1896.

Mackenzie and Mann, having determined the course for the railway line, also determined that the new townsite would be located on 10-25-19W., a section of land belonging partially to George Barker and partially to William Whitmore but being actively farmed in 1896 by Herb Chute as the railway was being laid. As soon as the wheat crop had been harvested in the fall, surveyors laid out

As soon as the survey was completed, lots went on sale on October 7, 1896. The honour of buying the first lot went to Thomas McLean, who bought property at the northwest corner of Gartmore Road (Main Street) and Front Street for two hundred and fifty dollars. Here, he built his Grandview Hotel, a landmark in Dauphin throughout its life, until it was destroyed by fire in the winter of 1932.

The sale of the other lots was brisk and it was obvious that the citizens of Dauphin Lake and Gartmore had determined to join forces and to move their respective properties into the new town where now, because they had access to the outside world, they could turn their entire energies to the realization of the full potential of the land. By December, seventy buildings had been moved into Dauphin.

It was against this background of optimism and renewed energy that so many Dauphinites turned out on December 23, 1896 to see W.A. Walker, engineer and "Dad" Risteen, conductor, bring in the first passenger train to the newest village in Manitoba.

Chapter 2 — Early Settlers

Books and Reports:

Ferguson, Eva. *The Story of Dauphin Pioneer Days.* Provincial Archives of Manitoba, 1955.
Hanna, D.B. *Trains of Recollection.* Toronto: McMillan & Comany, 1924.
Malcolm, James L. *I Took to the Road.* Provincial Archives of Manitoba, Microfilm #199.
Preston, Emmy, ed. *Pioneers of Grandview and District.* Pioneer Book Committee. Carillon Press, 1976.
Letters:
McKillop, Bruce, re The McKillops and The Gillies, John McKillop. Collection of A. Little.
Reid, Bernice, re The Gorbys. Collection of A. Little.

EARLY SETTLERS 47

PIONEERS OF THE DAUPHIN DISTRICT: 1883 to 1895
(Read left to right)

Adam, W.
Adams, George
Akers, A. & Mrs.
Alguire, William & Mrs.
Allin, James & Mrs.
Anderson, James Fraser
Armstrong, Adam
Armstrong, Andrew & Mrs.
Armstrong, Hugh
Atkinson, G. & Mrs.
Barker, G. & Mrs.
Bates, W.S.
Batty, Edward
Beach, Charles & Mrs.
Beauchamp, Dr. & Mrs.
Bell, John
Bielby, Robert
Bigham, Robert & Mrs.
Bigham, John & Mrs.
Birnie, Robert & Mrs.
Birss, Alex & Mrs.
Blackmore, James
Bogie, Thomas
Bole, A.H.
Bond, A.A.
Bonnett, A. & Mrs.
Boughen, F. & Mrs.
Bouvette, A. & Mrs.
Boyd, John & Mrs.
Boyd, Robert & Sarah
Bradshaw, E.A.
Brain, A.W. & O.H.
Brown, James Wilkins
Brown, T.L.
Brown, William & Mrs.
Bruce, David
Bryce, J. & Mrs.
Buchannon, James
Buchannon, William
Burke, William
Burrows, T.A.
Burton, George & Mrs.
Buzza, Joseph
Cameron, M.
Campbell, D.A. & Mrs.
Campbell, J. & Mrs.
Campbell, Robert
Campsall, B.W.
Cannon, William
Cardiff, Robert
Carmichael, W. & Mrs.
Cathers, J. & Mrs.
Cauldry, Lou & August
Chamberlain, W. & Mrs.
Chambers, George
Chapman, William
Chard, J.D. & Mrs.
Cheshire, William
Chute, Herb. & Mrs.
Clark, Joseph & Mrs.
Clarke, A.C.
Cleaver, William & Frank
Clementson, William C.
Clendening, Thomas
Cockerton, Robert
Cocks, John
Coles, J.J. & W.D.
Condon, Morris
Coombs, Alfred
Cosway, C.L.
Coulthard, Guy
Cox, Thomas
Craig, Thomas
Crawford, William

Cruise, Robert & Mrs.
Curle, R.E.
Dewar, Donald
Dickson, James
Drinkwater, W. & Mrs.
Durham, Thomas & Harry
Edwards, John & Mrs.
Esplen, Archie & Mrs.
Farrell, W.J. & Mrs.
Farquhar, John
Fee, Frank
Ferguson, Albert
Freeman, Joe
Fry, Charles & Mrs.
Fulton, Hugh
Gelling, W.R. & Jos.
Gilbert, W.
Gorby, Thomas & Mrs.
Graham, Capt.
Gray, Albert E.
Gunne, Robert & Mrs.
Hall, William M.
Halpenny, W.T.
Hartley, John
Hassard, G., J. & F.
Hayes, James
Hedderley, John
Herriot, A.
Hewitt, Edward
Hodshell, T.
Hoover, Henry
Horton, A.T.
Hueston, William
Inkster, James & Jane
Iredale, Thomas & Mrs.
Jardine, Gilbert
Johnston, Albert
Johnston Bros.
Jones, William

Curle, F.J.
Daniel, John
Dickson, D. & Mrs.
Domil, John
Dunfield, William
Durston, John & Mrs.
Elgert, John & Mrs.
Esplen, Alex & Henry
Farrer, W.F.
Fawcett, J.B. & Mrs.
Felker, Chris. & Mrs.
Ferguson, R.G. & Mrs.
Friend, James
Fulford, George
Geekie, Stuart
Gibson, Robert & Mrs.
Gillies, Mrs. Mary
Graeme, P.J.F.
Grant, Donald
Greaves, R.S.
Hall, J.H. & Mrs.
Halliday, John
Happell, James
Harris, James A.
Hassard, John & Mrs.
Hayes, Robert Mrs.
Henderson, A.J. & Mrs.
Hewis, W.H.
Hicks, C. & Mrs.
Hood, George
Hoy, Charles & Mrs.
Hosegood, Therese
Hughes, Henry & Richard
Inkster, John & Mrs.
Jackson, Andrew
Jensen, Chris.
Johnston, Alfred
Johnston, Sidney
Jones, William & Mrs.

EARLY SETTLERS

Kearns, John
Keats, Edward & Mrs.
Kennedy, J.
Kerr, James & Mrs.
Kitt, Mrs. Eliza Ward
Leigh, George & Mrs.
Lucas, Robert
Macneill, Harry
McClean, J.R. & Mrs.
McCorvie, Harry
McDonald, J. & Mrs.
McDowell, James & Mrs.
McInnis, James
McIntosh, John & Mrs.
McKeever, James & Mrs.
McKerchar, Alex.
McKillop, Dan & Mrs.
McKone, Thomas
McLaughlin, John & Mrs.
McLeod, Norman
McMartin, Edward
McNabb, Thomas & Mrs.
McNaughton, Harry & Mrs.
McPherson, Fred & Mrs.
McQuarrie, Charles & Allan
MacNeill, Donald
Mahoney, John
Mansfield, Joseph
Maynard, Alfred & Mrs.
Metcalfe, Thomas
Moore, Herbert & Frederick
Mullen, William
Newton, Frederick
Nex, Fred & Albert
Padfield, James
Parson, Thomas & Mrs.
Paynter, Henry & John
Perry, Samuel & Mrs.
Pitts, Isaiah & Mrs.

Keats, A.H. & Mrs.
Kelly, James & Mrs.
Kennedy, John & Mrs.
Kilty, Frank & Mrs.
Lee, Matthew & Mrs.
Liddie, W.F.
Lumsden, John & H.W.
McCallum Bros.
McCorvie, Archibald
McDonald, Angus
McDonald, N. & Mrs.
McFarlane, John
McIntosh, Capt. & Mrs.
McIntosh, William
McKenzie, M. & Mrs.
McKinnon, Don & Mrs.
McKillop, James
McLaughlin, Charles & Mrs.
McLean, Archibald
McLeod, Robert & Mrs.
McMunn, William & Mrs.
McNaughton, Clementine
McPherson, A.J. & Mrs.
McRae, William
Machan, R.S.
Macnutt, Stewart
Malcolm, A. & Mrs.
Marsden, Harrop
Melsome, Percy
Miller, William & Mrs.
Morrison, Leslie
Murray, William
Nicholson, J. & Mrs.
Ogilvie, H.G. & T.W.
Park, Rollie
Payne, Albert
Pepper, James
Pilgrim, H. & Mrs.
Playford, Chance, James & Thomas

Pollon, Thomas & Mrs.
Porterfield, Ed.
Race, Joseph & Mrs.
Rathwell, Joseph
Richards, Thomas
Rintoul, William
Roberts, G.J. & T.R.
Ross, Noel & Chester
St. John, Adam
Sandgren, Andy & Mrs.
Satterthwaite, Thomas
Seale, John
Shand, James & Mrs.
Short, Allan
Sinclair, Dan & Mrs.
Smythe, James W.
Spence, Thomas J.
Spillett, Isaac & Mrs.
Steenson, W.S. & W.J.
Stinson, William
Stuart, R.N.
Tennant, Enoch
Timm, William & Mrs.
Turrell, Samuel R.
Wakelin, George
Warner, H.E.
Watson, John Wesley
Whiteman, John & Mrs.
Whitmore, Thomas & Mrs.
Whitmore, Frank
Wilkinson, Robert
Williams, William
Willoughby, George & Mrs.
Winters, William & Mrs.
Wishart, Robert & Mrs.
Wood, Paul
Yeaman, George

Porter, Jake & Mrs.
Potts, J.
Rasmussen, R.J.
Rice, Joseph & Mrs.
Richardson, R.D.
Roas, Heriot C.
Robinson, James & Mrs.
Rosser, J.G.
Sangreen, A. & Mrs.
Sanderson, Ed.
Scott, A.E.
Sexsmith, David
Shaw, James & Thomas
Short, Herb.
Smith, Fred. C.
Sorenson, Jens
Spencer, A.U. & Mrs.
Stapleton, Arthur
Stewart, W.J.
Strang, Gavin & Mrs.
Switzer, Albert & Mrs.
Terry, Walter & Mrs.
Tucker, Joseph & Mrs.
Vance, J.D.
Walker, James
Warner, Thomas & Mrs.
Watt, H.O.
Whitmore, Harry & Mrs.
Whitmore, William & Mrs.
Wickes, Thomas & Mrs.
Williams, G.R.
Williamson, James & Mrs.
Winters, V. & Mrs.
Winterton, J. & Mrs.
Wood, P.C.
Wright, William

3

THE SEARCH FOR LIBERTY

Early Ukrainian immigrants to Canada honoured Dr. Josef Oleskow for his contributions to their welfare and his encouragement of their emigration to a new and promising farmland. Their sons and daughters have continued to hold him in the same esteem as a recognition that it was he, more than any other person, who laid the groundwork for a mass exodus of Slavic people from eastern Europe to the plains of Western Canada. He has been likened to a modern day Moses who led his people from the hardship and miseries of their Austrian provinces to a land free of aristocratic and bureaucratic suppression, where a chance to thrive depended on a man's willingness to work.

Other Ukrainians had reached Canada before Dr. Oleskow organized for large and frequent migrations. In the main, these immigrants were in military units or were diplomatic officials. A few were individual workers. None of them, however, formed any organized community and most were not permanent residents.

In 1891 the steamship *Oregon* brought Wasyl Elyniak and Iwan Pyllipiw, the two earliest settlers, to this country. After looking over several possible settlement sites and working for a short time in Gretna, Manitoba, Pyllipiw returned in the following year intending to bring the two families to Canada. His return to Canada was delayed, however, when he was harrassed for several weeks by the Austrian authorities and, finally, jailed for a month for actively encouraging emigration amongst his countrymen. The result of his "agitation" was that in the year 1892 a large group emigrated, arriving in Quebec nine months after Pyllipiw and Elyniak had first arrived. All of this group settled in Alberta.

"Cross of Freedom" and plaque commemorating the arrival of Ukrainian settlers who took up homesteads near Valley River, Manitoba, in 1896.

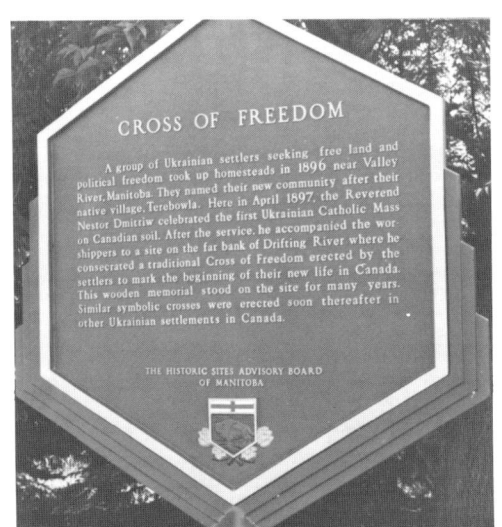 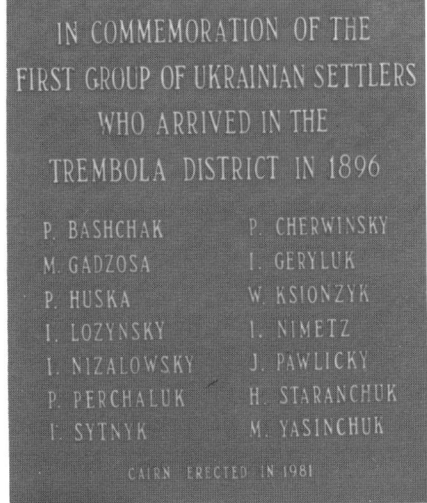

Commemorative plaque from the cairn to the first Ukrainian settlers in the Trembola District.

It fell to Josef Oleskow, a professor in a teachers' seminary in Lemburg, Austria (Lviv) to lay the solid foundations necessary for the successful transfer of large numbers of families from eastern Europe to the open lands of the Canadian west.

Dr. Oleskow had been acutely aware of the hardships being experienced by the farmers of his homeland, particularly in the eastern portion of the then powerful Austro-Hungarian empire. Overpopulation created serious problems. Land was subdivided so that more and more farmers could be accommodated on the same land holding, but as the farms diminished in size, they became incapable of enough production to feed growing families or to sell or barter with others. Heavy taxation took a large part of the returns from farming and, in some cases, after the harvest, the farmer was left in further debt than before his year's work.

Political situations for the peasant farmer grew worse as each year went by. The result of all these conditions was poverty, frustration, lack of education and a general sense of despondency. Profits from the labour of the peasants were enjoyed by the land-owning elite of Austria who encouraged their toil and discouraged their education. Bukovina and Galicia were two provinces in the western Ukraine where these conditions were most severe although all of the provinces were affected to a serious degree.

This unhappy situation was taken particular advantage of by the immigration agents of Brazil which, at the time, was encouraging immigration of European farmers. Unhappily, the immigrants were often given land in the middle of heavy jungle with no training in the ways of protecting themselves against heat, humidity, wild animals, poisonous snakes or tropical storms. In addition, the agents in Europe were extracting unreasonable sums from the emigrants or taking their land at rock-bottom prices in return for assisting with the emigration. For many, the Brazilian experience was a very unhappy one.

Dr. Oleskow had always opposed the removal of farmers and their families to Brazil. He opposed it, not only on the ground that he thought the charges were exorbitant or that the land was unfit for the European farmer but, also, because the vacated land in Europe was falling into foreign hands. It was Oleskow's wish, and also the wish of the emigrating farmers, that their lands should pass to other Ukrainian families so as to relieve the land congestion, even to a small degree.

Glowing reports of the availability and the quality of land in Canada had already reached Dr. Oleskow. He determined to seek out more information about the possibility of a large emigration to Canada. His plans were careful and far-sighted. To his thorough and honest research the Ukrainians and Canada owe a great debt. There was never any evidence of self-enriching or self-aggrandizing aspects to his motives or actions.

Oleskow knew that the average peasant family consisted of five members who possessed about seven acres of land from which a farmer could expect to harvest less than thirty bushels of grain. His enquiries about Canada led him to believe that each family, for a small homestead claim payment of ten dollars, could expect to get one hundred and sixty acres of land. This was more than twenty times as much land as they then held so that, even if only a portion of the land was productive, their chances for an improved economic well-being were very good. In addition, he believed that life in the new land would free them from heavy state bureaucracy and taxation and that in a new environment the chances of progress for them and for their children would be greatly improved.

Dr. Oleskow spoke and wrote "About Free Lands". He initiated correspondence with the Canadian government, both in Ottawa and in London, England in order to learn as much as he could about Canada's west and its agricultural potential. Secondly, he sounded out the government about its willingness to accept large numbers of Canadian immigrants and its views as to the practical aspects of land costs, transportation and its costs, provision of seed grains, alternate employment and its availability especially during the winters of the emigrés early years. Finally, he offered himself and other local representatives for a visit to Canada to gain first-hand information as to the land, the climate, the terms for immigration, the desirable areas for colonization and other considerations. He also agreed to return and report to the people about his experiences and findings and, if there was a desire for emigration, to organize and assist in the orderly movement of families from eastern Europe to western Canada.

Dr. Oleskow was a man of his word. Following a series of letters to Canadian officials and their satisfaction that he was, indeed, a man to be trusted, a visit to Canada was arranged for himself and I. Dorundiak. They left Lviv on July 12, 1895. They met with Sir Charles Tupper, Canadian High Commissioner in London, on July 29 and then continued on across the Atlantic, arriving in Montreal on August 12, 1895, just exactly one month after leaving Ukraine. They were treated hospitably by the Canadian authorities and their agents in Winnipeg and westwards. Oleskow, himself, impressed those who met him as a man of good sense and of high and sincere aspirations for his countrymen. He returned to Lviv full of hope that many immigrants would and could be absorbed into the wide expanses of land which he had personally viewed during his visit.

On his return he fulfilled his promise to report to the people and he began to organize for their departure to the new land. He organized a major conference in Lviv which set about to assist the emigrés; it also organized a credit institution to assist in purchasing land from departing farmers so that the land would remain in Ukrainian hands. He wrote another major brochure entitled "About Emigration" in which he described the country he had seen and the requirements for those who contemplated living in Canada.

Much of the land which impressed him lay in the new province of Manitoba, mainly in the northwest in the Dauphin Lake area and in a line extending north and west of it. The attraction of this land was that it was very similar to the land in and around the Carpathian mountains in Austria, from whence he expected to get many, if not most, of his emigrés. In particular, the Ukrainians who emigrated to Manitoba came from Galicia or Bukovina, two provinces in the Ukraine which bordered on the Carpathian mountains. The land was wooded and undulating. Dr. Oleskow was impressed that the land in Manitoba, sheltered by the Riding mountains on the south and by the Duck mountains on the north and west was also wooded and traversed by several small rivers and streams. It was so much like the Ukrainian lands that he felt reassured about the security of the future emigrés.

During and coincident with all this activity, the Emigration Relief Committee, which had been established as a result of the Lviv conference, organized a group of one hundred and seven persons who left on April 30, 1896 under the care of Vladymir Oleskow, the doctor's brother. This group settled at or near Edna, Alberta and began the colony named "Ruska Svoboda" (Ruthenian Freedom). Other groups followed in rapid succession and, in the majority, came to Manitoba. In July, 1896 a group settled near Stuartburn and established "Rus", the first colony in Manitoba. Some twenty-seven families and some single men arrived in August, 1896 and settled eighteen miles east of Dominion City, later expanding their colonies to Gardenton, Tolstoi, Vita, Rosa, Caliento and other southeastern Manitoba points.

Very soon afterwards Dr. Oleskow wrote to the Canadian High Commissioner in London saying:

> I am sending a party of settlers, about thirty families, who will leave Hamburg on April 11 for Canada through Messrs. Spiro & Co. This party I will direct to Lake Dauphin district, please to inform me whether there is enough space, especially on the south shores of the Valley River for a greater number of Settlers. The failure of this first expedition would close forever the flow of emigrants from this country.

A memo directed to the High Commissioner to assist in framing a reply to Oleskow's question mentioned that although many lands were already occupied in the area, there were some vacant sections in townships 24, 25, 26 and 27 in range 21 W. On further investigation, however, it was determined that melting snow and heavy, early, spring rains made the country virtually inaccessible. It was recommended that the party of immigrants be directed to Whitemouth, east and slightly north of Winnipeg. By this time the party was already on the high seas. Dr. Oleskow had serious reservations about Whitemouth because of earlier experiences. The group, also, when it arrived in Winnipeg, was unenthusiastic about the Whitemouth area. The result was that most of the group went to join their countrymen in the Edmonton area and three families settled in the Beausejour area of Manitoba.

Contrary to Dr. Oleskow's prediction, immigration did not "close forever". Another group, arriving in Canada on August 21, 1896 split up on reaching Winnipeg. Some went to Dauphin. In that group going to Dauphin was Basil Ksionzyk, from the village of Zwale in the district of Trembowla, who sent reports back to Dr. Oleskow about farming possibilities in the area. Basil

Ksionzyk took out a homestead on N.E. ¼ 19-26-20 in the Valley River area and other settlers had homesteads nearby, all in township 26, range 20. Those early pioneers included P. Bastchak, P. Cherwinsky, M. Gadzosa, I. Geryluk, P. Huska, W. Ksionzyk, I. Lozynski, I. Nimetz, I. Nizalowsky, J. Pawlicky, P. Perchaluk, H. Staranchuk, I. Sytnyk and M. Yasinchuk.

In the spring of 1897, Father Nestor Dmytriw of Philadelphia, visited the colony, probably on April 12, 1897, where he sang the first Ukrainian mass in Manitoba and where he dedicated a "Cross of Liberty" which the settlers had erected on a hill to commemorate the liberty they attained in 1896. *The Dauphin Pioneer Press* reported his visit in August of 1897, but this may simply be the result of slow communication in a new settlement especially during and following the spring thaw and early spring rains.

Another of Father Dmytriw's duties while in the Dauphin area was to marry Caroline Zarowny, the daughter of a Ukrainian pioneer, herself born on Kosiv in Ukraine, to Frederick Nex, a printer for the *Dauphin Press.* Nex was a Londoner who sought his fortune in Canada. He attempted to publish an English-Ukrainian newspaper in Dauphin about the turn of the century but the enterprise failed for lack of subscriptions. He later operated a store in Sifton.

The district settled by Ksionzyk was named Trembowla and a school, erected in 1897 but organized as a school district in 1899, was also called Trembowla in honour of the home district in Ukraine. These settlers were the only Ukrainian settlers in the area in the winter of 1896-97.

In the spring of 1897 many more Ukrainians came to Canada, a considerable number of whom went to the Dauphin area. Some of them left Hamburg on April 10, 1897. After a stormy and frightening Atlantic crossing on the *Arcadia,* an old steam and sailing ship, they arrived in Quebec after twenty-one horrendous days at sea. In that group were Paul and Katharina Potocki with two children, Nicholas and Michael, the latter of whom was to practise medicine in Dauphin for many years, until his death in 1970. Following a further trip to Winnipeg, four hundred and seventy-five of the group left by special train for Dauphin where they were among the first immigrants to be received and sheltered in the new

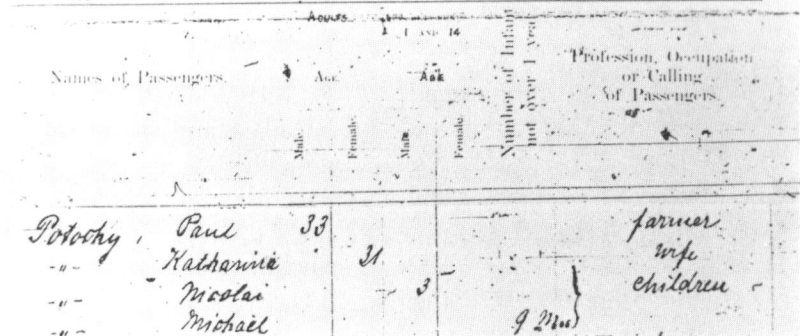

Extract from the passenger list of the S.S. "Arcadia".

A pioneer Ukrainian home.

Ukrainian woman winnowing wheat with a homemade sieve.

immigration hall which had been built close to the railway tracks at the corner of Mackenzie Avenue and Vermilion Street. Most of these immigrants came from the provinces of Galicia and Bukovina. The Galicians were usually Greek Catholics while the Bukovinians were usually of the Greek Orthodox persuasion. *The Dauphin Press* of May 5, 1897 notes that J.N. Mouat, the supervisor of the immigration "sheds" had "his hands full looking after the Galician immigrants". Paul Wood, having sold his land to Bill Buchannon, moved to Sifton where he performed a valuable service as an interpreter for the new immigrants.

It wasn't long before racial prejudice raised its head in the new town, since a further remark in the same newspaper of May 26, 1897 states, "It might be well for our merchants to keep an eye on their goods when the Galicians are around as there is good evidence to the effect that there are sneak thieves among them". D.B. Hanna, in his *Trains of Remembrance* relates several other acts, by the businessmen of Dauphin, which were distinguished by their lack of understanding or charity towards the new immigrants.

By June 2, 1897, four hundred more Galicians arrived by train. The immigration sheds became one of the busiest spots in town for many months as more and more immigrants arrived. Each new wave of immigrants arriving at Halifax or Quebec during 1897 brought many whose destination was Dauphin or Trembowla. On the *S.S. Prussia,* which arrived in Halifax on May 22, 1897, there were thirty-nine families who gave Trembowla as their destination. Most of these immigrants settled on land at Valley River or on land extending north and west of the Valley River colony on townships 26, 27, 28 and 29 in ranges 19, 20, 21 and 22.

Many of the immigrants were exposed to and survived difficulties from the time they entered Canada. Some immigration agents, railway employees and others took advantage of the poorly eductaed immigrants who had landed in a country where they did not understand the language, the money system or the customs. Charging a fee for services which were to be free, short-changing after a purchase, taking exorbitant fees for advice and other sharp practices were perpetrated on newcomers frequently.

Although most of the settlement in the Dauphin area occurred north and west of the town, one group, housed in the immigration sheds, had a different idea. As the land around the Valley River colony filled up and the desirable properties north and west of this colony were taken, attention turned to land along the northern edge of the Riding Mountain. Much of this land was in the Riding Mountain Timber Reserve but that did not deter some of the immigrants who chose to squat on the land pending a later survey. Although they were advised the land was in the timber reserve, it seems true that some of the land agents did not press the point forcibly and may have been guilty of an unwitting and tacit agreement to the settlement. Most of the land in question was in Tsp. 23, Rge. 20. Subsequently it was determined that all of the odd-numbered sections were legally the property of the C.P.R. as part of the federal government's land deed to that company. In the end, after a great deal of delay and much anxiety for the settlers, the Canadian government, in 1902, removed the land from the timber reserve and arranged for an exchange of other crown lands with the Canadian Pacific Railway. Thus the lands in question were freed for those who had "squatted". This settlement was not accomplished, however, before some of the wardens of the forest reserve had burned some of the buildings on land which had been "squatted" upon. The district became the district of Keld, receiving its name some fourteen or fifteen years later when the name was given to its first post office.

Many of the Ukrainian settlers came to Canada with few resources, certainly not enough to sustain them through the years required to build homes and farm buildings, to clear and break the land and to plant and reap their first harvests. They lived in primitive log and sod homes; sometimes even in riverbank caves. Most of them looked for work, especially winter work, in neighbouring or distant towns. Some travelled long distances by foot to find work. This often necessitated living away from home for long periods while their wives and children kept the home together. Much of the work that was found was in railway construction or maintenance, lumbering, saw-milling, road building or other such work. Frequently, the farm work came after a day's work was done elsewhere.

It was a hard life, in a rough climate, in a country where the language was strange and where the attitude of many of its people towards the Ukrainian immigrant was unhelpful, if not openly hostile. In October 1899, a disastrous prairie fire swept through much of the Dauphin country, including all the Ukrainian settlements at Valley River and Keld and much of the land surrounding Dauphin. In many cases, buildings and animals were lost. The provincial government gave financial aid to all farmers who suffered significant loss but, initially, refused aid to the Ukrainian settlements on the grounds that the Ukrainian settlers were "wards" of the federal government. Eventually, some help was offered by the provincial government on the condition that a lien against the property would be taken. Most of the settlers refused this arrangement and sought help from neighbours and friends and other sympathetic to their dilemma.

Through all these difficulties, the Ukrainians never stopped thanking God for their freedom. They never stopped working hard to improve conditions on the farm. They never forgot that a major reason for leaving Ukraine was to give their chidren an education and the chance of a better life, and they did so. In the main, they never failed, through two world wars, to come to the defence of the country which had opened its doors to them. They ignored the slights directed at them, they preserved a great part of their wonderful culture, they passed on a pride which had seen them through difficult times. They were great pioneer settlers.

By the end of 1901 in Dauphin, Ethelbert and Sifton there were 5500 Ukrainains of whom Immigration Commissioner McCreary said, "They are among our very best settlers". This sentiment was supported by Paul Wood, the official interpreter, who had so much to do in helping the Ukrainian settlers adjust to their new homes. In the *Dauphin Press* of July 21, 1897, an editorial comment quotes Paul Wood as follows: "The amount of substantial and permanent improvements they have made on the land is, considering the time they have been settled, quite surprising — nearly all have neat substantial buildings in course of erection or finished. All have good crops of potatoes and corn, some have put in wheat, oats and barley in small patches, while here and there tobacco and flax, though in most instances too late, appear to be doing well.

Some settlers have in as much as half an acre of corn or nearly an acre of potatoes. Those who have no cookstoves have constructed most ingenious and well-finished bake ovens. These are so constructed that very little fuel is used while giving good heating and baking results. It would "be well if some of our Indians and even white settlers were to copy these. The majority have one to three cows, and some here and there have oxen, wagons and ploughs. I was everywhere met with great courtesy and hospitality. If some of our Canadians and other settlers, who seem to object to any but Canadians or rich Europeans as settlers, would go and see for themselves what these poor but energetic immigrants, all true farmers, as shown by neatness and care in cultivation, are doing, it might tend to dispel their unreasonable and misplaced prejudices."

As years went by the Ukrainians, their children and their grandchildren began to take a larger and more prominent place in Dauphin's business, professional and cultural life until now it is known as Canada's "Ukrainian Capital".

Notes for Chapter 3

Books and Reports:

Czumer, William A. *Recollections About the Life of the First Ukrainian Settlers in Canada.* Edmonton: Canadian Institute of Ukrainian Studies, 1871.

Ewanchuk, Michael. *Pioneer Profiles: Ukrainian Settlers in Manitoba.* Michael Ewanchuk, publisher, 1981.

Kaye, Vladimir J. *Dictionary of Ukrainian Canadiaan Biography: Pioneer Settlers of Manitoba 1891-1900.* Toronto: Ukrainian Canadian Research Foundation, 1975.

Piniuta, Harry. *Land of Pain, Land of Promise.* Saskatoon: Western Proaducer Prairie Books, 1978.

Polloway, Vince. Memo re early days in Dauphin. Provincial Archives of Manitoba, Microfilm #203.

The Ukrainian Canadians: A History. Winnipeg: Ukrainian Academy of Arts & Sciences, 1982.

4

FROM VILLAGE TO TOWN

    The establishment of a new community on section 10, township 25, range 19, west of the first meridian, the site of a wheatfield in the very summer of 1896, created an intensity of activity in the area that was never to be seen again. The railway had chosen a route midway between the earlier settlements and proceeded to lay its tracks in a southeast to northwest direction across the new townsite. Avenues ran parallel to the tracks and streets at right angles to them, so that the main street of the town, named Gartmore Road, ran in a southwesterly to northwesterly direction. The railway effectively divided the town into a "north end" and a "south end", a division which took on some social significance in the minds of some of the later citizens of the town. In the initial village plan both the avenues and the streets were given proper names. It was not until 1908 that most of the avenues were numbered while most of the streets retained their proper names.

    It was evident to everyone in Gartmore village and in Dauphin Lake that survival for business and the opportunity to establish new businesses lay in procuring land and doing business close to the railway lines. Consequently, the fall of 1896 saw the physical removal of the two villages to the newly surveyed land lying along the railway lines in the new townsite. *The Pioneer Press* of 1896, reported that when Joseph Clarke moved his Dauphin House to the new townsite, there was still a roomer in the bed in one of the rooms. He was so upset with the motion that he stayed in bed during the entire move.

    The new town sprang up overnight. Everywhere one looked in the first few months, there were mounds of earth, like giant ant hills, where excavations were being completed; over these, old buildings would be set or new buildings erected. As *The Dauphin Pioneer Press* reported, "the hum of the hammer and saw" was heard in all quarters. By the late fall of 1896, some seventy buildings were already in place and many residences had been moved and were being occupied. It was in that fall, also, that the first Ukrainian settlers, led by Basil Ksionzyk, came to Valley River district. They went little recorded by *The Dauphin Pioneer Press*.

The torrid pace of the building and moving activities and the numbers of people coming into the area to seize the opportunities for business or for land speculation, required that some order be maintained on a communal basis. Building standards, sanitation, public safety, traffic, water supplies and fire safety were amongst the concerns of the first citizens. The next few years were crucial to the development of the village and a sane and rational approach to these common problems was essential for solid progress.

The businessmen of Dauphin lost no time in promoting a Board of Trade. A meeting was held as early as January, 1897, for that purpose. The first meeting, however, resolved itself into the formation of a Citizens' Committee to establish priorities for improvements and to obtain the right to proceed with the necessary action for eventual incorporation as a legal entity such as a village or a town. George Barker, whose farm had become the original townsite; Noel Ross, who operated a store at Gartmore; J.B. Nicholson, who had come to the Dauphin area in 1890 with his father; J.A. Maughan, one of Dauphin's early solicitors and J.F. Hosegood, who became a leading merchant in the new village, carried on the business of the community for eighteen months, until the first election in August, 1898, just four weeks after a village charter had been granted, on July 11, 1898.

Their first action was to raise $800 by assessment, to be spent as follows:

Sidewalks	$500
Fire Protection	$125
Streets	$100
Secretary & Overseer	$50
Incidentals	$25

By March, 1897, the committee learned that incorporation as

a village required a population of at least five hundred people. They, thus, continued their work, awaiting that day.

A volunteer fire brigade was formed in 1897 with R. Hunt as the chief and Frank Morrison as the assistant chief. Frank Morrison will be remembered as one of the best ice-makers, skating or curling, that Dauphin had in those early days. Most knew him as "Dad" Morrison. He was also a cement maker who built many of the cement foundations in the early town.

Wooden sidewalks were built along Main Street from the tracks to Barker Avenue in 1897 and also from the Manor House to the Massey Harris warehouse on Main Street South. Within a year the committee had determined to install plank sidewalks all over town. Some were to be built by residents; some by the town. A bridge across the Vermilion River at Burrows Avenue was completed in 1897. At the time it was the only traffic crossing from the west and the north. Another bridge, to cross the river at Wakefield Avenue, was started.

Land was bought from Harry Whitmore for a cemetery but arrangements had yet to be made about its financing. The formation of the Rural Municipality in 1898 made it possible for the two councils to share the cost of upkeep. There was a major problem for the committee in attempting to keep the lanes in town in a decent state of neatness and cleanliness. Some were described as filthy. This condition, and the presence of outhouses, contributed in a major way to the presence of typhoid fever in the community. It was to be a continuing problem.

Much of the time of the Citizens' Committee was occupied by the desire for incorporation. Initially, the incorporation was prevented by lack of sufficient population. The influx of settlers and business people with their families soon ended that problem. In May, 1898, it was said that incorporation was proceeding well. Within weeks, however, legal entanglements caused delays. The petition for incorporation pleaded that all of section 10 be included in the townsite. This meant the inclusion of the quarter section homestead of William Whitmore which occupied the southwest quarter of 10-25-19W. By August of 1898, however, all legal tangles had been resolved and elections were held for the council of the new village. The first mayor was George Barker. He had four councillors to assist him in his work: H.P. Nicholson, Albert Williscraft, David Sutherland and Robert Hunt. A secretary-treasurer, William Murray, was to be paid ten dollars a month for his services, while James. G. Harvey, Dauphin's first lawyer, was appointed village solicitor at a salary of twenty-five dollars for the balance of the year.

During all this time Dauphin found itself in the midst of a building boom. The new immigration hall at MacKenzie and Vermilion was built at a cost of three thousand dollars. This hall and the town hall on Burrows Avenue were fitted with bunks in preparation for a large group of Doukhobors which was expected at any time. Three hundred Doukhobors arrived in January of 1899 and another four hundred in March of the same year. Almost all of them moved further west to Saskatchewan.

Residences were erected at a record pace, as quickly as supplies could be found. Businesses, also, arose or were enlarged. The appetites for building materials seemed insatiable. A site had been found on Burrows Avenue for a new post office. That was fortunate, as a disastrous fire in mid-May of 1900 wiped out several buildings along the south side of Burrows Avenue west of Main Street. A new post office was rapidly constructed on Burrows Avenue, a site retained until the 1960s.

Fire had been a serious threat in the business centre for years. It was only in September of 1899, however, when a fire protection by-law was passed by the voters. This set aside six thousand dollars for a new chemical-pump fire-wagon and a firehall site. The site chosen was at the northwest corner of Vermilion and Front Streets.

Already many of the names of those who remained in Dauphin and built a solid base for the prospering community, had made their appearances. Those who had come earlier to farm the land has already proven their worth. The Durstons, Malcolms, Esplens, Cruises, Birss's, Winters, Cathers, Dunfields, Wisharts, McKillops, Boughens, Gillies, Chutes, Buchannons, Gorbys, Hassards, McDonalds, Nicholsons, Playfords, Spilletts, Whitmores, Lees, Millers, Pollons and many others were established on their farms. They needed merchants, tradesmen and professional men to match the farming community.

And they got them.

They got some of them from the business and professional men already in the area and many more from the flood of the people who, after the railroad reached Dauphin, seized the opportunity to add variety and volume to the enterprises to be found in town.

Amongst those who were already serving the community and who simply moved their premises to Dauphin were Captain David McIntosh who, in partnership with J.F. Hosegood, opened the Pioneer Store, a hardware store, at the corner of Gartmore Road and Burrows Avenue, a site which for many years was considered the prime real estate location in Dauphin. For most of Dauphin's life the business section centred around this corner. Advertisements for McIntosh & Hosegood are found in the first issue of the *Dauphin Pioneer Press* of April 1, 1896. J.H. Bigham moved his saddlery and harness shop from Dauphin Lake into town where it prospered for years. This was the same J.H. Bigham who had established such a fine reputation in the pioneer settlement as a very good man with an adze. Charles McLean of Dauphin Lake moved his Leland House into Dauphin where it occupied the southeast corner of Gartmore Road and Burrows Avenue for several years, until replaced by the Clarke Block. Joseph Clarke, another early hotelier, moved his Dauphin House to the northeast corner of the same intersection where it later became known as the King's Hotel. George Irwin, a private banker and broker, moved his bank from Dauphin Lake to Dauphin and started the chain which resulted in the Union Bank and, subsequently, the Bank of Nova Scotia, coming to Dauphin.

Mark Cardiff brought his tinsmith and hardware shop from Gartmore to Dauphin. Others from Gartmore who transferred their business locations to Dauphin were Adam & Company, general merchants; Chester Ross, who with his brother Noel, operated the Cash Store, another general store; J.B. Nicholson who bought the Hudson's Bay Company store in Gartmore and moved it in December 1896 with the help of eleven teams of horses and the necessary drivers and guides; James Walker, a boot and shoe maker and Mortimer Gossett Jackson who brought his real estate and insurance office into town.

Professionally, the people of the Dauphin area had, for years, sought medical advice from Philip J. Beauchamp who came to the Dauphin district in 1886 as a pioneer farmer. He had some training in pharmacy, as a result of which he was often called upon for support of the sick or dying. These demands were so frequent that farming became difficult for him so he continued his medical work in the pioneer settlement for many years. He was always referred to as "Dr." Beauchamp. He became locally famous for his own "Chain Lightning", a medication for horses or humans!

The first qualified doctor in Dauphin was a native son. Dr. J.R. Gunne was the son of Robert Gunne, the first land commissioner in the Dauphin area. After graduating from the Manitoba Medical College Dr. Gunne began his medical practice in Dauphin in 1894. He had a drug store in association with his practice. In the same building was found a jewellery store, operated initially by A.H. McIntyre and later by Dodimead & Company. Dr. Beauchamp opened a drug store in 1898 where the Pollon Block was later built. It was totally destroyed in a fire on Christmas Eve, 1901 and never reopened.

Dr. Gunne continued his practice in Dauphin until 1905 when, at least partially for health reasons, he left Dauphin. He undertook post-graduate studies in London and in Vienna the following year and returned to Rat Portage, Ontario where he practised with his brother until 1910. In that year he returned to Europe for further studies in diseases of the eyes, ears, nose and throat. On his return on this occasion he entered practice in Winnipeg in association with Dr. A.W. Moody. He kept in close contact with his friends in Dauphin and frequently came to Dauphin to consult in his specialty. In 1919 he returned to Dauphin permanently to become a founder of the Dauphin Medical Clinic. He remained until his death in 1935. He was one of Dauphin's staunchest citizens and a strong promoter of its welfare.

Dr. Gunne was joined in practice in 1897 by Ernest E. Bottomley. A small, prim man, Dr. Bottomley, born in England, graduated in medicine from the Manitoba Medical College in 1895 and came to Dauphin soon afterwards. In 1899, as a result of an epidemic of typhoid fever, he turned his home into a hospital for the very ill patients. It was this beginning which promoted the drive for a hospital in Dauphin. In July of 1900 a third doctor, Dr.

Samuel Duncan Cameron, began a practice which, although successful, was short-lived, as the doctor left a year later to work with the North-West Mounted Police in the Yukon. He was succeeded by Dr. W.J. Harrington who arrived in Dauphin in July, 1901 and was to spend the rest of his life there.

T.T. Malcolm, son of Andrew Malcolm, left Dauphin in 1896 for Toronto, where he pursued his studies in pharmacy. By July, 1897 he was back in Dauphin where he was engaged by Dr. Gunne in his drugstore. Soon, he and Dr. Gunne had formed a partnership which was given a new name, "The Medical Hall", and managed by Tom Malcolm.

Dauphin was still being served by intinerant dentists, although Dr. G.C.J. Walker expressed the intention of settling permanently.

The legal needs of the community, until the railroad came, were provided by Mortimer Gossett Jackson, a monocled, wax-moustached, prim man who stood out on the streets of Dauphin by the added virtue of a gold-headed cane. Gossett Jackson had been appointed a notary public in 1896 so was able to satisfy many of the routine legal matters of the community. In August of 1896, Mr. J.G. Harvey located in Dauphin for the purpose of establishing a legal practice. He was, therefore, the first fully qualified lawyer in the area. He was followed, before the close of 1896, by Mr. J.A. Maughan who opened another law office in town. Mr. Maughan was appointed legal counsel for the new railroad company. By March, 1897, A.E. Wilkes had joined the legal group in Dauphin. Another lawyer, Mr. J.A. Campbell, joined Mr. Maughan in the firm of Maughan & Campbell in 1899. Shortly thereafter Mr. Maughan left Dauphin, and Campbell practised alone for several years. A county court was established at Dauphin. It was housed in a building belonging to Thomas Whitmore at the corner of Gartmore and Clifford. Thomas Whitmore was the county clerk. John A. McKinnon was bailiff. Joseph Ryan of Portage la Prairie was the county court judge who visited regularly to hold court.

The Shaw brothers, Thomas and James, had a sawmill and a grist mill in the area.

The problem the new town faced was to attract more businesses of a greater variety so that supplies and repairs, further education and cultural amenities might come with the increased economy of the district. As an agricultural community it was without peer. Those who came when the area was just opening reported very positively about the farming prospects. There were good hay lands of natural grasses, which provided abundantly for those with dairy cattle. The dairy commissioner for Manitoba at that time stated that the Dauphin area was one of the very best dairy districts in the whole of Canada.

Early farmers reported heavy yields of wheat, oats and barley from the land that had been cleared. *The Dauphin Press* reported wheat yields of forty to forty-five bushels per acre in 1895. The very land on which the town was built yielded thirty-five bushels of wheat per acre in its last crop of 1896. Many farms had heavier yields. In the same period oats often ran to one hundred bushels to the acre, barley to sixty bushels and flax to twenty-two bushels to the acre. Some of the early settlers came to Dauphin precisely for the reason that there were such high praises for the crops in the Dauphin district. Andrew Malcolm came over from Minnedosa on the strength of crop reports from the Pollon and Esplen families and from Jack Daniels.

The natural resources of the area were abundant and very important to the settler in an isolated environment. The slopes of the Riding Mountain contained plentiful timber growth for the building of log or frame houses and barns. There was an adequate supply of firewood within relatively easy distances for most farmers, either on their own land or on the mountain slopes or along river courses. Edible game and game birds were in good supply. While berries were abundant and many pleasant days were spent by families, in those times, on summer picnics which included the picking of cranberries, wild strawberries, wild raspberries, chokecherries, pin cherries, blueberries and "saskatoons".

Fish were plentiful in lakes and rivers. Amongst the species common in the waters of the Dauphin area were pickerel, whitefish, perch, goldeye and northern pike. Salt was available from the salt springs and evaporating pans at Winnipegosis and was sold throughout the district. Salt Creek, west of Dauphin, was so named because of salt deposits near its course.

Against this background of agricultural and resource bounty one had to weigh the relative lack of good roads to the outside. The

FROM VILLAGE TO TOWN

provincial government built a road, the Cameron Trail, in 1889, across the Riding Mountain, but it had been little used since it had many steep grades and sharp turns. Most people used the Strathclair Trail which passed about twenty-five miles west of Minnedosa, from Strathclair through the Elphinstone area, across the Riding Mountain about eight miles west of Clear Lake, past Lake Audy and then down the northern slope of the mountain into what is now the Keld area and on to Gartmore and the Dauphin Lake district.

In addition to those trails over the mountain, a road was built in 1890 to Neepawa, often referred to as the "Burrows road", a reference to its superintendent, Theodore A. Burrows. Although this road gave easier access to the outside world, it was in no way an all-weather road.

The advent of the railway, then, was the transportation boom that Dauphin required for its growth as an agricultural and resource area. It needed the railway, not only for passenger service, but even more importantly, for freight service in and out of Dauphin. Initially, the passenger train schedule was a bi-weekly service. Trains left Dauphin Tuesdays and Saturdays at 12:30 p.m. arriving in Portage la Prairie at 7:00 p.m. There the passengers stayed overnight and changed trains to Winnipeg or found other forms of transportation. Return trips depended on trains that left Portage la Prairie on Mondays and Fridays at 11:00 a.m. and arrived in Dauphin at 7:00 p.m. A new train schedule in June, 1897 allowed passengers to reach Winnipeg without staying overnight in Portage. By June of 1898 there were three trains per week. Within the first year of running, rail passenger traffic had doubled. A freight shed to handle the increasing volume of freight was built on Front Street just east of Main Street. In addition, a car shop was to open near the west yards. The railway had agreed to build some cottages west of the river for some of its employees. The stockyards in the east railway yards were completed in 1897.

Shortly thereafter, in 1899, the railway was renamed. The Lake Manitoba Railway and Canal Company, often called the "Dauphin Lake Railway", became the Canadian Northern Railway. A new passenger train schedule was adopted, having the train from Dauphin to Portage la Prairie leave at 5:00 a.m. In 1901 it was announced that the Canadian Northern Railway and the

Northern Pacific Railway were to merge.

What the town needed, in addition to the railroad, were the people and the enterprise to seize the opportunities and to forge a desirable community from its diverse resources and people. The response to the need was gratifying.

Postal services in the early settlement were scanty and sporadic. Prior to 1890, mail for Dauphin and district was sent to Elphinstone, on the south side of the Riding Mountain. There it remained until someone who was making the trip to Dauphin would, obligingly, take the mail with him. There were great delays in delivering with this arrangement. In 1890, on completion of the Strathclair Trail, a mail service was established to bring mail to the settlements of Gartmore and Dauphin Lake, Rigby and Gilbert Plains. David McIntosh was named postmaster at Dauphin Lake; Percy Chipman held the same position at Gartmore. It was David McIntosh's responsibility to drive a four-horse stagecoach to Strathclair and return each week. Often the interval was longer, especially in winter and spring. In 1897, Thomas Iredale was named postmaster for the new village of Daupin and mail came much more quickly by the new railway. David McIntosh for Dauphin Lake and Percy Chipman for Gartmore, relinquished their positions in favour of Mr. Iredale. After the move of the post office to its large quarters on Burrows Avenue, Thomas Iredale "put up a notice requesting the users of chewing tobacco not to spit on the office floor". The editor of the *Dauphin Press* felt that this was "a very reasonable request and one that should be complied with".

The activities of the new settlement were so numerous and varied and the agricultural and commercial opportunities so promising, that it was not long before a need for a community newspaper became evident. *The Dauphin Pioneer Press* was initiated on April 1, 1896 by George Perry who published the first number in the village of Dauphin Lake. In 1897 *The Dauphin Pioneer Press* became simply *The Dauphin Press* when it was bought by a syndicate which included Dr. J.R. Gunne, Bob Malcolm, Theodore Burrows, J. Hedderley, J.B. Hanna, and George King. W.T. Shipley was the editor for a year and was then suceeded by George King.

In 1899 a second newspaper, *The Weekly News*, was started

by Fred Nex and Thomas Odger. George Barker obtained a major interest at a later date and then the newspaper passed to Mr. S.A. Slocum who called his paper *The Spectator* but who published intermittently. Slocum, being a free-spirited soul and perhaps partial to his spirits, published exactly twenty-three issues of his newspaper. He then left town, leaving the business to Fred F. Moore who took over as editor. He, in turn, renamed the paper *The Dauphin Herald*. The *Dauphin Press* was as solidly Liberal-supporting as *The Dauphin Herald* was Conservative-leaning. In June of 1907 Moore sold out to a syndicate comprised of J.G. Harvey, Robert Hunt, R.G. Ferguson, W.H. Arnett and W.D. King, son of George King of *The Dauphin Press*. Within a few years W.D. King became the sole owner and was joined, in 1911, by his father who had left *The Dauphin Press*. The *Dauphin Press* changed hands a few times and in 1917, because of wartime exigencies, it was sold to the owners of the *Herald*. The amalgamation resulted in *The Dauphin Herald and Press*. Later, from 1921 to 1923, *The Dauphin Progress* was born but died in two short years after World War II.

Thomas McLean had the honour of buying the first lot in the newly surveyed village in October, 1896. On it he built the Grandview Hotel, a landmark in Dauphin until it was destroyed by fire on a very cold December night in 1932. The Grandview Hotel was, for years, Dauphin's largest and most popular stopping-off place. It housed several stores on the ground floor and twenty-three bedrooms and a parlour on the second and third floors. Business was so brisk in the first years that a 40' x 20' addition to the full three storeys was added in 1899. Being on the northwest corner of Gartmore Road and Front Street it was exactly opposite the original railway station which was located on the north side of the tracks just west of Gartmore Road. E.W. Johnson tells of a stop-off in Dauphin in the spring of 1898. He went from the train station across the street to the Grandview Hotel. The hotel was filled with people of all descriptions and of many costumes. The rooms were completely booked. He left to find another stopping place and found the "streets were thronged with persons who had either been to the Swan River valley or were going or who were seeking for adventure or speculation in and around Dauphin". He commented also

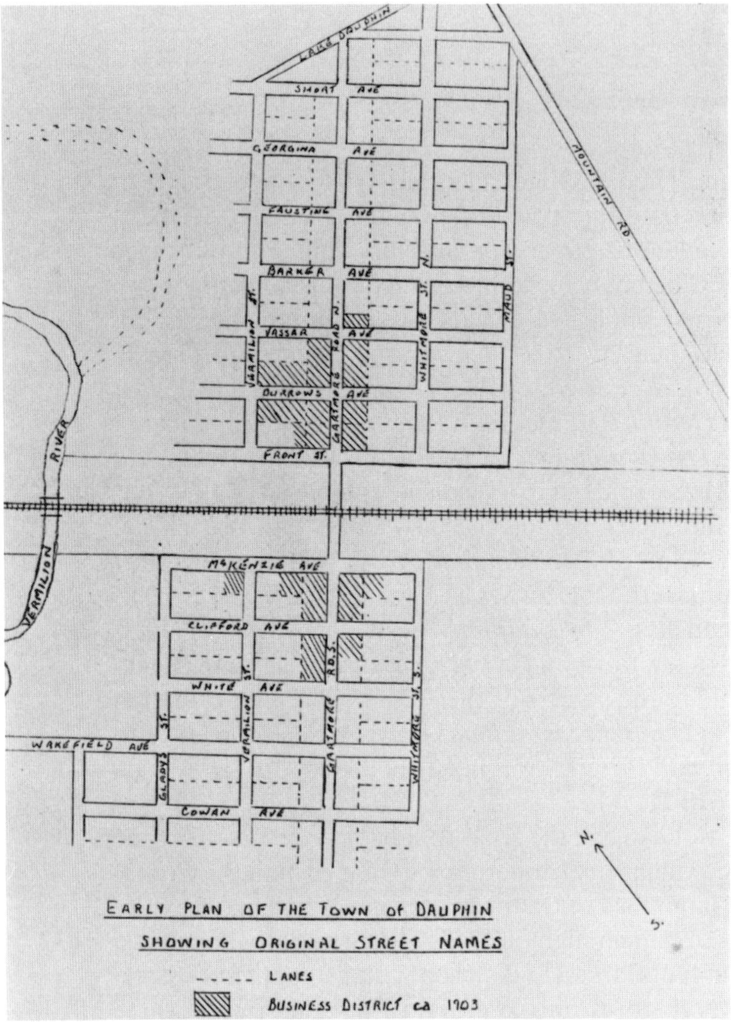

Plan of the commercial centre of Dauphin, 1903, showing original street names.

Manor Hotel, built in 1897 by Pioneer William Whitmore. An addition was built c.1900.

that there was a great deal of sticky mud on the streets. This was a state of affairs well-known, especially in the spring of the year, to anyone who lived in Dauphin, before the post-war paving of the streets. Many a shoe rubber or a boot remained behind when one stepped out into Dauphin's mud.

The business section of the town grew rapidly in the early years. The buildings from Gartmore and Dauphin Lake had been moved into the new townsite. New stores and residences, hotels and boarding houses were seen to be rising in all areas. All the activity centred originally around the intersection of Gartmore Road and the Railway tracks but, as more and more people arrived, lots were taken up further from the centre of town. An approximate plan of the commercial centre of Dauphin is shown in the accompanying diagram.

There were many merchants who started their businesses early in the life of Dauphin. John Bryce, a confectioner and baker, erected a building on Gartmore Road South, between Mackenzie and Clifford in 1897. For many years, with a short break in the early years of the century when the McLean Brothers and Cruise and McGaffen operated the bakery, the Bryce family ran this business and eventually expanded to a successful career as bakers in Winnipeg. The Dauphin store continued operation until the mid-50s.

Halsey M. Park started his jewellery business in Dauphin very soon after the incorporation of the village, in 1897. Dodimead & Company also had a jewellery shop for a short time. Halsey Park remained in business in Dauphin until 1922 when he sold to E.F. Fox. During his time in business he contributed appreciably to the musical and social activities in town. Within a short time James Wait established as a watchmaker and jeweller in a small building just south of John Bryce's building on Gartmore Road between Mackenzie and Clifford Avenue. He remained in that building until his retirement in the 1930s. Jimmy Wait was an avid supporter of the Boy Scout movement, giving a great deal of his time to both the Wolf Cubs and the Boy Scouts for many years. For much of this time, meetings were held in the original railway station which was then located on the railway right-of-way just off Vermilion Street South.

Robert Lilly came to Dauphin in the spring of 1898. He established a general department store, with his partner, under the name of Lilly & Carter. The store was located on Mackenzie Avenue just west of Main Street. The partnership lasted a short time before Mr. Lilly struck out on his own in the Up-to-Date Store in the same location. Later, with other investors, he initiated the Dauphin Mercantile Company Ltd., a firm that was eminently successful in supplying men's and ladies' wear and notions to the Dauphin market. Tragically, he died by his own hand in April, 1914. He was said to have been an unusually competent merchant who did a great deal for his community in its early days. He was, at the time of his death, chairman of the school board. He led the drive for school buildings and improved education in town.

Frank Turner and Sandy McPherson opened the first hardware store in Dauphin, although they were followed closely by W.J. Bigham, a Dauphin pioneer. Turner and McPherson eventually sold out, in 1906, to the Malcolm brothers who had already bought David McIntosh's store at the corner of Burrows and Main. David Sutherland, who had been employed by Turner & McPherson, left the employ of that firm in 1898 and joined with A.H.F. Stelck who had come to Dauphin as a tinsmith with McDonald & Voigt, to form a hardware firm. They bought out J.H. Bigham's hardware store and over the next five decades built a hardware business which was said to be the best in the rural west.

Jake Buckwold arrived in Dauphin in 1898 at the age of twenty two years. He began his career by clerking in T. Finklestein's general store which was located on the west side of Main Street between Clifford and White Avenues. In September, 1902, he married Bessie Finklestein in the first Jewish wedding held in Dauphin. The wedding took place in the firehall where a canopy had been erected at the north end of the hall. It was a wedding of great interest to the people of Dauphin. Later, with Sam Corman, Jake Buckwold ran a general store in the Barker Block, where the Dauphin Hotel stood in later years. Still later, he operated a liquor store but when the province went dry in prohibition days, he branched out into fur-buying, horse-trading and in the fuel supply business, principally wood and coal. He was one of Dauphin's most generous merchants, carrying many farmers during the depression of the thirties for the cost of their machinery; at that time he had added an implement agency to his business concerns. This family business thrived in Dauphin for many years.

During the pre-railway days, when farms were small, when houses were built from logs or lumber made from the local trees, when settlers grew their own vegetables and supplied their own meat and milk, when hunting and fishing resulted in productive yields and when barter was a way of life, money was not an essential commodity. With the arrival of the railway there were businesses to establish, crops to be shipped, machinery to be imported and larger buildings to erect. The increase in population stressed the urgency of schools, a larger and more modern hospital, a water supply, road maintenance, electrical energy and other amenities. Money became a necessary commodity in the life of the town and much of it had to be borrowed. Dauphin's first bank was a private bank, owned and operated by Mr. G.L. Irwin who served the settlers well until the coming of the railroad. Such was the demand at that time, however, that Mr. Irwin's private resources were insufficient to meet the needs. He then arranged for his bank to become a branch of the Bank of Ottawa in 1897. Mr. Irwin remained the manager of the Dauphin branch until 1916.

The Manor House, built in 1897 on the southwest corner of Main Street and Second Avenue South was the first of several hotels on that site and even today is the site of the Tower Hotel. The Manor House was built by William Whitmore, a brother of Tom and Harry who, with his wife Emma, came to Dauphin in 1886 after having lost, by fire, everything they owned in Gladstone. William Whitmore died in 1902.

Tom Whitmore built a two-storey block on Main Street, kitty-corner from the Manor House which contained the county court offices. It was later replaced by the Pollon Block, built by Tom Pollon who had come to Dauphin to farm in 1887. The Leland House, operated by Thomas McLean and the Dauphin House, operated by Joseph Clarke, were opposite one another on the southeast and northeast corners, respectively, of Main Street and Burrows Avenue. Just behind the Leland House, the three Eagle brothers from High Bluff, opened a blacksmith shop. William Ross opened The Cash Store at Gartmore Road and Vassar Avenue.

The old town hall at Dauphin Lake was moved to the new

town. First, however, it had to be sawed in half and each half transported separately to the new town. It was placed on the north side of Burrows Avenue West.

George Barker built a two-storey building near the northeast corner of Main Street and Front Street which was later replaced by the Wallace Block. Massey-Harris had a warehouse south of the tracks on the southwest corner of Main Street and First Avenue Southeast. The Shaw brothers erected a lumberyard and office just east of Main Street on First Avenue Southeast. It remains a lumberyard today having passed to Theodore Burrows, Monarch Lumber Company and Revelstoke Lumber Company. The first grain elevator to be built in Dauphin was the elevator of the Northern Grain Company on the railway right-of-way west of Main Street on the south side of the tracks. When it opened Frank Chase came to Dauphin to manage it and raised his family in a fine house on Front Street West. Frank's son, Darwin, managed the same elevator much later.

The majority of pioneer settlers prior to the coming of the railway were single men or married men with young families. They were not long in the area when they recognized the need for educational, religious and social amenities. These had been forged, to some degree, in the original settlements of Gartmore and Dauphin Lake where schools, churches and social groups had existed for years. In the new town, however, the process had to be repeated. The Dauphin village school district was organized and chartered in 1897 by Inspector Maguire with teachers Miss E. McWilliams and Miss Beatrice Gunne. School trustees were William McIntosh, Tom Pollon and John McKinnon. A temporary schoolroom was located on the top floor of a frame building on the west side of Main Street between Third and Fourth Avenues North, the lower part of which was a carpenter shop. It was soon replaced by a four-room frame building on the site of the present Mackenzie school. That school came after much debate about the site and little debate about the cost. A meeting on June 19, 1987, just six months after the coming of the railway, approved the borrowing of four thousand dollars to build a school. There were delays because the school could not be started until after incorporation; then delays again occurred due to alleged construction defects. When the frame was strengthened the new school opened in May of 1899. It wasn't long before this school was overflowing with students.

Dauphin's boom year was the year of 1898-99, notwithstanding the great outburst of building and moving when the new townsite was thrown open. By 1900 the school population had increased to 264 pupils. The number of residences and business blocks had shown a rapid growth as well. There were now five grain elevators in Dauphin. Frank Chase ran the Northern elevator, J.B. McIntyre managed the Lake of the Woods elevator, J.N. Mouat had the Dominion elevator, W.B. Nicholson operated J.E. Hedderley's elevator and the Dauphin Milling Company's elevator was managed by S. Gable.

In addition to the Shaw Brothers lumberyards there was a lumberyard along the north side of the tracks, across from the firehall site, at Front and Vermilion, known as Sinnott's lumberyard.

The Steenson Block, on the west side of Main Street, between Burrows and Vassar Avenues, housed George Cameron's drug store which had opened in opposition to the Medical Hall. Shortly thereafter Steenson erected a billiard parlour in the lot between his block and Bigham's harness shop.

Pressure for a grist mill in Dauphin bore fruit in November, 1898 when Sam Code established The Dauphin Milling Company along the railway siding on Mackenzie Avenue West. Unfortunately, the mill had no sooner opened when Mr. Code died of typhoid fever.

The Manor House required enlargement by a 24' x 26' two-storey addition on its south side. The lower floor was to serve as sample rooms. It had been planned originally by Stuart Geekie and built by W. McDonald for William Whitmore.

Theodore Burrows announced plans for a two-storey business block at Gartmore Road and Burrows Avenue in Septmber, 1898. The excavation began in July, 1899. Ramsay and Philip moved their department store into the Burrows Block in June, 1901. Drs. Gunne and Bottomley took offices on the second floor. The Dominion Land office moved to the Burrows Block and Mr. Burrows had his own office there.

The first Chinese laundry in Dauphin came into being in Dauphin in February of 1897. It was operated by Fong Dong and later by Wing Lee. The business was announced in the *Dauphin Press* as being operated by a "native of the Celestial Empire". Wing Lee became the first Chinese to own land in Manitoba and possibly in Canada, outside of British Columbia. Their laundry was on Burrows Avenue just behind Turner's hardware store on Main and Burrows Avenue.

J.G. Harvey built a brick veneer block in 1901 on the east side of Main Street just north of the Dauphin House. Joseph Clarke, now owner of the Leland House, made an early decision to replace his establishment with an up-to-date brick three-storey block.

John Sumpton started as an auctioneer and a livery stable operator in early 1897. His first location was on White Avenue but he later took over the Roseberry Boarding House and Livery Stable on Vassar Avenue West.

W.C. Turner erected a large store on Gartmore Road in 1897 next to the Medical Hall. He had previously had space in the store of his brother, C.F. Turner. The former had a men's wear store, the latter a hardware store. The *Dauphin Press* moved from the McKenzie building to the town hall building on Burrows Avenue in March, 1897.

Several businesses changed hands. The McKenzie brothers sold out to Lilly & Carter. Archie Hoy bought James McKinnon's blacksmith shop on Front Street. Archie Hoy's father, Charles Hoy, had operated a confectionery and ice cream parlour on the east side of Main Street, north of Harvey's law office. He bought the Cruise bakery and moved it to the Lilly store on Mackenzie Avenue. R.B. Cockerton, a pioneer farmer, moved to town to become an implement dealer for Cockshutt. The Grandview Hotel was sold to E. Widmeyer of Gretna. These were only some of the many transactions taking place in the hectic enviornment of a burgeoning village.

From the beginning of the village settlement, disease threatened the community. Public health knowledge was in its infancy, the village lacked adequate sewage disposal, many of the residents were careless about the cleanliness of their properties or had little knowledge of the importance of personal hygiene. The result of all this was that typhoid fever, small pox, diptheria and other communicable diseases were frequently present, often in epidemic proportions. Some of Dauphin's residents recognized the need for a hospital and pushed for its establishment. Many meetings were held. The weekly press pursued the issue in editorials and news items. Discussions were had with private sources who, it was hoped, would fund a hospital in the district. At the end of all this activity nothing resulted until the eventual occurrence of a major threat to the community.

    A serious outbreak of typhoid fever in 1899 resulted in a more serious movement to obtain a hospital for the area. The need was increased by the arrival in Dauphin of a trainload of seriously ill typhoid patients; no beds had been available for them in Winnipeg, which was their intended destination. Something had to be done. It was then that Dr. Bottomley agreed to open his home as a hospital for very ill patients. His home served as a temporary respite but the need for a permanent hospital was made more apparent. The means for raising the necessary funds were examined. The target of nine thousand dollars was set and the village and the surrounding municipalities made grants toward it. Local groups sponsored teas, dances, musical evenings, plays and other activities. The entire community pitched in with voluntary efforts. Mrs. Emma Whitmore spear-headed the drive amongst the women's organizations. Private donations swelled the hospital building fund. Lord Strathcona, himself, made a donation of two hundred dollars. A large tract of land in the southwest portion of the village was donated by the Whitmore family and some adjoining property was purchased. Construction began in the summer of 1900 and in September the first hospital board was elected. George King headed the first board, R.C. Brown was secretary, William Blackadar was treasurer. The rest of the board were J.E. Hedderley, G. Irwin, Harry Macneill, Robert Hunt, Thomas Shaw, Sam Code and A.E. Wilkes. A charter was granted in February, 1901 and the hospital of twenty-four beds was opened for patients in the fall of that year.

    Miss Sarah Picken was the first matron. She almost lost her position soon afterwards when a donation of two thousand dollars from the Victorian Order of Nurses became the basis of pressure to have Miss Picken replaced by a nurse from the V.O.N. To its credit the hospital opted to refund the donation and retain Miss Picken's service. On the opening of the hospital a training school for nurses was started and Miss Winnifred Malcolm, daughter of Andrew Malcolm, a pioneer of the district, became Dauphin's first nurse trainee. The medical staff of the hospital on opening day included Dr. J.R. Gunne, Dr. E.E. Bottomley, Dr. S.D. Cameron, and Dr. W.J. Harrington who had just arrived in Dauphin. Public ward rates were one dollar per day while a private ward could be had for two dollars a day.

The Anglicans, the Presbyterians and the Methodists were represented in Dauphin in 1896, although only the first two had church buildings in the early village. Presbyterians first met in David McIntosh's building but by April, 1897, they had a temporary church building at Vassar and Vermilion while they built a fund to finance a new church. Excavation for the new Methodist church started in September, 1897. The building was to be 40' x 50' with an annex for classrooms measuring 20' x 30'. The cornerstone was laid on September 16, 1897. The church was dedicated on February 20, 1898.

Looking back, a few years later, the A.E. Iredales recalled some very early church activities of interest. "The very first church service in the settlement, according to Mrs. N. Bigham, was held at the home of Tom Whitmore, now the Rampton farm, in the district later to be known as Gartmore.

"The date was March 18, 1888 and the minister was Rev. Allmack, a Methodist Missionary, a relative of the late R. Argue. He had come from Newdale to perform the marriage ceremony of Tom Whitmore and Minnie Bigham the day before, and stayed over to hold a service the next afternoon. Word of the service spread around surprisingly fast. Some had been "in" for three years without any church service. Practically all the settlers, irrespective of creed, turned out and filled the house. Seats for all were provided by boards and benches, and after the service, tea was served.

"The organist was Mrs. Charles Hoy, mother of the late Archie Hoy. She brought her own little organ in the sleigh. Those who led the singing were Tom and Jane Iredale and Mrs. Shand, brothers and sisters of the late A.E. Iredale and Tom Whitmore. The first hymn was "Nearer My God To Thee" and the closing hymn was the minister's choice, "God Be With You".

"The first entertainment in the district, held to raise church funds, was on February 16, 1889. All the young people of the district helped and they drove miles to practice for the two plays which were the main part of the program.

"The first play was called "The Country Cousin" and the following took part; a Mr. Robinson, Carrie McIntosh, Laura Hoy (the late Mrs. Bottomley) and Mary Barker (Mrs. R.G. Ferguson). The second play was "Advertising For A Husband". The cast included Tom Iredale, Duncan McDonald, Billie Ward and Annie Ward (Mrs. N. Bigham).

"The first Thanksgiving celebration was held at the home of Mrs. Wm. Whitmore, about where the Whitmore school now stands, and took the form of a dinner, held under the auspices of the Anglican congregation, and the first Christmas tree concert was held by the Presbyterians in the newly completed general store of Capt. McIntosh, with about twenty children present".

The Anglicans, at this time, made a decision to build a new church on property they obtained on Wakefield and Vermilion. The Baptists, in 1897, were in the process of raising funds for their own building. The Anglican minister, the Rev. H.G. Wakefield, was the first minister in the district although several student ministers and lay ministers had served in the area for variable periods.

The first fraternal organization in town was the Knights of the Maccabees which was organized in December of 1896. Soon after, in February of 1897, the I.O.O.F. established a lodge which met in the upper floor of the Mountain View Hall, situated on Main Street North between Third and Fourth Avenues North. It is noted that the organizational meeting was followed by "a great meal" in the Grandview hotel. In the same month and the same year the Foresters formed a court at Dauphin and the Royal Templars formed a lodge. A chapter of the St. George's Society was formed in February of 1898. The Freemasons also established a lodge in Dauphin in 1898.

Entertainment was simple. Soccer was popular even before the village was formed. George Lynch, a pioneer farmer who later moved to the Gilbert Plains area, tells of two soccer teams in the area, one at Dauphin Lake, the other at Rigby. They "used to play on a ridge on the Jack and Harry Macneill farm, later sold to Art

Boughen. I cannot remember what year the Mountaineers started to play football in the district called Spruce Creek. They played on the Miller farm". He goes on to tell of a team in 1895, representing Dauphin, 14 men in all, who left, with "three teams of horses pulling democrats and buckboards", for Neepawa. They carried food which the people of Old Dauphin had donated, and carried a large tent for camping along the way. When the game was played "we surprised the town by holding them down to a tie game of two goals each. They told us they thought we would all be Indians coming from so far north". The team members are listed as Bill Jones in goal; Jack Macneill and Dr. Gunne, fullbacks; Peter Macneill, Donald Gunne and a preacher, halfbacks; Joe Gelling, Sid Tate, George Lynch, Bob Cardiff and Mark Cardiff, forwards. Although George Lynch was not sure when the Mountaineers started playing football, we do know that it was early in the history of the community. On one occasion they defeated Gilbert Plains 2-0 with a team consisting of McDonald, V. Law, A.E. Kydd, G. Tucker, J. McLaughlin, E. Fulkerson, R. Miller, J. Rennolds, H. McCorvie, V. Love and F. Law. Archie McCorvie was the referee.

A curling club was organized with Will McIntosh as president, F.K. Herchmer as first vice-president and R.C. Brown as secretary-treasurer. The first rink was located on Mackenzie Avenue, west of Main Street. It was prepared for flooding in November, 1897. The ice surface measured 186' x 85'. The centre, under arches, was 35' wide and held two curling sheets. On each side was 15', and at the one end 20', of ice surface for skating.

A lacrosse club started in 1897. Baseball and hockey were not as popular at that time although a baseball club was organized in the spring of 1898. A cricket club started at that time as well. There were tennis courts on Vassar Avenue and Whitmore Street. A rifle club was organized early in the life of the village.

The early rink had a short life. In 1900 it was out of action. McKinstry & Son operated an open air rink in the winter of 1900-01. At the same time shares were being sold for a new curling rink.

In the cultural types of entertainment, Dauphin's citizens had no lack. Private dances were not uncommon. The Hosegood Ball and the Iredale Ball were two examples of the private sponsorship of public dancing. A "Dramatic Society" had a busy schedule and a successful life in the early days. A Shakespeare Club was active for many years. The Dauphin Band was well received on many public occasions. A Quadrille Club was popular for those who enjoyed ballroom dancing and the Bachelors' Ball was an annual event anticipated with great pleasure.

Several companies and individual entertainers visited Dauphin. Pauline Johnston made several trips to entertain the local populace. The Nelson Stock Company had seven days of performances with packed houses each night. The Dominion Concert Company had a three-night stand in the Orange Hall with similar success. Cornyn and Lindsay, an operatic troupe, closed out nine days of *The Exile of Erin* at the Orange Hall and was well received after each performance. *Trial By Jury* had its Dauphin premiere in the Orange Hall.

The many public occasions and special events were usually marked by large parades and sports days. These were well attended, as the revelry was a welcome break from the arduous tasks of the day. Much of the downtown celebration centred around a bandstand situated on Gartmore Road and Front Street East, before the east end of Front Street was opened.

In August 1898 the pioneers of the district had their first meeting. Listed as present at that meeting were John Edwards, Neil McDonald, Harry and Thomas Whitmore, James Blackmore, Tom Parsons, Joseph Buzza, George Barker, William McIntosh, Thomas Iredale, William Whitmore, Charles Hoy, R.D. Gibson, David McIntosh, Archie Gillies, R. Ferguson, Harry Hughes, Peter Gillies, John Daniels, Angus McNeil, M. Cameron, Thomas Pollon, Noel Ross, D. McKillop and Chester Ross. The pioneers met again in March of 1899, at the Manor House.

A serious and widespread prairie fire raged through the district in October of 1899. It wasn't long before many were out cutting hay again on land that was spared. Farmers in the district paid a great deal of attention to the improvement of their livestock. In most seasons champion stallions or bulls were available for breeding purposes.

The *Dauphin Press* of June 22, 1897 reported that there were already one hundred buildings in Dauphin "exclusive of outbuildings". Fifty-five of these buildings were residences in most of which the lower storey was utilized for business and the upper storey as a residence.

In October, 1897 the population of Dauphin was 586 persons. By 1901 the population had almost doubled to 1000 souls. The village was now eligible to apply for a town charter which would give it a better credit rating, an improved status amongst other growing towns in Manitoba and the chance to compete as a marketing and railway centre for northern Manitoba. The application for a charter was accepted and in the fall of 1901 an election for the new council of the town of Dauphin, to take office on January 1, 1902, took place. George King of the *Dauphin Press* became mayor while R.C. Brown, an insurance agent; Stan Coxworth, a pump maker and distributor; J.S. Hedderley, a grain merchant; R.G. Smith, harness maker; James Wait, jeweller; Thomas Whitmore, farmer; John Walton, furniture salesman and undertaker, and C.F. Turner, merchant, were elected as first councillors.

Four years after the first train arrived in Dauphin, the two settlements of Gartmore and Dauphin Lake had moved, physically to a new site; had built the commercial centre and many residences, its hospital and its school. The school population had risen from seventy-seven children in 1897 to three hundred and seven children in 1900. Surely the future looked bright. There was an optimism in the air and an energy amongst the citizens which bode well for this new, northern centre of population. There appears to have been little thought in this corner of the world for the insurrection in Africa known as the Boer War.

Notes to Chapter 4:

Books and Reports:

Berton, Pierre. *The Promised Land.* Toronto: McClelland and Stewart, 1984.
Curelly, Chas. Trick. *I Brought the Ages Home.* Toronto: Ryerson Press, 1956.

Newspapers:

Burrows, T.A. "Dauphin's Unwritten History," *The Dauphin Herald,* September 28, 1911.
The Dauphin Pioneer Press, April 1, 1896 to January 6, 1897.
The Dauphin Press, January 13, 1887 to December 23, 1915.

5

THE FOUNDATION

The incorporation of the town of Dauphin was a cause for great celebration. The charter was dated November 21, 1901. So it was that as Christmas approached in that year, the people of Dauphin felt fortunate indeed. In general, crops in the area were bountiful; the railroad had made it possible to develop a good market town and goods were flowing in and out of Dauphin regularly; the isolation from outside towns and especially from Winnipeg had ended; their hospital had opened; their school was operating; they had doctors and lawyers and merchants; they had established places of worship and they enjoyed an area of generous resources and scenery. They had two roads out from Dauphin — the Strathclair Trail over the Riding Mountain and the Burrows Road to Neepawa and beyond.

They had problems as well which occupied the close attention of the new town council. Foremost among these problems were those of fire safety, water supply, electrical power supply and street construction and maintenance. It must be remembered also that the town lay on land that had been farmed and, as a consequence, would require the planting of trees and shrubs to create the beauty that many foresaw for their home town. At that time the land along the river was well treed but the rest of the townsite had only a few clumps of growth.

As to the first of these problems, it was apparent that fire might easily destroy a great part of the commercial area if it got started. Most of the buildings were frame buildings and would serve as good fuel if fire established itself. Since there was, as yet, no water supply except that provided by wells, the council, in one of

BOB GARDNER

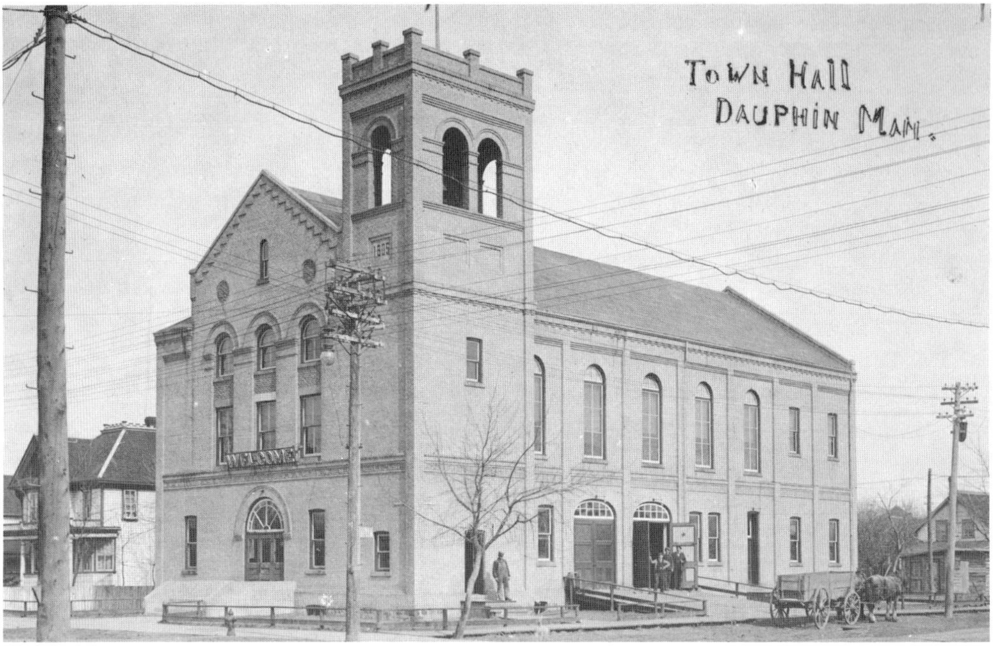

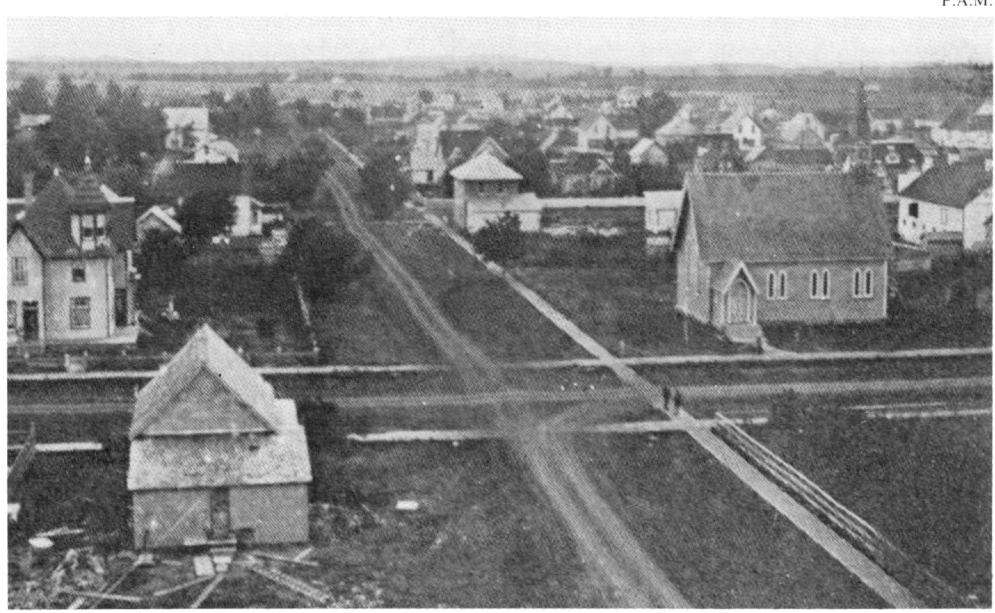

The town hall, built in 1905 at the cost of $27,000. c.1920.

P.A.M.

A view of Vermilion Street, 1906, taken from the new town hall. In the foreground St. Paul's Anglican Church. In June of this year tenders were called to replace the wooden sidewalks with "granolithic" sidewalks.

its earliest resolutions, authorized expenditures for a new pump wagon and the installation of water tanks, about twenty-two feet underground, at strategic locations in town. Four such tanks were installed within the main core of the town along Main Street. The first was at Barker Avenue (now Fourth Avenue North) and Main, the second at Burrows and Main, the third at Mackenzie (now First Avenue South) and Main and the fourth at Wakefield (now Fourth Avenue South) and Main. It can be concluded from this that any building more than a block away from the tanks or outside the eight block limit on Main Street, continued to have almost no fire protection. This system of fire-fighting, although woefully inefficient by today's standards, served Dauphin for many years and was manned by a volunteer fire brigade whose members began a heritage of voluntary fire-fighting of which Dauphin became very proud over a long period of time. Two of the dedicated fire chiefs in the early days of Dauphin were Robert Hunt, a harness maker, who started his business in 1896 in Dauphin and Edward Batty, one of the pioneers of the Dauphin district.

One of the buildings the fire brigade was unable to save was the first town hall, located on the north side of Burrows Avenue, west of Main Street. On New Year's morning of 1905 fire broke out in the town hall, destroying the building. Interestingly, the fire was probably caused by the overturning of a stove when the fire hose, which had been hung to dry after a fire of the previous evening, fell from its place sometime in the early morning, tipping the stove. At any rate, the council was faced with the problem of rebuilding a town hall. They chose to develop the firehall site, a site on the northwest corner of Front Street and Vermilion Street, to erect a two-storey brick building which served as the municipal and cultural centre of Dauphin from 1905 until after World War II. It more than repaid its twenty-seven thousand dollar cost which, at the time of its erection, was criticized for being inordinately expensive. The Love Brothers laid the three hundred thousand bricks in the new town hall. This was the beginning of a family business which continued for many years and involved at least three generations.

Electrical power came to Dauphin in February, 1906 when the town erected an electric light plant at the west end of Front Street near the Vermilion river. The cost of the plant was accepted by the ratepayers in April, 1905 by a vote of 86-4. It was a wood-fired steam plant which served the town until the end of 1944. The original contract for the electrical installations was let to Westinghouse. The dynamo for the plant arrived in February, 1906 and was immediately installed. That the town was thrilled by the result can be read in the newspaper accounts of the day. "We have never before seen such lights in a country town" and "never have we seen a more brilliant light". The total cost of the plant was twenty-five thousand dollars. One of its features was a steam whistle which for years sounded at exactly noon and which, in the case of fires, blew the ward number — one blast for ward one, two blasts for ward two, and so on.

During its life the electric light plant served the town well and usually returned a profit which alleviated some of the costs of other undertakings. Over the years, and especially in the early years and during the depression of the thirties, it provided work and income to its direct employees and also to a great many men who cut and delivered the large wood supplies needed to generate the steam to power the turbines. Although never intended as such, it was also a good indicator of the severity of spring flooding in the Vermilion river, as it was amongst the lowest of Dauphin's buildings. It was affected by the rising waters earlier than most other buildings and thus served as an early warning system for river flooding.

The supply of water in Dauphin had not been a problem, at least in respect of household requirements. Wells could be sunk anywhere in town and water found not too far down. It was inconvenient, however, and, in addition, people hoped for indoor water supplies and a modern sewage system to minimize the risk of typhoid fever, one of the day's major killers. Winter not only accented the discomforts of outdoor "privies", it frequently froze the pumps or even the water in the well. The story is told that when the first Mackenzie school burned in 1909, the firefighters could not use their equipment because of a frozen well. A new supply of water and a proper waterworks system therefore seemed desirable.

Meetings began as early as 1907 to discuss the possibility of a water and sewage system. Studies were made of various water sources and eventually a report in 1908 suggested that the best source was Edwards Creek, the creek along which John Edwards sowed his first potato crop. By July, 1910 tenders were accepted to begin the waterworks system from Edwards Creek at the foot of the Riding Mountain to Dauphin. The combined waterworks and sewage systems were to cost two hundred and sixty thousand dollars. By February, 1910 a waterworks bylaw had been prepared and given first reading. Debentures were sold to raise the funds to dam the stream on the north slope of the Riding Mountain to develop a reservoir and assure a constant supply of water for the system.

Trenching for the water and sewer pipes in town began in the summer of 1911 and both systems were in operation by 1913. The reality of having the system built was a major factor in the land boom and prosperity which was felt in Dauphin, especially during 1912 when property values increased rapidly. Many businesses enlarged their premises and many new businesses came to Dauphin.

The water supply system worked well in usual times but often in spring the people of Dauphin were treated to muddy water which entered the system when the sluice gates were damaged by spring floods. Generally this change was accepted stoically by the citizenry which was grateful for the system, even with its faults. Occasionally there were stories of living things in the muddy water but this must have been a relatively rare occurrence.

The sewage system which was built at the same time as the waterworks system was a boon to the people of Dauphin although for many, many years outdoor "backhouses" were in evidence in many areas. It was not until after World War II that the town fathers prohibited any further use of such accommodations and forced the use of the indoor sewage disposal system.

The building and maintenance of streets and lanes in Dauphin was fraught with numerous difficulties. The harsh winter weather, with deep frosts, resulted in a multitude of "frost boils" in the spring. Some of these were immense and seemed to swallow up large parts of the road surface. Grading was helpful but there was so little gravel on some roads that the machinery became mired in the viscous gumbo of Manitoba mud. Sand and gravel seemed to disappear miraculously. When the snows melted the water collected in the lower parts of the ditches and roads, submerging the road completely in some areas. The provision for run-off of the melted snows, and the rain in summer, was primitive. In fact, in the early spring, it was almost non-existent because of the frozen ice and snow blocking the culverts. This necessitated the use of a steam boiler, mounted on a sleigh drawn by horses, and having a steam hose, directed by a long pole, pushed into the culverts to melt the ice and snow so that the water could escape. It was always one of the joys of spring for young boys to follow this sleigh and watch the freeing of the waters. Often, if the water did not flow away, it would refreeze. This made a perfect hockey surface. If it froze partially, but not too solidly, it provided the great pleasure of sliding on "rubber ice". That was a ball!

When spring had turned to summer and the streets had been graded, the problem of dust became an annoying one. Main Street and other business streets were watered, sometimes twice or three times daily, and later oiled, but the residential streets got this treatment much less frequently. If the summer rains were heavy the streets and lanes became slippery, sticky messes again and what little traffic there was, slowed or stopped altogether. Sometimes good, strong teams of horses failed to pull a load through the mud, so deep and sticky was it. These were occasions when the townspeople measured the skill and kindness of the teamsters, some of whom whipped and swore and failed, while others coaxed and cajoled and helped their horses and succeeded in getting through.

The need for sidewalks and improved road surfaces, in these circumstances, was evident to all. In addition, the state of the lanes in the early town was a common source of complaints and editorial wrath. Much of the basis of the pleadings for a cleaner townsite was the prevalence of disease, especially typhoid fever. So far as the sidewalks were concerned, council called for tenders in June, 1906 for the construction of "granolithic" sidewalks on both sides of Main Street to the north end of town, on Mackenzie Avenue from Main to Vermilion, on Front Street from Main Street to the powerhouse and on Georgia Avenue from Main to Maud Street. These sidewalks replaced some of the earlier wooden sidewalks installed in 1902, many of which remained in use until the mid-1920s.

Some idea of the cost of municipal government in those days

is reflected in the tax returns for Dauphin in 1901. The mill rate was 25 mills on a total property assessment of about $390,000, yielding $8,095 to cover both the general municipal costs and the school costs. This was only possible because the council members served without recompense, the town solicitor was paid twenty-five dollars per month and the town constable was paid forty dollars per month. The Misses Gunne and McWilliams, Dauphin's first teachers were paid twenty dollars per month for the school term.

On the commercial side, changes were in evidence constantly. New businesses opened, old businesses changed hands and national and provincial governments opened offices in Dauphin. With many of these changes young families arrived in Dauphin at a rapid pace. In the ten years between 1901 and 1911 the population of the town rose from 1100 to 3687 and the property assessment rose from $390,000 to $1,884,679.

Robert Lilly's Up-to-Date Store was selling sugar at 5¢ per pound, peas and beans were 25¢ for three tins. Men's hair-lined larrigans (boots) were on sale for 50¢ a pair. The tailor, J.A. Ball, was selling men's tweed suits at $25. W.C. Turner, the haberdasher, advertised sixty suits and twenty-five overcoats at $7.50 each. Scotch ginghams could be bought at Ramsay & Philip's for 10¢ per yard. Advertisements in the *Dauphin Herald* in February 1906, included one from Dr. G.C.J. Walker, Dauphin's first dentist, who had set up shop in the Burrows Block at Main Street and Burrows Avenue. Dr. Walker came to Dauphin in 1904 and, with the exception of one short break, he served his entire professional career in Dauphin. His father also served Dauphin as a dentist for several years in the early part of the century.

Recreational activities were well supported in the town. In the interval between the inauguration of the town and the beginning of the Great War many sporting and cultural events filled the evenings and the weekends of the community. Hockey quickly became dominant in winter sports. The game utilized the seven-man team consisting of goal, point, coverpoint, rover, centre and right and left wings. The game was played in two halves rather than three periods, as it is today. In 1906 there was a hockey league with Dauphin, Grandview, Neepawa and Gladstone. During the summer months tennis was very popular. There were, at one time, six different tennis clubs in Dauphin, even at this early date.

Dauphin had a brass band in the very early years and later a "town band" led by William McMurray who, for many years was "Mr. Music" in Dauphin. Not only did he stimulate his family to pursue musical hobbies but his inspiration to hundreds of young people in Dauphin who first learned music from him was an immense contribution to the community.

There were many other athletic clubs. Badminton, soccer, baseball and track and field sports were well supported. Pigeon racing, horse racing and curling bonspiels were popular events in early Dauphin days. Billiard halls and bowling alleys were both found in the young town, one of which was operated by George Barker.

Lodges flourished. Freemasons (1897), Oddfellows (1897), Orange lodge (1890), Brotherhood of Locomotive Firemen and Enginemen (1907) and others were active in the first decade and later. The Masonic Ball was always a glittering affair. The Turf Club leased the race track from the Agricultural Society. It improved the track, built another barn and laid out a baseball diamond in the oval of the track. A Literary Club was organized in 1906 with Harry Macneill as president. It met regularly until the Great War. Touring entertainers frequently included Dauphin in their itineraries, especially after the building, in 1905, of the new town hall with its large auditorium and modern stage.

As early as 1901 some members of the community were looking toward Lake Dauphin as a suitable recreational area for those who wished to picnic, enjoy water sports or to develop summer cottages. Particularly attractive amongst several sites was one on the lakeshore almost directly east of the townsite which became a popular camping area as early as 1901. Dauphin Beach has been popular since, although it suffered a downturn during the drought of the depression years, at a time when the new Riding Mountain National Park came into being. Sunday excursions to Dauphin Beach were frequent and so concerned the "men of the cloth" that many a Sunday sermon was preached on the evils of such activity. In spite of these rebukes the habit continued and before World War I many families spent camping holidays and several built summer cabins or cottages at the beach. Boating became one of the excitements; sport fishing thrived as well and prize specimens of pickerel, whitefish, perch and jackfish were taken from its waters.

It was about this time (1901-2) that the first petitions were made to government to lower the level of Lake Dauphin. Farmers whose lands bordered the lake wanted the level lowered so that they could till more land or have greater hay lands to feed their cattle. Cottagers and fishermen, on the other hand, wanted to maintain a high level of water in the lake for their particular purposes. The history of the water levels since that time demonstrates the persistence of opposing views and the vacillation and irresolution of successive governments in dealing with the matter.

Telephone service was first promoted in 1903 when the Bell Telephone Company began to survey the town to ascertain the need for their service. Debate followed in meeting after meeting as to whether or not the system should be privately or publicly owned. There was considerable support for granting a franchise for telephone service to Robert Malcolm and, in fact, in February of 1905, the town council did grant a franchise for a ten-year period with an option to purchase at the end of that time or to extend the franchise for another five years. Telephone rates were established at two dollars per month for commercial phones and one dollar per month for residential phones. When three hundred phones were in use the promoter was to provide twenty-four hour service. Initially, the exchange would remain operative for twelve hours a day. It is not clear what happened to Bob Malcolm's franchise. It is clear that in mid-January of 1905 the *Dauphin Herald* announced that the Bell Telephone Company intended to start work in Dauphin in the spring of that year. A month later, however, the same newspaper reported that the town council had granted the franchise for a ten-year period to Mr. Malcolm. By mid-April Bell Telephone was still insisting that it was coming to Dauphin. The debate over public or private ownership of the telephone system continued. Evidence that the people of Dauphin favoured public ownership was demonstrated in a September referendum on the subject in which public ownership won a 100-28 victory. The Bell System, however, had already begun a program of erecting poles on Main Street a month earlier and even after the referendum they continued to develop their system which became operative in the fall of 1905, with fourteen subscribers. By early 1907, the problem became a provincial concern when the government of Manitoba held a province-wide referendum which again supported the idea of public ownership of all telephone systems. The wish became fact in December, 1907 when the government purchased all the Bell and other systems in Manitoba. Bell was paid $3.3 million for their system. By September, 1908 there were 190 phones in Dauphin. Subscribers were urged to learn to use the "new-fangled gadgets". They were also warned not to use the telephones during a thunderstorm. In fact, orders were issued to "central" to cut off all service during a storm.

Growth continued over the next few years and by 1914 tenders were called for a new telephone office. In the same year a long distance line between Dauphin and Neepawa was completed, ensuring further rapid contact with outside points. The completion of the new telephone office was delayed by the advent of World War I. It eventually opened in 1918 on the west side of Main Street between Third and Fourth Avenues North. This building served the system until 1953 when newer and more commodious and badly needed space was made available on Third Avenue Northeast. From the inauguration of service in 1905, until automatic dialing systems took over after World War II, the "telephone girls" provided a friendly and much needed service in the community.

The professional life in Dauphin increased after the incorporation of the town. The two early doctors, Gunne and Bottomley, were joined in 1900 by Dr. Samuel Cameron who had his office in George Cameron's drugstore on the west side of Main Street, just north of the corner of Burrows Avenue. Dr. Cameron was in Dauphin only a short time. He came about mid-January 1900 and stayed until July, 1901. Taking his place in the late summer of 1901 was Dr. D.M. Lineham who had been practising in Swan River. Dr. Lineham and Dr. Gunne formed a partnership for a short time until Dr. Gunn left Dauphin in 1905 for health reasons and to pursue specialty training in diseases of the eyes, ears, nose and throat. It was 1901, also, when Dr. W.J. Harrington arrived in Dauphin. He had graduated from the Manitoba Medical College in 1900 but had taken a year of special training in surgery before coming to Dauphin. As a result he became, and remained for many years, the major surgeon in northern Manitoba. He was the first coroner in

Dauphin. He remained in Dauphin, raising his family, representing Dauphin in the provincial legislature, contributing to the social and sporting life of the community and raising his practice skills to a high level in his efforts to serve the community as a doctor, until his death in 1941.

In 1902, Dr. R.B. Culbertson began practice in Dauphin in association with Drs. Gunne and Bottomley. Dr. Bottomley took advantage of his coming to leave for further studies in England. He remained in England for eighteen months and returned to Dauphin in the spring of 1903.

Dr. Mecklenberg, an alleged ophthalmologist, fitted for eyeglasses and examined for eye diseases on frequent trips to Dauphin from Winnipeg. It would appear that he provided satisfactory service to the community since there seems no evidence to the contrary. His services stopped abruptly, however, when he was charged with having practised medicine without a licence.

The influx of doctors into the area, the building of the new hospital in 1901 and the move on the part of two of the doctors to upgrade their training was the result of several influences. Chief among these was the rapidly increasing influx of settlers and business people into Dauphin and its surrounding communities. Adding to the urgency of the matter was a major outbreak of smallpox in 1901 and the continuous threat of typhoid fever in a community without adequate sewage management and with a raw water supply. Contributing to the need for improved medical care were the risks of childbirth in an isolated community, the increased frequency of serious trauma, and accidents in the more primitive circumstances of a pioneer settlement. The obituaries of the day demonstrate, in a striking way, the high death rate in the newborn period. Often, the birth and the death of the newborn were reported in the same issue of the local newspapers. Equally striking was the number of deaths in children and youths from the common infections: tuberculosis, rheumatic fever, nephritis, diphtheria and scarlet fever. "Blood poisoning" was an ever-present threat as were such conditions as boils, carbuncles and erysipelas. The complications of rheumatic heart disease and chronic Bright's disease claimed the lives of many young adults and working people. The great killers among adults, however, were lobar pneumonia, fatal burns, gunshot wounds, drownings and farm accidents.

The major causes of death and the number of doctors caring for the sick and injured remained fairly constant in the period prior to the Great War. Dr. Culbertson left Dauphin in 1904 to practise in Clanwilliam but by May of 1905 he had returned. Dr. W. Ross left Grandview in March of 1910 to practise in Dauphin in partnership with Dr. Lineham. He came with good qualifications, having won the gold medal in obstetrics in the graduating class of the Manitoba Medical College in 1908. The partnership lasted only a short time; Dr. Lineham left for Winnipeg in February, 1911 where he subsequently became an alderman. Dr. Culbertson left a year later for post-graduate study and Dr. Ross, in January, 1914 sold his practice to Dr. W.G. Rogers who remained in Dauphin and served the community well and faithfully until his death in 1943. Dr. Ross moved north to The Pas where he established a fine reputation for his medical prowess.

The hospital itself, having first opened in Dr. Bottomley's home as a response, in 1899, to the crisis of a typhoid epidemic, was soon unable to respond to the needs of the community. Nine thousand dollars were raised for a hospital building, which opened in October, 1901, on property donated largely by the Whitmores. That hospital had room for twenty-four patients but was often filled to overflowing. Within a few years some relief of the patient congestion was obtained when another wing was added in 1905. This annex brought the bed capacity to a level of thirty-two and further strained the energies and the ingenuity of its board and supporters in managing its financial problems. Miss Hyde, who had succeeded Miss Picken, resigned from her post in March of 1906. In May of that year, Miss Brereton came to take her place as Lady Superintendent in the Dauphin General Hospital. In 1908 an isolation unit was built behind the main hospital. This unit had a capacity for eight patients and was restricted to those with infectious diseases.

In the early days of its existence the hospital, being the only modern hospital in northern Manitoba, north of Neepawa, served a very large area with a rapidly growing population. The demands on its services were heavy from the day its doors opened. During 1904 the hospital admitted 334 patients. In spite of the fact that these patients stayed in hospital an average of twenty days, the total expenditure for the year was only $7,102. This amounted to a per diem cost for hospital care of only slightly more than a dollar a day! Despite that, only about one-half of the patients made any payment for their hospital care. This necessitated appeals to the community for supplies and provisions. The newspapers of the day document in detail the donations of meat, chickens, vegetables, bedsheets, books, preserved fruit and cheese that came from the citizens of Dauphin and the surrounding countryside. The town and the municipalities gave small annual grants when they could afford the money. Provincial and federal governments gave nothing.

The bulk of the financial support came as the result of the efforts of the Women's Hospital Aid. Ice carnivals, fair booths, formal balls, teas, theatre, dances, craft fairs and competitions of various types formed the basis for the collection of money. Without these funds the hospital might well have been forced to close. The women in this group made an enormous contribution to the health of the entire community. They continued their work as the hospital and the community grew, except for the wartime period of 1940-45 when the priority for the women turned to wartime voluntary work.

Dental care, originally supplied by itinerant dentists, had been regularly supplied by Dr. G.C.J. Walker who, with his father, interchanged practices between Dauphin and Carberry from 1901 to 1904 until the younger Walker made his permanent residence in the town in 1904 and remained there until the late 1930s. Dr. H.E. Bewell, a graduate of the Toronto dental school, came to Dauphin in 1906 to establish a practice which continued until 1945. He was the first dentist in Dauphin to install an electric motor in his drilling machine. Dr. Bewell's interest in the educational system in Dauphin was apparent from his early days in the area. He devoted many years of his life to the voluntary work on the school board. He and Harry Macneill had twenty-two years of continuous service as members of the school board, from 1912 to 1934. Dr. Bewell was an avid gardener, as was his wife. Between them they nurtured one of Dauphin's finest home gardens. Throughout the early years in Dauphin's history, Dr. Walker and Dr. Bewell provided the dental care for the town and, indeed, for the entire northern area of settlement in Manitoba.

Supporting the medical group of the day were the pharmacists, some of whom had come to Dauphin in its earliest hours. Dr. J.R. Gunne had established the first drugstore in Dauphin in late December of 1896. This establishment, referred to initially as J.R. Gunne & Co. was joined in partnership in 1901 by T.T. Malcolm who had recently returned from Toronto, having graduated in pharmacy there. T.T. Malcolm was one of the sons of Andrew Malcolm who had brought his family from Minnedosa in 1887. At the beginning of 1902 the partnership dissolved and T.T. Malcolm carried on the business under the name of The Medical Hall.

Philip Beauchamp, in addition to his medical practice, established a drugstore in the new village at the corner of Main Street and Second Avenue Southwest. This store was destroyed by fire on Christmas Day of 1901 and was never in business again. "Dr" Beauchamp later became the immigration agent and census enumerator for the federal government in Dauphin.

George H. Cameron came to Dauphin in April of 1899. He managed an active drugstore until the end of 1906 when he sold his business to W.H. "Ikey" Morrison who had apprenticed with T.T. Malcolm and had recently graduated in pharmacy. "Ikey" Morrison was apparently a very well-liked young man who quickly established a thriving business in Dauphin. He sold it two years later, in 1908, to Charles Teeple who renamed the business "The Red Cross Pharmacy". Charles Teeple sold out in a few months to T.T. Malcolm. Morrison returned in 1909 to open another store and in 1911 he became associated with the Rexall chain of drugstores. He sold out for the second time, in 1914, to Wilfred Robson. Bruce Goodhand, who was working for Ikey Morrison at that time, stayed on with Wilfred Robson until he joined the armed forces.

A.E. Munson established a drugstore in April, 1907 but sold out to T.T. Malcolm in 1909 when he received an appointment as magistrate in April of that year.

In early 1913 the "Dauphin Pharmacy" opened its doors on Main Street South between First and Second Avenues. The proprietor was the first lady druggist in Dauphin, a Miss

Carmichael. About the same time, T.T. Malcolm, who had taken a course in optometry in Toronto, opened an optometric "parlour" in his drugstore. Fred Wright came to town to manage the drugstore component of Malcolm's business.

The Dauphin Pharmacy changed hands in a very short time when Otto Heaslip bought the business in May of 1913. He changed its name to Heaslip's Drugs. All of these moves meant that at the end of 1913 there were three drugstores in Dauphin: T.T. Malcolm's Medical Hall, Robson's Rexall drugstore and Heaslip's Drugs.

The explosion in population, the building boom which accompanied it, the increasing demands for careful civic management and the need for a proper system of law and order, brought with them demands for a growing legal profession and for an improved and more convenient court and penal substructure. Dauphin had been well enough served by its early lawyers, Maughan, Wilkes, Harvey and Campbell, but the courts were serviced by a judge from Portage la Prairie for hearings and for incarceration if convicted. The condition of the roads, the weather and the distance made the administration of justice a cumbersome duty. In addition, land registrations were handled by a part-time office and the proceedings were slow and often confused.

J.G. Harvey, Dauphin's first lawyer, built an office for himself in 1901 on the east side of Main Street north of the King's Hotel. He added a second floor in 1902. He practised alone until 1908 when he engaged, as a partner, Mr. A.W. Sutherland. Harvey, himself, had become very active in both civic and provincial politics for the Conservatives. He was on the town council for several years and served as mayor for the three terms of 1907-09. The partnership with Sutherland was a brief one, as Sutherland ended his own life in January, 1909. Within a few weeks a new partner was found in the person of C.H. Edwards and a few months later they were joined by James L. Bowman. Tragedy struck again in October 1909, when Edwards died of typhoid fever and the firm became Harvey & Bowman. In 1913 Mr. Harvey left Dauphin. J.L. Bowman bought the building from him at that time.

J.A. Campbell, also one of Dauphin's early lawyers, was as much a Liberal as J.G. Harvey was a Conservative. They frequently opposed each other on political questions. They both added materially to the welfare of their community and, especially, to the legal side of their community's life. Campbell, like Harvey, established a reputable law firm. His first partner, Mr. E.J. Bawden, had served as principal of Dauphin schools until 1902 when he left to study law. He returned in the fall of 1906 to join Mr. Campbell in the firm of Campbell & Bawden, with offices in the Burrows Block. The partnership lasted only a year, however, when Bawden left in 1907 to take over the practice of A.E. Wilkes who had practised law in Dauphin since 1897. Wilkes went to Neepawa as the land registrar. Campbell lost no time, after Bawden's departure, in inviting Mr. F.E. Simpson to join him in 1907. That invitation introduced one of the giants in Dauphin's legal history to the people of Dauphin. Campbell and Simpson were joined later in the year by Mr. McKim and in the following year by Harry Macneill, a recent member of the bar. McKim left shortly after having joined the firm because of serious eye problems which required treatment. Macneill left to accept an appointment as magistrate but this appointment was also short-lived, for he became land registrar in Dauphin's new Land Titles office.

Early police magistrates include William Rintoul who operated a stationery shop in Dauphin; William Murray, who had been secretary-treasurer of the Rural Municipality; A.E. Wilkes, H.N. Macneill and A.E. Munson, a druggist. Only Wilkes and Macneill amongst them were lawyers.

As the town increased in size it became apparent to the lawyers and to others affected by the working of the law, that Dauphin lacked certain facilities which were essential to good legal care. The most important of these were a land titles office and the formation of a new judicial district for the northern part of Manitoba, centred in Dauphin. Discussion of these services began in the early years of the town's existence and by 1907 had developed into the petitioning of the government for them. Unfortunately, the priorities of the provincial government did not include consideration of these petitions. Many delays and frustrations were experienced by the petitioners.

Difficulties remained in the transport of prisoners, the registration of lands, the availability of courts above those of the local magistrate who could adjudicate on only the simplest of matters. Dauphin's newspapers joined in the pressure for action by editorial comments. Some of these reflected poorly on the district, although well-intended for the purpose; such as the fact that 80 percent of the prisoners in the Portage jail came from Dauphin! As one election succeeded another, candidates promised to work for a land titles office and for the establishment of a northern judicial district. Finally, in 1911, construction began on a land titles office on the east side of Main Street between Third and Fourth Avenues South. Harry Macneill was the first land registrar in this office.

In March, 1912 another delegation waited on the government about the possibility of a judicial district. Leading this delegation was J.L. Bowman who, in early 1913, received assurances from Premier Roblin that a county court would be established, with Dauphin as its centre. Within a very short time, however, the country was at war and Premier Roblin's government was embroiled in scandal about the construction of the legislative buildings; this eventually caused the government's downfall. The question of the judicial district had to await another day.

In the meantime Dauphin's legal community was increased by the addition of Bertram Ryan, son of Joseph Ryan who had presided at the country court sessions for many years. Jack Ramsden, having completed his bar examinations, took a position with J.L. Bowman only to leave shortly afterwards when war broke out and he enlisted. Hugh Brayfield, another lawyer, announced the opening of an office in Dauphin toward the end of 1913 but nothing more is heard of him nor of Bertram Ryan, both of whom likely stayed only a short time.

During the first decade of the century the common charges against those appearing in court were laid for game law infractions, drinking and disorderly conduct, assault, cattle theft and robbery. More serious offences of murder and rape were not uncommon.

If one could characterize the dominant forces in the daily lives of Dauphin's early citizens and of the community generally, one would certainly consider religion, politics and education as three of the most prominent. One or another, and often all three of these areas were entered into with great zeal by many of the townspeople. The clergy, individually and as a group, were a dominant force in the community. They frequently brought their influence to bear on matters of politics and business practices. The Sunday sermons usually appeared in the weekly newspapers, if not in full at least in summary.

The early churches in the settlement — Presbyterian, Methodist and Anglican — had their starts in the small communities which preceded the organization of the town in 1896. They were active congregations who accepted the challenge of establishing their presence in the new village and town. A Presbyterian church opened in the first month of the new century and stood on the west side of Main Street between Third and Fourth Avenues. The Rev. Robert Scott was its minister at the time. It received the name of St. James Presbyterian church in 1910. Other ministers who succeeded Scott up to the beginning of the 1914 war were the Rev. R.H. Gilmour and the Rev. David Fleming, both of whom had a major impact on their congregations and on the community generally.

The Methodists, who had originally worshipped at the log church in Cumberland (now Spruce Creek) began the excavation and laid the cornerstone of Grace Methodist church on the northwest corner of Main Street and Fourth Avenue North in September, 1897. The Rev. Fawcett, who had been the first teacher in the Dauphin district, was also the first minister for the Methodist church but it was the Rev. Hopper who presided during the construction of the church. His successors in the early days were the Revs. A.E. Smith, W.A. Lewis, W.W. Adamson, A.E. Smith for his second term, S. Wilkinson and J.G. Bethel. Of these the Rev. A.E. Smith was probably the most energetic and provocative of the group. He later entered politics and is said to have given up the church and espoused atheism and communism. He was all hell-fire and brimstone when he preached. The Methodists built the church manse, next to the church on Main Street in 1910.

The Anglican church, too, had an early start in Gartmore and Dauphin Lake. The Anglicans moved their churches into the new village during December of 1896. With the increase in population they built a larger frame church in 1899 to replace the old log church which had been brought in from Gartmore. This church, at the corner of Vermilion Street and Burrows Avenue served the congregation for many years. It was eventually sold to serve as the first Ukrainian Catholic church building in Dauphin. The sale was made possible by the decision of the congregation of St. Paul's, in 1913, to purchase land at the corner of Wakefield Avenue (Fourth Avenue South) and Vermilion Street, where they erected a fine brick church to seat three hundred people. The congregation began worship in this church on January 25, 1914 when the building was dedicated by Archbishop Matheson. Ministers of the Anglican church prior to the first war were the Revs. H.G. Wakefield, C.N.P. Jeffrey, A.W. Goulding, William Walser and A.S. Wiley. Of these ministers, Wakefield, Walser and Wiley appear to have made the most notable contributions to their congregations.

The Salvation Army was represented in Dauphin at least as early as 1906 when Captain Elliot was its commander. By the end of 1907 a decision had been made by the Army that a barracks would be built in Dauphin. Land was obtained on the north side of Second Avenue Northeast at Whitmore Street (First Street Northeast). The barracks were officially opened on August 7, 1909. Hardly a Saturday evening passed, winter or summer, in the early days of the town, when the ring of Salvation Army singers did not gather in the town centre to bring their message of salvation to the townspeople.

In December, 1905 the Roman Catholic congregation of nine families dedicated their new chapel, named St. Viator's chapel. Catholic services had been held at the homes of some of its adherents for several years. It was following the receipt of a gift of four lots that in 1904 the members of the church felt it possible to build a chapel. It was not until 1909 that Father Lauzon became the first resident priest in Dauphin. Those who succeeded him prior to the war were Fathers Duffy, Kelley, and Joseph Halde. The erection of a larger church had to await a later day.

The early Baptists worshipped initially at the Orange Hall on Main Street South. During that time they erected a temporary church building at the northeast corner of Main Street and Fourth Avenue North. While in this building they initiated plans for the gathering of funds for a larger and more permanent church building. The church became a reality within a few years so that on

Sunday, February 11, 1906 the new brick church, costing eight thousand dollars, was opened. At the time the minister was the Rev. J.C. Bowen who, after leaving Dauphin, moved to a church in Strathcona, Alberta and went on to become Alberta's sixth Lieutenant-Governor. After Mr. Bowen left in 1907, the church was served by many pastors, each only a short time in Dauphin, until after World War I.

The many ministers who served Dauphin in the first decade of the century were God-fearing men of Victorian upbringing. Their sermons brought the realities of the community up against the blandishments of the Holy Book. They did whatever seemed necessary to brook the weaknesses and transgressions of their parishioners at very turn. The effects of their wrath were felt by the business and professional communities, by the courts, by politicians and by their flocks. There were times when the intensity of their preachings reached white heat. They joined in the criticism of the hotels in Dauphin for "poor hygiene, bum meals and too much attention to the booze end of the business", as outlined by the editor of the *Dauphin Herald*. Many a sermon mentioned the undesirable situation developing when young children were allowed to stay out late "learning to smoke cigarettes, chew tobacco and swear". In this connection the *Dauphin Herald* reported the case of a Dauphin boy who "sent fifty cents to Toronto in response to an ad to learn how to keep from swearing. The answer came back, 'Keep your mouth shut'. The boy has been swearing ever since".

Partially, if not totally, due to the efforts of the clergy, the town council, in May of 1908, passed a curfew bylaw by which all persons under 16 years of age had to be off the streets by 9:30 p.m. In addition, there was an anti-loitering bylaw and a bylaw to prohibit spitting or vomiting on the streets. The Rev. Gilmour of the Presbyterian church was the first to advocate a mid-week half-holiday for the commercial establishments so that the clerks "will not desecrate the Sabbath as they do when it is their only day off".

The fervour of the clerical effort reached its peak in that decade, however, when a letter to the editor of the *Dauphin Herald* in March, 1909 complained of certain "houses of ill repute" within the town limits. The writer alleged that twelve to fifteen women were using accommodations on the west side of the Vermilion river for immoral purposes. He alleged, also, that about a dozen young men had lost their jobs as a result of frequenting the establishment. He urged the clergy and the newly formed Board of Trade to do something about the situation. The town council made a decision to hire more constables to "raid the houses from time to time". About two weeks later Mrs. Bella Thorne, said to be the madam of the establishment, was charged with selling intoxicating liquors. The hearing was held in camera and the defendant was acquitted by magistrate H.N. Macneill. The *Dauphin Herald* and the clergy were irate about both the decision itself and the fact that the hearing had been held in camera. Subsequent actions resulted in charging all the ladies of the establishment on the grounds of immoral conduct. On the day of the hearing, however, none of the ladies appeared in court to answer the charges. They had all cleared out of town during the night, leaving only an "old roustabout" in the house. He was charged and given hard labour. About two years later, however, reports came to the surface of further immorality of the same type. No note is found about the action of the clergy in the second case. In recounting these events, some years ago, J.B. McIntyre told of a similar activity in the old settlement of Dauphin Lake. The house in use at that time burned to the gound quite mysteriously one night to bring an end to its function. J.B. McIntyre suggested that there was a strong suspicion that the ladies of the community had set the fire deliberately. Of course, there is no evidence to substantiate the story.

In addition to the daily round of visitations, the Sabbath activities and the theological-political activities of the clergy generally, there was, especially between the Methodist and the Presbyterian churches, talk of church union. This is noted as early as 1902 and continued intermittently until union actually occurred in 1929. One editor described church union as "undoubtedly the most prominent public question in Canada today".

There must have been other denominations in Dauphin, at least temporarily, for in the *Dauphin Press* of June 27, 1901 is this note: "The Mormons are with us, but the chance of them making many converts is slim. Most of the bachelors here would be glad to have the opportunity of securing one wife, let alone half a dozen".

An earnest concern of the churches in early Dauphin was the provision of adequate services for the burying of the dead. A cemetery had been established on land bought from Harry Whitmore on the east bank of the Vermilion river at the south end of the town. It had been named Riverside Cemetery as the result of the competition to find a suitable name. The competition had been won in 1904 by Robert Cruise, a pioneer farmer who had been reeve of the rural council and Dauphin's third member of parliament. Throughout Dauphin's early years the cemetery was acknowledged to have great potential beauty but it required considerable urgings by the clergy and others to get the voluntary help needed to realize its potential.

Somerville and Wallace were the town's first undertakers. E. Sanderson first cared for the cemetery. Lawrence and Thompson had an early furniture store and were undertakers as well. Their partnership broke up in 1910, after which Thompson carried on alone in the business.

Finally, so far as the clergy of those days is concerned, there was always a constant vigil kept over church attendance. The problem was more acute in the summer when outdoor activities lured even the faithful. If absence wasn't all the problem, tardiness was the remainder. It may have been for that reason, therefore, that in the early months of 1914, town council was urged to "ring the town bells on Sunday morning to bring people to church on time but, if not on time, at least to be there for the taking of the collection." So much for pastoral economics!

The second dominant communal interest was politics. Even then, politics seemed a game for lawyers more than any other single group, although the early years in Dauphin were marked, in a political sense, by the person of Theodore Burrows. It was Theodore Burrows who represented Dauphin in the provincial legislature from 1892 to 1903. There was no one who was more knowledgeable about the district. He came to the area early in its history as a surveyor's helper before any permanent settlement had occurred. He was responsible for supervising the construction of the only two roads leading into the area and he had joined himself to the early community by establishing himself in the lumbering business. His service to the community while he was an M.L.A. appears to have been extensive and satisfactory so far as one can judge from the local newspapers. It was during the time that he represented the Dauphin constituency in the House of Commons that his career was marred by hints of scandal about his dealings in the procurement of timber licences.

The Dauphin federal constituency came into being in 1904. In 1905 Burrows, representing the Liberal party, became its first elected representative. He was the mover of a motion in the House of Commons that gave Manitoba its present northern boundaries. It was only a short time until rumours abounded about his dealings in connection with his timber leases and their possible relationship with Sir Clifford Sifton, Burrow's brother-in-law and then Minister of the Interior. It was this matter, more than anything else, which caused his electoral defeat in 1908 and brought to the seat another very controversial figure in the person of Glenlyon Campbell of Gilbert Plains.

Glen Campbell was the young man who had first ridden into the grasslands of Gilbert Ross's territory from Elphinstone and had vowed to return for a homestead. He did so in an area now called Glenlyon in his honour. He took a keen interest in the development of the community and became a local legend for his abilities as an outdoorsman and hunter. He was a well-educated man who, although born in Canada, received his education in Edinburgh and Glasgow. Fluent in many Indian tongues, he was a solid eccentric in many ways. He was also an early and serious critic of Theodore Burrows. Since he was also of a solid Conservative stripe, he relished the challenge of defeating Burrows and taking his seat in the House of Commons. The wish became fact in the federal election of 1908. Campbell was probably not a very effective member since his eccentricities, which included a very rough tongue, turned many members against him. The result was a defeat in the general election of 1911 in spite of the Conservative victory in the country. Dauphin moved to the Liberals by electing Robert Cruise, a pioneer farmer, who held the seat for the Liberals until 1921.

Campbell and Burrows were bitter political enemies. Campbell suffered two defeats at the hands of Burrows in the provincial elections of 1892 and 1896. He won his 1908 victory by 217 votes. After defeat Burrows returned to his lumbering interests.

In October, 1926 he became Manitoba's Lieutenant-Governor, a post he held until his death in January, 1929. Glen Campbell, after defeat, became the Superintendent of Indian Agencies for the federal government. At the outbreak of war he was made a Lieutenant-Colonel. He recruited two battalions for overseas service, one of which he commanded.

On the provincial scene, Theodore Burrows, who had held the seat continuously from 1892 to 1903, resigned in the latter year to run for a seat in the new federal constituency. The provincial election of 1903 saw the Dauphin seat won for the first time by the Conservatives whose representative was a native son, Dr. J.R. Gunne. He served for one term until 1907 when the seat returned to the Liberals under J.A. Campbell, head of the legal firm of Campbell & Simpson. Frank Simpson, himself a newcomer to Dauphin in 1907, lost no time in identifying himself with the Liberals. For years he fought hard in the Liberal cause without ever becoming a candidate, although many thought of him as the strength of the party in Dauphin while he was active in politics. J.A. Campbell held the seat for only one term. He was defeated in the election of 1910 by his chief adversary, J.G. Harvey, of the firm of Harvey & Bowman. Mr. Harvey served the constituency from 1910 to 1914 at which time he left Dauphin, transferring much of the Conservative party's future in Dauphin into the hands of his partner, J.L. Bowman, who remained for years, the chief protagonist and the favourite candidate of the local Conservatives.

All of these men served their constituency in times of great activity and general prosperity. It was a time when western Canada was booming. World markets were hungry for the grain and primary resources of the west. Immigrants from Britain, Europe and American were pouring into the prairies. In Dauphin and in the area extending northwest towards Swan River, this flow of people was extensive. With it came new problems. Some of these problems involved a railway policy to protect the citizens against high freight rates and to control railway costs; the Manitoba school question; the prohibition question, which pitted many frontier societies against the Victorian mores and the churches; the question of compulsory school attendance, especially as it affected the children of immigrant Europeans and the question of juvenile delinquency amongst those children not attending schools, especially in Winnipeg; the Manitoba boundary disputes. The problems relating to the grading, storage and shipment of grains which resulted in the organization of the grain growers; public buildings such as hospitals, mental institutions, sanatoria, schools, colleges and universities were only some of the issues tackled by the men from Dauphin and other constituencies of the province. It was a time of bitter rivalries in politics but it was also a time of gratifying accomplishments. The newspapers of the day and, indeed, the citizens took their politics seriously and divided on very partisan lines.

The schools of Dauphin have provided some of its proudest history. That education was an important feature of communal life is evidenced by the organization, from as early as 1888, of rural schools to meet the desires of incoming families with young children. When the villages of Dauphin Lake and Gartmore were moved to the railway side they formed a community of about five hundred persons. For a few months it was necessary for the children to attend at their old district schools. The oldest of these was on the "old lake road" which went one mile north from the north end of town and then directly east toward Lake Dauphin. A school district, #531, had been established there in 1888 with J.B. Fawcett as its first teacher, to serve part of the community of Dauphin Lake. On the N.W.1/4 of 16-25-19 the school building of the Vermilion School District, #613, was erected in 1890. It was consolidated with the Dauphin School District in January of 1902 and amalgamated in 1907. The third school, #629, at Gartmore, had been built of logs in 1891 on the northwest quarter of 29-24-19. Miss Jane Iredale was its first teacher.

The long trek to school for the children of Dauphin lasted only a few months. By May of 1897 a new school district known as the Dauphin School District #905 was formed and a two-room school was built on block 33, where the Mackenzie school now stands. The enrolment in September of 1897 was 77 students. Miss E. McWilliams and Miss B. Gunne were the first teachers. Albert E. Kydd was its first principal, earning a salary of five hundred dollars annually. The school was called the Central School and was the successor to the frame building on Main Street which had served as a school temporarily.

Still the population of Dauphin continued to rise. Vermilion school district was consolidated with the Dauphin school district in 1902 making temporary classrooms a necessity until 1904 when a new wing was added to Central School to make an eight-room school for 387 pupils. This school, again, was unable to handle all of the students arriving in Dauphin with their parents. Rooms in the municipal hall were used for the overflow and a determination was made to build a new school in the south end of town where homes were being erected at a fast rate.

Land was set aside in block 43 where a four-room, two-storey school was built for fourteen thousand dollars. It opened in 1908. It looked then as though Dauphin had adequate school space, at least for a time, but in the early days of January, 1909, the Central School burned to the ground. Classes were dispersed to all available space in town and before long a 12-room brick schoolhouse, costing sixty thousand dollars, was built on the same ground. A public competition was held in 1910 to name the new schools. After some months the school in the northend, in block 33, became the Mackenzie School in honour of the early railway building, while the school in the southend, on block 43, became the Whitmore School in honour of the Whitmores, who first came to the Dauphin area and on whose original homestead the school stood.

As the population of the northern area of Manitoba continued to rise and school districts formed with increasing frequency (in sixteen years between 1889 and 1906 about 1100 new school districts were created in Manitoba), the need for qualified teachers became more and more urgent. Full-time "Normal" schools had been established in the southern part of the province at Winnipeg, Brandon and Portage la Prairie. It was evident that a further facility was needed. Attempts had been made since 1904 to bring such a school to Dauphin. Eventually, in 1911, the school board doubled the size of the Whitmore school to eight rooms and added a third floor auditorium to house the "Normal" school which began its operations in the fall. For several years there had been a "winter session" normal school in Dauphin but it did not give permanent and full teachers' certificates. Some of the pupils who attended in the winter session of 1905 were Roger Watson, Florence Merrell,

Isabella Strang, Christine Hicks and Lydia Steckley.

During these early years the district was well served by teachers like Beatrice Gunne, A.C. Crosby, D.S. Woods and A.B. Fallis. Several went on to play leadership roles in educational fields provincially and nationally. The early inspectors, also, such as Hooper, Maguire and Walker, set an excellent standard for the teachers to match. In no less manner, the residents who served on the school board, especially Robert Lilly and William Smith-Jackson, made a lasting contribution to educational well-being in Dauphin.

School attendance was not compulsory at this time. By the end of the decade a good primary and secondary education could be had in Dauphin. A high school department had been established at the Mackenzie school in September, 1905, under the principalship of Mr. A.B. Fallis. In 1908 a Collegiate Institute was formed and was to occupy the top floor of the original Mackenzie school. All of these departments were of high quality. Dauphin was carving a reputation for itself in the field of public education. Grade XII, however, was not available in the town until a much later date. It is of interest to note that Miss Ethel Cadman first joined the Dauphin school staff in the fall of 1902. She left Dauphin in 1908 to study music and returned to co-ordinate the teaching of music in the Dauphin schools, a position she maintained until the late 1930s.

Commercially, Dauphin enjoyed the same boom times of the first decade of the century which were felt throughout the west. A rising population, markets hungry for its produce, a boom in land sales and in residential and commercial construction lent an aura of unreality to some of the activity which was experienced at the time. Land was bought and sold frequently, a modern day "flipping"; businesses started and failed quickly or were sold for profit after short intervals. The result was a constant movement in and out of town or in and out of commercial concerns for many individuals. The transient population was always high but, in spite of all these conditions, a hard core of permanent entrepreneurs were successful and stayed on permanently. Through their efforts they were largely responsible for the creation of a stable community where opportunities abounded for those with a will to work and the desire to build on a permanent basis.

Amongst this group were hardware merchants such as David

Sutherland and A.H.F. Stelck, D.D. McDonald and Jimmy Oliphant. They replaced the pioneer hardware men such as Sandy McPherson, C.F. Turner, W.A. Bigham and the Malcolm brothers, Robert and John. The early jewellers, Dodimead & Company were replaced by W.H. "Skimpy" Wallace who was the first to build a major business block in Dauphin in 1903, Jimmy Wait, and Halsey Park who placed a large street clock in front of his establishment which remained until the 1930s.

H.P. Nicholson, who had come to Gartmore with his family in the pre-railway days, started out as an auctioneer and grain buyer. Shortly after he added real estate to his business which he called "The Dauphin Land Company". He took his brother, G.A. Nicholson into the business with him until the latter's retirement. In 1906 the brothers took into their employ a young accountant named Robert (Bob) Hawkins who, subsequently, became a partner in 1909. Bob Hawkins became head of the firm which has continued until the present. Much was to be heard of Bob Hawkins in Dauphin's later history.

Also in real estate dealings in the early town was Albert E. Iredale, the son of Thomas Iredale who became Dauphin's postmaster when the post offices of Dauphin Lake and Gartmore amalgamated with the new post office at Dauphin. Albert Iredale succeeded his father as postmaster in 1907 and remained in that office throughout all of the early days until 1942.

W.S. Marsh opened a fruit and confectionery store in Dauphin in 1908. He continued in this business until 1923 when he was employed by the town for a short time after which he became the editor of the *Dauphin Herald*.

In 1903 the Love brothers, Thomas and Herman, made their presence felt in Dauphin by winning the contract for the construction of the new town hall and fire station. They remained Dauphin's major bricklayers, passing on the business to sons and grandsons. Another set of brothers, Dan and Gavin Craig, established a reputation, beginning in 1908, for first quality contracting and building. Dan was still active in Dauphin in 1951.

Another fine tradesman who came to town in 1904 was Joe Barker, a shoemaker and shoe repairer. Joe Barker was an enthusiastic sportsman who, for many years along with Mr. H.J.

Miles, refereed most of the soccer games played in Dauphin. Joe Barker was, for a time, the owner of the most up-to-date skate sharpener in town. He sharpened the skates of hundreds of "would-be" hockey stars in his day. A.J. Hunt was the foremost painter and decorator in the early days of the century.

Nelson Griffin and Archie Hoy were early blacksmiths, the latter remaining at his work in Dauphin until his untimely death in the mid-30s. Archie Hoy was one of the prominent figures in the history of the volunteer fire brigade. He also served on the town council for six years. His father, Charles Hoy, ran one of Dauphin's earliest ice cream and confectionery shops. His brother, Ernie, was the first pilot to fly across the Rocky Mountains from Calgary to Vancouver. Nelson Griffin sold his business to Wallace Weir who later went to work for the Canadian National Railway when the roundhouse and the shops were built.

Mark Cardiff was a tinsmith in Gartmore who moved his shop to Dauphin. He later had his shop at his house at the northeast corner of Wakefield and Vermilion, opposite to St. Paul's church. Ed Mitchell came to Dauphin to manage the tinsmithing department of Sutherland & Stelck's business. In 1908 he bought out that end of the business and struck out on his own. He established a plumbing and heating and tinsmithing business which carried on in Dauphin throughout its formative years and into the period following World War II. Frank Bumstead, also an employee of Sutherland & Stelck when he arrived in 1911, struck out on his own in 1912 to create a family plumbing and heating business which continued until the 1960s.

Fred Race barbered in Dauphin from December, 1896 until his death in the late 1930s. W.B. Poucher was Dauphin's early plasterer but left Dauphin before long when much of the plastering contracting was done by the Justice brothers. An early and successful builder in the early town was Isaac Hafenbrak. Many of the early homes and commercial structures, including the first piers at Dauphin Beach, were the work of Isaac Hafenbrak. In 1910 he was joined in a sash and door manufacturing plant by C.B. Steen. That business thrived, with different partners, throughout Dauphin's history, at its location on Front Street East.

Department and clothing stores prospered throughout the

B. REID

Mrs. Steckley's Boarding House.

P.A.M.

Canadian Northern Hotel, Main Street South, 1912.

decade. Ramsay & Philips served the community for several years before becoming Steen & Copeland and, later, Ramsay-Wright. Thomas Caldwell and Anthony Reznoski ran a thriving general store for years. W.G. Murphy and Robert Lilly had strong businesses, as did W.C. Turner. Martin & Fagen catered in men's clothing and J.A. Ball established his tailoring business in 1903. He sold the business in 1909 to take on the agency of the Singer Sewing Machine Company. In turn he sold that business to Louis LaFleur when he became customs inspector for the Dauphin area. Jake Buckwold ran the Commonwealth Store until 1910 when he attracted Eli Bay to the business. From that time until recent years Eli Bay's name has been associated with men's fashions in Dauphin. Jake Buckwold ran a liquor shop, did some horse trading and then settled into the fuel and farm implement business which was later run by his sons, Percy, Alf and Harvey. Tom Jordan supplied ice and wood to the community. He built a small business block at the corner of Main Street and Third Avenue Northeast, where he later carried on a wholesale liquor business. This ended when prohibition arrived. The block was sold to W.G. White. Out of his ice and fuel business, he developed Jordan's Draying, which he sold in 1907 to Shanks and Edwards.

The nature of the community, being mainly attuned to an agricultural setting, necessitated services for that industry. By 1903 Dauphin had seven grain elevators with a combined storage capacity of 114,000 bushels. The elevators of that year were the Northern, the Lake of the Woods, the Export, the Dominion, the Dauphin Milling Company, Morton Pearson's elevator and H.F. Forrest's elevator.

Hotels and rooming houses provided space for the single men in town and for temporary lodgers. The Dauphin House (later the King's Hotel), the Leland House, the C.N. Hotel and the Grandview Hotel were the major hotels. George Sumpton had The Roseberry House and Livery Stable. The Cockerton House and the Coxworth House were other boarding establishments. There were, in addition, two private boarding homes, the Riverside and Mrs. Steckley's home. There were many livery stables, among them the Windsor Stables run by J. McKinstry, Caldwell & Willis Stables and the Roseberry Stables which later became Kelly's barns. There were five or six flour and feed stores.

By the end of 1913 Dauphin had four banks. G.L. Irwin's private bank had become the Bank of Ottawa in the early days. In 1902 the Bank of Commerce came to Dauphin on a site just north of the Dauphin House. Later it erected one of Dauphin's finest buildings on Main Street, south of the Clarke block. In 1906 the Union Bank went into the new McDonald & Voigt block and remained in business until 1936. In 1912, Dauphin's fourth bank, the Bank of Montreal, began business in town.

A major and much needed business opened in Dauphin in 1906. This was the Dauphin Steam Laundry and was under the ownership of Mr. W. Vanderdaasen. It proved a great boon to the community. The ownership changed frequently but it remains one of the oldest businesses in Dauphin. It chose a site at the west end of Front Street, adjacent to the powerhouse to assure itself of a ready supply of steam and hot water. Robert Smith ran a thriving business on the east side of Main Street. Several butchers, Archie Bennett, Lampard & Baird, Mr. Durham, Webb & Rankin supplied meat; the McLean brothers, John Bryce, Mrs. I.C. Montgomery and Harold Lepper supplied much of the bread and pastries.

Throughout the decade the Agricultural Society remained active in encouraging improved farming methods and organizing an annual agricultural exhibition and fair. The Dauphin newspapers always contained informational material relating to farming — how to stack hay, how to build a chicken house, or how to construct a barn. All of this information was designed to be helpful to the novice farmer. Horse auctions were a weekly feature of life in Dauphin during the summer and fall. McKinstry brothers and, later, Dan Hamilton, would frequently dispose of 150 horses in the course of a week. Participants and on-lookers were present in plentiful numbers. From the beginning the livery barns served as the locale for the "standing at stud" of prize stallions. Purebred chickens and cattle were continually purchased to improve the flocks and herds. Heavy horses were favourites of the time and some fine Percherons, Belgians and Clydesdales were seen in Dauphin. The first annual seed fair was sponsored by the Dauphin Agricultural Society in 1906.

The movement of people and goods in and out of Dauphin and northward to the districts opening around Swan River and The Pas was handled, in large part, by the railroad which grew as the area grew. By July, 1903 a daily passenger train service was begun to replace the thrice-weekly service which had been in effect previously. In 1904 Dauphin was made a divisional point on the railway and in 1907 a decision was made to build a roundhouse and railway shops. A 15-stall roundhouse was opened in March of 1908, just a month after an announcement had been made that a new railway station would replace the original station alongside Main Street. By 1910 traffic was heavy enough to warrant an extension of the railway yards. In January of 1912 the railway station burned to the ground, necessitating the rapid building of a new one. The railway company raised a storm by announcing that it intended to close off Vermilion Street and keep the Gladys Street crossing open. In spite of many objections that is what happened. Traffic on Main Street was frequently blocked, sometimes for long intervals, by trains passing through or being made up. Such is the power of railways that this problem still remains.

There were criticisms of the level crossing as a safety hazard for pedestrians as well as for vehicular traffic. It was not long before suggestions were being heard about the desirability of a subway for pedestrians, if not for vehicles. In fact, there were few vehicles on the streets of Dauphin prior to World War I, which were not horse drawn. Cars were just becoming commonplace before the war. T.T. Malcolm's Reo was one of the earliest cars in Dauphin. It had a thirty horsepower motor and a seating capacity for six persons. In June, 1909, a motor trip from Winnipeg to Dauphin, in a McLaughlin-Buick, demonstrated the conditions of travel. The group left Winnipeg at 3:00 p.m. on Friday and reached Gladstone by late evening, where they stayed overnight. Leaving Gladstone early the next morning, they reached Dauphin at 9:45 p.m. on Saturday. They calculated their direct costs at two cents per mile. Many other motorists took days to make the same trip, their time dependent, to a great extent, by the weather and the driver's ability to judge the roadway. Dauphin's first automobile accident occurred in early October, 1910, when J.W. Johnston hit a horse at Main Street and Fourth Avenue North. Edward Batty was one of the earliest car salesmen in Dauphin, selling for McLaughlin-Buick. W.J. Drinkwater, Thomas Jordan and the firm of Campbell & Simpson were three early customers.

The first rat to be seen in Dauphin was observed near the railway station in August of 1913.

In general, times were good throughout the foundational decade. There was an economic lull in 1905 but business increased following that year and by 1912 Dauphin was in the midst of a land boom. There had been losses, of course. Some of these were material in nature and most often due to serious fires in the business centre necessitating relocation and rebuilding. Some never recovered from the loss, some made splendid progress in spite of the difficulties.

The greater losses were those of life. There had been epidemics of scarlet fever and smallpox. These and the hazards of childbirth accounted for many of the deaths. Tuberculosis, drownings, burns and other accidents were frequent. The pioneers, also, were beginning to decrease in number as many reached the ends of their lives. J.H. Bigham, the harness maker; Will McIntosh, who had cut the stakes for the original town survey; William Whitmore, who built the Manor House; Thomas Iredale, Dauphin's first postmaster; Mrs. Andrew Malcolm who, with her husband and family had crossed the Riding Mountain in 1889 to settle in "Skillagalee"; Mrs. Alex McKerchar who had come in 1888; Robert Wishart who had homesteaded in 1890; Jane Iredale who had come with her family in 1887 and Mrs. Mary Gillies, another 1887 pioneer, were some of those who were missed.

Chapter 5 — The Foundation
Books and Reports:
Dauphin the Plentiful. Dauphin Board of Trade, 1912. Provincial Archives of Manitoba.
Hall, D.J. *Clifford Sifton: A Lonely Eminence.* Vancouver: University of British Columbia, 1985.
Newspapers:
The Dauphin Press, January 13, 1897 to December 23, 1915.
The Dauphin Weekly News, January 10, 1901 to December 27, 1915.
The Dominion, June, 1912. Provincial Archives of Manitoba.
The Dominion, July, 1912. Provincial Archives of Manitoba.
The Spectator, June 2, 1904 to Dec. 30, 1904.
Letters:
Personal Communication, George Lynch to John Gardner, undated.

6
THE GREAT WAR

"The greatest war in the history of the world is now in progress", the editor of the *Dauphin Herald* wrote on August 6, 1914. He went on to say, "In this war Great Britain is a participant. As part of the Empire, Canada is also at war and is ready to take her part in whatever way she may be called".

While these sentiments well expressed the views of the great majority of Canadians, there were to be some dissenters. In any event, the statement defined the colonial view of Canada which was evident at the time.

This news of war was the first that many in the district had of World War I. News of previous months, at least in the local publications, contained few comments about forthcoming conflict. The realization of war seems to have come, in Dauphin's case, to a largely unsuspecting populace. The *Dauphin Herald* of the previous week, July 30, 1914, made no mention of the possibility of war, nor had the newspapers of earlier months discussed such a possibility. Indeed, as late as March 26, 1914, the *Dauphin Herald* carried a news item reporting a speech by Philip Scheidemann, the first vice-president of the German Reichstag. Scheidemann was quoted as saying that "there will never be another war in Western Europe because working people are organized as socialists in opposition to war and are resolved not to fight each other at the command of their rulers".

Scheidemann's prophecy was inaccurate in all respects. Not only did war in Western Europe occur within a few months of his prediction but working men from all walks of life, both in Germany and the Allied countries, flocked to their flags to fight one another.

The response in Dauphin to the news of war was quick and spontaneous. Within the next week young men of the district were applying for service and by August 13, 1914 it was reported that Garth Johnston, Neville Munson, Frank Bumstead, H.H. Moore, E.C. Herrick and Neil Birss had made application to go to the front. By the end of August they were posted for training to Valcartier, Quebec and by early November some of these men were already on their way overseas.

War news and wartime activities began to occupy the major attention of the townspeople. War news dominated the newspapers. A great deal of what was written was propaganda intended to stimulate recruitment of young men and to encourage investment in war bonds for the national effort. Dauphin responded to these approaches to a high degree. By February, 1915 one hundred and eight men from Dauphin and district had enlisted. There were reports of fierce battles in France and rumours that ten thousand men on each side had been killed. The rumours of the Kaiser's illness with pneumonia in late 1914, the "saving of Calais" by the British in April, 1915, the German sinking of the *Lusitania* by submarine in May of the same year, the battle of Ypres and the report of the use of poison gas in the trenches in 1915, all helped to spur the organization of patriotic groups, soldiers' welfare societies and bond drives. Recruiting was active and the war effort was carried on with fervour and sacrifices on the parts of many of Dauphin's citizens.

Apart from the eighty-two men from the Dauphin district who died in service, no greater contribution was made to the war effort than that by "Billy" Barker, the son and grandson of pioneer Dauphin families, and Glen Campbell, the man who had represented Dauphin in the House of Commons from 1908 to 1911. Each contributed in his own special way.

Bill Barker was born in Dauphin Lake district in 1894. His grandfather came to the Dauphin area to live in 1888 and to ply his trade as a blacksmith. The blacksmith shop was located in Dogtown, a mile north of the present town. When Gartmore and Dogtown moved to the new townsite in 1896, George Barker Sr. became the first village mayor. His son, George Jr., married Jane Alguire in 1893. She was also the daughter of a pioneer family. They farmed

P.A.M.

William George Barker, V.C., D.S.O., M.C., D.F.C. "The most indestructable of all Canadian war aces."

R. GARDNER

The July 1, 1919 parade down Main Street, Dauphin. Baptist church in background, left.

in the Dauphin area, and for a few years near Russell, Manitoba. George was a pioneer in the use of the new steam engines to run the threshing machines and to break the land. There was a family of nine children, seven sons and two daughters, amongst whom was William George Barker, an air hero of World War I of 1914-18.

Bill Barker initially enlisted in a calvary unit in 1915 but soon transferred to the Royal Flying Corps where he distinguished himself in action in France and Italy in the late war years of 1917 and 1918, flying Sopwith "Camels". His exploits as a machine gunner in the air over the Somme, and as a fighter pilot along the Peave river front in Italy, are legend. He is credited with having destroyed fifty-two enemy aircraft and nine enemy balloons. He flew with #28 Squadron. He earned a Military Cross with Bar, a Distinguished Service Order and the Victoria Cross, presented to him by King George V in March of 1919. He has been described as "the greatest of them all" by Edmund Cosgrove in "Canada's Fighting Pilots". Stephen Franklin, writing about heroes of the high skies says, "The most indestructible of all the great Canadian air aces, however, undoubtedly was Major William G. Barker who flew a greater variety of sorties for a longer period of time than any of his countrymen and won the Victoria Cross on October 27, 1918 in the most lop-sided air battle in history." The battle referred to took place about twenty-one thousand feet above Cambrai when Barker attacked a German reconnaissance plane only to find that nearby were three squadrons of German Fokkers, sixty planes in all. Before the battle was over Barker had downed five enemy planes, had suffered severe wounds in his right thigh, left leg and left elbow and had brought his bullet-riddled plane in behind allied lines. He himself was critically injured, dazed and bleeding.

Sadly, Billy Barker lost his life in an aircrash over Uplands airport in Ottawa in 1930 while he was test-flying a plane.

Glen Campbell made his contribution in a different way. When war broke out in 1914, Glen Campbell was almost fifty-one years of age. He had already proven himself as a competent soldier when he served with Boulton's "Rangers" in the Northwest Rebellion of 1885. He was a competent farmer, having established his homestead on land bought from Gilbert Ross on Gilbert's plains. He had some share of his father's keen enterprise when he left his farm in 1898, together with others from the area, to seek a fortune in the Klondike gold rush of the late 1890s. He made major contributions to the political life of the area by representing Gilbert Plains in the provincial legislature as a Conservative from 1902 to 1908 in the Roblin government. From 1908 to 1911 he represented the Dauphin constituency in the federal house and made a distinct impression on the House of Commons. Following his defeat in 1911 at the hands of Robert Cruise, the Liberal representative, Campbell was appointed Chief Inspector of Indian Agencies for Canada, a post he held until his death. He was a very large but gentle man who guided the formation of two battalions for service overseas.

The first battalion he organized was a Brandon battalion, the 79th, with Colonel Clingan as commanding officer. The second battalion, which he personally accompanied to the battlefields of France as its commanding officer, was the 107th battalion with 32 officers, 136 non-commissioned officers and 856 men, for a total strength of 1024 men. By this time he had been promoted from Major to Lieutenant-Colonel. The battalion embarked from Halifax on the S.S. *Olympic* on September 18, 1916.

In England the battalion was made a Pioneer battalion and distinguished itself in several encounters. Several men from the Dauphin area enlisted to fight with Glen Campbell, Garth Johnston, John May, Dave Justice and George H. Hall were amongst them. His men's love for him carried them through many dangerous encounters. His many letters home include those in which he tells of the bravery of his men in battle and, in particular, of the bravery of a seventeen-year-old from Winnipegosis. The battalion had more than five hundred Italians on its roster, from most of Canada's regions. Two Indians from his battalion were awarded the Military Cross for "conspicuous gallantry in action". Campbell himself spoke many Indian languages and dialects and sometimes gave the word of command in an Indian tongue. The battalion fought at Hill 70 and at Passchendaele in France where Campbell earned the Distinguished Service Order.

Unfortunately, a kidney ailment which had been troublesome prior to his wartime activities continued to plague his health while in France and he succumbed in a hospital in France in late October of 1917. And so a man of great personal popularity, of remarkable energy and courage, died, a representative of his people of whom they could be proud.

When war was declared in August of 1914 it quickly and understandably became of first importance to the country. The topic of war was on every tongue. There were suggestions that the war would not last long. Churches held special services to offer spiritual and tangible aid to the soldiers individually and to the country as a whole. Rumours abounded that Canadians would see limited overseas service. Estimates of British war dead reached one hundred thousand by September 3, 1914. The price of bread doubled overnight and wheat was selling at a high of $1.11 per bushel. A National Prayer Service was held in early September. Heavy fighting was soon reported on all fronts and General Sherman's dictum that "War is Hell" was recalled with apprehension. This apprehension waxed and waned as the news from France favoured or discouraged the Allied cause. Recruiting remained active but never enough trained men were ready to meet the awful demands of war. The price of flour continued to rise and throughout the year almost all the news in the local papers concerned the war in one aspect or another. There was a minor political battle about the issue of rum to the soldiers. Captain Sir Victor Horsley, an eminent British physician, stated that rum lowers resistance to infections such as penumonia, typhoid and dysentery. His remarks went unappreciated in many circles.

News travelled slowly and it was not until April of 1915 that the details of the first battle of Ypres in the previous October, with the horrors of poison gas, were reported in the *Dauphin Herald*. About that time Malcolm's drug store was selling patriotic notepaper covered with flags, while Robson's drug store was giving "German Iron Crosses" with each ten cent purchase. In April, 1915, one store advertised the following prices:

Sugar —	20 lbs. for $1.55
Tea —	3 lbs. for $0.85
Corn Syrup —	5 lbs. for $0.30
Toilet Soap —	7 cakes at $0.25
Strawberry Jam —	5 lbs. for $0.65
Dairy Butter —	11 lb. for $0.30

The intensity of the struggle in France appeared to increase through 1915 and 1916. Pages of news and reports of heavy fighting along all fronts continued throughout these years. Dauphin received the reports of injuries and death with the same degree of shock and determination that characterized all Canadian communities. There was particular shock by such reports as occurred in January, 1916, when it was learned that four brothers were killed together in a bomb blast in France. Surely, war was hell.

January of 1917 ushered in a very cold spell as temperatures dropped to -40 degrees F. One hundred men from the Dauphin area had enlisted. There were reports of "wonderful fighting in the air" by Canadian members of the Royal Flying Corps, amongst whom was Bill Barker. Archie Chute and Jack Ramsden were leaving Dauphin for active service, one to report to his battalion, the other to enlist after having passed his law examination for entrance to the bar. Enlistment had so reduced availability of local labour that work on the Hudson Bay railroad ceased. Soldiers, as well as available townsmen, pitched in to help reap the harvest in the fall. Many Sunday church services became memorial services as the list of wounded, missing or dead, lengthened. As local citizens and organizations pitched in to help in the war effort, they were successful in over-subscribing all the war bond drives and in donating in liberal amounts to those who were sending clothes, cigarettes and treats to the men at the front and to the wounded in hospitals. Neighbour helped neighbour through crises resulting from the war action. But the struggle was long. As time elapsed news came of Ypress, St. Eloi, the Somme, Arras, Hill 70, Lens, Amiens, Vimy Ridge and Passchendaele.

The speed of enlistment was not sufficient to keep pace with the number of casualties. Canada faced the knotty problem of conscription. By September, 1917, a "Win the War" meeting was held in Dauphin to support the cause of conscription. By October of that year conscription was a fact by dint of the Military Services Act, promulgated by the Borden Government. Exemption boards were established and young men, not already in service, began to receive their calls. Names of allowed and disallowed appeals against conscription were published weekly. In November a "First Victory Loan" was advertised with 5.5% interest. Merchants of Dauphin

MRS. M. CAMPBELL

Dauphin Pioneers Banquet in the Pollon Block, 1916.

L to R: 1. Not identified, 2. Martin Playford, 3. Tom Playford, 4. Albert Iredale, 5. Bill Murray, 6. Jack Daniels, 7. George Barker, 8. John J. Inkster, 9. Morley Park, 10. Theo. Burrows, 11. Tom Shaw, 12. Jim Shaw,, 13. N.i., 14. Jack Whitmore, 15. Jim Kerr, 16. Geo. Tucker, 17. Ed Gorby, 18. Robert Lee, 19. R.I. Rintoul, 20. N.i., 21. Donald McKillop,, 22. N.i., 23. John Gorby, 24. N.i., 25. Jos. E. Inkster, 26. T. Malcolm, 27. N.i., 28. no. #28, 29. Frank Whitmore, 30. Dan McKillop, 31. Bob Malcolm, 32. Jimmie Campbell, 33. N.i., 34. Jim Malcolm, 35. Alf Coombs, 36. Jack McKillop, 37. Wm. Durston, 38. Dan Wishart, 39. Sam Boyd, 40. J.B. Fawcett, 41. A.J. Hendeson, 42. Bob McLeod, 43. Dunc Dickson, 44. J. Seale Sr., 45. Lorne McKillop, 46. N.i., 47. N.i., 48. H.P. Nicholson, 49. N.i., 50. Jim Neill, 51. Jimmy Friend, 52. Chas. Durston, 53. Jim Nicholson, 54. N.i., 55. N.i., 56. Alton Nicholson, 57. John Hassard, 58. Angus Durston, 59. Harry Durston, 60. N.i., 61. N.i.

urged the purchase of these bonds; the goal was one million dollars, to be raised in the northern districts of Manitoba. Dauphin raised four hundred thousand dollars. A committee consisting of J.W. Bossons, R.M. McCall, Dr. G.C.J. Walker and Thomas Little was established to take applications for service in the Royal Flying Corps. A Dauphin War Committee was very active in obtaining food supplies and in urging on the townspeople, conservation of all goods and materials.

At the Gay Theatre, local patrons were seeing such movies as "The Kaiser, Beast of Berlin" and documentaries of the Battle of the Somme. Coal was in short supply and local fuel merchants were advising citizens to "buy now or freeze". In August of 1918, the Governor-General, the Duke of Devonshire, visited Dauphin; Charlie Chaplin was playing at the Gay Theatre; and memorial services were being held for one of Dauphin's sons, Lieutenant Willis Code, whose father had brought Dauphin its first creamery. Such were the valleys and peaks of Dauphin's emotional life.

In April, 1917 America entered the war against Germany. Spirits were buoyed by this fresh infusion of men and war materiels. Subsequent offensives in the Aisne-Marne area marked a turning point in the war and subsequent actions at Cambrai, Mons and Verdun and the second battle of the Marne brought the war to an end on November 11, 1918. On that evening the citizens of Dauphin joined in a Thanksgiving service and a night parade to celebrate the end of a terrible ordeal for so many men and women, some of whom would never return, and to anticipate a return to a more normal way of family and community life.

On the civil side of the town's life, however, the picture was not as bright as it had been earlier. The general economy of the town, which in prior years had reached boom-time proportions with the rapid influx of settlers and merchants after the coming of the railway, was now beginning to show a definite decline. The rate of increase in new building, both residential and commercial; the rate of increase in population and in the assessed value of property, slackened from its former pace. Farm mortgage sales increased at the same time. In the face of wartime exigencies, Canadians had turned their minds and energies to the war effort while local matters, necessarily, assumed a second level of importance. But things did not stand still.

In January of 1914, provincial politics necessitated nominations for an election expected later that year. The Roblin government, which had taken office in 1900 and had been re-elected at all provincial elections since that time, narrowly escaped defeat in the election of 1914 when they formed a minority government. William Buchannon, a pioneer farmer of Dauphin, represented his constituency for the Conservatives in that government. He defeated J.A. Campbell, the Liberal nominee, but found his tenure to be short when in May, 1915, Sir Rodmond Roblin, deluged by the political storm and the public reaction to irregularities in the construction of the Legislative buildings and the Law Courts in Winnipeg, offered the resignations of himself and his government to Manitoba's Lieutenant-Governor, Sir Douglas Cameron.

In the campaign following Roblin's resignation, William Buchannon again contested for the Conservatives. He was opposed by Dr. W.J. Harrington, the popular medical doctor from Dauphin. Dr. Harrington won that election to replace William Buchannon as Dauphin's M.L.A. During the ensuing term a vote was held in Manitoba which resulted in the prohibition of alcohol sales throughout the province. Dauphin supported this vote, with the "Drys" collecting 494 votes and the "Wets" collecting 207 votes. Within a short time T.T. Malcolm, O.E. Heaslip and Wilfred Robson applied as Dauphin's pharmacists, for liquor dispensing licences under the Manitoba Temperance Act. It wasn't long before a prominent barber was charged with theft of liquor from a railway car when 115 bottles of liquor were found in his shop. Shortly aferwards, the Rev. Haw of the Methodist church, berated the doctors and the pharmacists about their compliance and their cooperation with the Temperance Act. He bolstered his remonstrance by announcing that in December of 1918, four doctors had issued 1019 prescriptions for spirituous liquors. Of these prescriptions 440 were from one doctor and 727 prescriptions were for more than twenty-four ounces of liquor. There is no evidence that doctors, pharmacists or citizens were greatly upset by these revelations. It probably didn't matter too much, as by September of 1919 the government was considering the establishment of liquor dispensaries throughout the province.

During 1919 the return of the men from the services re-united families and added much-needed strength to the labour force. Dauphin welcomed them in many public ways. Churches held services of welcome and thanksgiving. They were honoured in a banquet in the town hall on the first anniversary of the armistice. Three hundred to four hundred veterans joined in an evening in which, a reporter stated, "the tables were groaning under the weight of good things". The Great War Veterans' Association resolved to build a recreational and business facility for their members. They were, at the time, meeting in rooms in the Lilly block.

In the political arena, the community noted the withdrawal of J.L. Bowman as Conservative candidate so that Robert Cruise could represent Dauphin in the federal coalition government of Robert Borden. Mr. Cruise was confirmed as Dauphin's coalition candidate in November of 1917.

In January of 1914, the new St. Paul's Anglican church, erected on the corner of Fourth Avenue Southwest and Vermilion Street was officialy consecrated by Archbishop Matheson, the first Anglican Archbishop of Rupertsland and Primate of Canada. The first minister to be called to the new church was Dr. A.S. Wiley who remained in Dauphin until the end of 1915 when he was succeeded by Dr. de Mattos. Other rectors up to 1950, have been H.P. Barrett, A.E. Cousins, W. Brailsford and H.E. Bridgett.

In other churches congregations remained active. The Methodists were able to burn their mortgage in 1919 at which time R.E. Spence had succeeded T.E. Bethel in the pulpit. The Presbyterian congregation made a decision on their thirteenth anniversary to increase the size of their church. The Baptist church celebrated its eleventh anniversary in 1916.

The weekly newspapers carried many of the Sunday sermons from the main churches. A large part of the community's social life, for both young and old, centred around the church. The church influenced the day-to-day tenor of life and, by entering into the debates about local issues, either by preachings or by a direct approach to the council or its committees, made its views known. A great deal of what they said fell on sympathetic ears.

Much of the effort of the church was directed against the use of alcohol, both in private and in public. From time to time, criticisms were made on Sunday mornings about the consumption of liquor at one or another social event. Those who served the liquor were attacked as having a baneful effect on the community and as being sinful persons. Fortunately, the scales were held in balance, at least to some extent, by the tolerant views of Dan Hamilton, who operated the C.N. Hotel. Dan proclaimed for all to hear that, in his view, a bartender "is as good as any church member so long as he keeps himself respectable".

By the end of the war considerable discussion had taken place in Dauphin, as across the country, as to the advisability of church union between the Methodists, Presbyterians and the Congregationalists. Of course, opinion was divided and the major debate was left to the next decade.

In medical circles, Dr. Walter G. Rogers came to Dauphin to associate with Dr. Harrington while Dr. Ross left Dauphin for The Pas in early 1914. The report of the Dauphin General Hospital for 1913 showed that 450 patients had been treated. Two nurses graduated from the nursing school. It wasn't until 1932 that the nursing graduands exceeded more than three per year except for the unusual years of 1910 and 1921 when there were four and five graduands respectively. Miss Laidlaw, later Mrs. Harrington, resigned her position as Lady Superintendent in 1913. She had been preceded, in order from the start of the hospital by Miss Picken, Miss Hyde, Miss Brereton and Miss Johnston. Fortunately, her successor failed to take up her appointment and Miss Laidlaw stayed on until 1917, eventually being succeeded by Miss Foyer. It was in 1914 that a proposal for a new hospital to replace the old was made. Nothing came of this idea for another fourteen years.

Dr. Harrington continued an active role in his medical practice while attending to his duties as the M.L.A. for Dauphin. He served from 1915 to 1920. He was opposed in the 1915 election by William Buchannon, Conservative, and by Mr. W.J. McQuay, Independent. Their election expenses were $309.11, $333.00 and $117.25 respectively.

Dr. Heaslip arrived in Dauphin to enter partnership with Dr. Culbertson. That partnership ended later when Heaslip volunteered for military service and Dr. Culbertson left Dauphin, after a severe illness, to practise later in the milder climate of the west coast.

Before he left, however, he invited Dr. N.G. Trimble to associate with him. Dr. Trimble remained in Dauphin for several years, leaving for The Pas in 1928.

A smallpox outbreak in Ochre River and sporadic cases elsewhere prompted the first major vaccination program in Dauphin when the school board made it compulsory for the school children to be vaccinated. There was much opposition to this decision and for some weeks the debate raged. One writer expressed a common feeling when he wrote to the *Dauphin Herald* as follows, "In the mind of the writer, vaccination is an accursed practice and should be stamped out, and in the name of humanity we should cease poisoning and polluting the pure blood of the helpless child with putrid matter from a diseased calf". The *Dauphin Herald*, with liberal quotes from the Encyclopedia Brittanica, supported the program and it went ahead.

Dauphin's population, at the beginning of 1914, was 4421. The increasing number of citizens, the nature of the work in a pioneer agricultural area and the increasing chance of infections and infectious diseases with an increasing movement of people, all conspired to keep the doctors busy. An explosion in an acetylene plant with consequent loss of a leg, frequent cases of "blood poisoning" and of boils and carbuncles, of scarlet fever, diphtheria, smallpox, typhoid fever, sawmill accidents resulting in finger, hand or arm amputations; shotgun and rifle wounds; drownings and a high birth rate all combined to increase the demands on medical manpower. The addition of an influenza epidemic in the fall of 1918 and early 1919 was an aditional burden which robbed the doctors of whatever rest they needed.

The months of the influenza epidemic were hectic months for many. In order to stem the spread of the disease, schools, theatres and other places of gathering were closed. Travel was discouraged. Many working people were advised to use face masks to prevent the acquisition or the spread of the disease. Most of the ill were cared for at home but when complications appeared, and there were many, admission to hospital frequently became necessary. The hospitals were under great pressure to provide the care needed for so many.

After the flu epidemic had largely subsided the doctors of

Dauphin decided to pitch their lots in together to form the Dauphin Medical Clinic in April, 1919. T.T. Malcolm was to manage the business affairs while Dr. J.R. Gunne (diseases of the eyes, ears, nose and throat), Dr. Harrington (Surgery), Dr. Rogers (Medicine & Surgery), Dr. Trimble (Pathology) and Dr. Bottomley (X-Ray) did the medical work. T.T. Malcolm would also do optometry. The clinic was housed on the second floor, up a very long flight of stairs, in the Burrows block. The elderly, the feeble and the lame had difficulty making the stairs.

B.S. O'Grady, a dentist, was in Dauphin for a short time in the early war years. Dr. W.I. Bell, a dentist from Souris, came to Dauphin in early 1919. He had his office above Bowman & McFadden's office on Main Street. Later he, too, moved to the Burrows block. This brought to three the number of dentists in Dauphin. Dr. Bell practised dentistry until his death in Dauphin and his practice was eventually taken over by Dr. A.D. McKee in the early 1930s.

In September, 1914, an ad appeared in the *Dauphin Herald* announcing the association of J.T. Thorson and J.N. McFadden the practice of law. Their offices were to be above Humphrey & Wilson's store. Advice was also given that they were to open a branch office in McCreary. Later they opened an office at Winnipegosis as well. It appears that the association in practice, in this case, meant that J.N. McFadden would handle the firm's affairs in Dauphin while Thorson was the Winnipeg arm of the partnership. Whatever the relationship, it did not survive much longer, for in August 1916, J.N. McFadden joined Mr. Bowman in a partnership which lasted a long time and contributed significantly to the affairs of the region. Both Bowman and McFadden spent the rest of their days in Dauphin and both made enormous contributions in differing ways, to the welfare of the town and its surrounding area.

In another office, J.A. Campbell, who first opened a law office in Dauphin in 1899, was joined by Frank Simpson in 1907. Campbell left Dauphin in the early years of the first war, leaving Simpson to practice alone until 1916 when he joined forces with Ernest N. McGirr, a lawyer having recently passed his law exams with honours. This partnership was formed in August, 1916, the same time that Bowman & McFadden had formed theirs. For a short interval in 1916, R.C. Smith worked with Simpson but left in August to work on his own. Toward the end of 1918 Simpson & McGirr took Neville Munson into the firm and at that time moved their offices into the new Clarke block on Main Street North. Also in October, 1918, Alex Katz, then a member of the Royal Flying Corps, came home to recuperate from an injury suffered in an air accident. He was later to join the firm, after Munson's leaving, which through the next thirty years would be familiar to Dauphinites as Simpson, McGirr & Katz. That firm earned a solid reputation in Manitoba's legal circles.

Before the end of World War I it had become evident amongst those concerned with the administration of justice in Manitoba, that a reorganization of the judicial districts in the northern part of the province was an urgent need. A strong and successful drive had been made to convince the authorities that the burgeoning population of the Dauphin area and the surrounding towns would be better served by the division of existing judicial districts into more manageable and efficient precincts and the establishment of courts and a jail within the Dauphin area. It is likely that this would have occurred earlier but for the war, which caused the postponement of many plans for a time. However, the decision was made to create a Northern Judicial District, with its administrative centre at Dauphin, in 1913. The erection of the courthouse and jail, which was built by Sam Brown of Winnipeg, was given the go-ahead when the provincial government, in early 1916, voted eighty thousand dollars for the purpose.

Planning began immediately and a site chosen at the head of Main Street North. Contracts were let in July of 1916 and by March, 1917 Judge Gregory Barrett, newly appointed for the Northern Judicial district, held court for the first time in the new court house. Mr. Simpson and Mr. Bowman made opening remarks to welcome the first judge. Present also on that day was Thomas Little, the first court reporter in the judicial district. He was later to make a very solid contribution to his chosen career and to the town. At the beginning of 1918, Judge Barrett was succeeded by Judge A.L. Bonnycastle, who remained in Dauphin for many years and whose sons brought the family name into prominence in Canadian business life. The lower courts were presided over by Robert Hawkins who had been appointed police magistrate in September, 1915. Robert Hawkins came to Dauphin in 1903 and had established a reputation in real-estate and insurance fields.

The business and commercial life of Dauphin was affected to a great extent by the war. The demands which the war effort put on the manpower situation and on financial resources limited the availability for non-military purposes. Still, many changes occurred during the war years in this aspect of the town's activities.

The last issue of the *Dauphin Herald* in 1913 carried advertisements and professional cards for eighty different businesses and professional establishments in Dauphin. These consisted of five lawyers, four doctors, two dentists, two veterinarians, three banks, three drug stores, three watchmakers and jewellers, one architect, three butcher shops, six contractors and builders, two florists, one livery stable (although there were several more), two fuel dealers, two photographers, five department stores, one theatre, two stationery and book stores, three hardware stores, four bakery, confectionery and fruit stores, two grocery stores (there were many more), five plumbing, heating and tinsmith shops, a steam laundry, a maternity home, a harness shop and five clothing shops; the rest were a mixture of services such as draying, a wholesale liquor store, auctioneers, furniture and undertaker, custom sawing, and real-estate.

One of the early pioneer merchants, W.C. Turner sold his grocery business to A. Alton as he moved further west. An eastern magazine flooded Dauphin with salesmen who offered a lot in British Columbia free with each subscription paid for! Although the general economy was said to be turning down, Dauphinites were encouraged by reports that tenders had been called for a new telephone exchange building and that Standard Lumber Company of Winnipeg was said to be soon establishing a branch in Dauphin.

A major blow to the business community in Dauphin in the spring of 1914 was the sudden and unexpected death at age 41, by suicide, of Robert Lilly who had come to Dauphin in the spring of 1898 and had been a leader in the town's development since that time. After his death the remaining partners arranged a closing out sale. His new home on Fourth Avenue Southwest and Hospital

Street was subsequently sold to F.E. Simpson and then to Eli Bay; it was next a nurses' home and the Lodge's Funeral Home.

Another name which was prominent in Dauphin's history was that of A.E. Prentice who, in Mayof 1914, purchased a livery stable from Merritt Spillett. It was situated across the lane behind the C.N. Hotel (later the Hamilton). A year later he added another livery barn to his businesses when he bought out the Willis Livery Stable at the northeast corner of Front Street and First Street Northeast. He ran Prentice's "barn" behind the Hamilton Hotel until the barn burned on a summer evening in 1936 and, tragically, brought to an end the life of Tom Scrase, one of Dauphin's best loved young men and, as a very good hockey player, an idol of many of its boys. In June, 1914, George Barker, the son of Dauphin's first mayor opened a livery business in a lot opposite the King's Hotel on Second Avenue Northeast. Barker's livery business was soon taken over by Harry Esplen and Sam Boyd in November of 1914 and in 1916 by Dr. Gofton. Another livery stable which was very active in those days was Kelly's Feed & Livery Stable, situated on the east-west lane between Burrows Avenue and Third Avenue Northwest. This barn also burned in a spectacular fire in November of 1928.

It was also in 1914 that E.J. "Teddy" Mayo took over the indoor electrical wiring responsibilities previously handled by the town. He entered a partnership with Wallace Waters but later, and for many years, he handled an electrical contracting business out of a small building at the corner of Main Street and First Avenue Southwest. Other new businesses included H.C. Purdy & Co. who operated a ladies' and children's clothing store; G.A. Hunter, the "Home of Good Clothes", opposite the bank of Montreal; Plumm's Consolidated Store for groceries and clothing which later became "The Farmers' Store" on First Avenue Southwest, just off Main Street. Stewart Baird Co. opened as an independent auctioneer and H.C. Purdy & Company opened a furniture dealership on Main Street.

A.J. Sherwood opened the first chiropractic office in Dauphin, in the Pollon block. Mrs. I.C. Montgomery and Son of the Royal Fruit Store on Front Street, opened a branch of her store in "Winterton's old stand on Bond's Beach" (Ochre Beach)., A.F.

Farrell started business as a funeral director and licensed embalmer and sold furniture as well. He was Dauphin's busiest funeral director, operating on the north side of Burrows Avenue for many years. W.R. "Bill" McCormick opened his stationery business on Burrows Avenue, immediately east of the post office, in 1914. He remained in that business, at that site, for thirty-five years before his retirement. A new restaurant, the Dauphin Restaurant (later the Rex Café) opened on Front Street across from the new railway station and was run by Charlie Hong. The Nelson Furniture Company took over the furniture business of W.C. Turner in 1915 and closed out the following year. In 1918 W.G. White opened a fabrics and millinery shop which thrived for many years at the southeast corner of Main Street and Third Avenue North.

It was during the war years that cars first began to appear in appreciable numbers on Dauphin's streets. Merritt Spillett, late of the livery business, opened an agency for McLaughlin-Chevrolet cars. His warehouse and office were on Main Street next to the C.N. Hotel. A 35-horsepower McLaughlin Buick sold for $960. In 1917 Charlie Stewart opened an agency for Canadian Briscoe Motors Company Ltd. which sold a 4-cylinder touring car for $895 and an 8-cylinder touring car for $1185, both f.o.b. Brockville, Ontario. At the same time, A.B. Buie opened the first Studebaker agency in Dauphin and a new kind of business, "Madden's Automobile Livery" opened at Gofton's stables opposite the King's Hotel. A.P. Rowat handled Chalmers, Saxon and Maxwell cars and T.T. Malcom had the agency for Gray-Dort cars. Sutherland and Stelck, the early hardware merchants, became the selling agents for Chevrolet cars when the agencies were divided. Merrell & Smith were selling Willys-Knight and Overland cars by 1917 although Sutherland & Stelck obtained that agency later. Merrell & Smith originally had the Ford agency in Barker's bowling alley. A 1917 Ford runabout (roadster) cost $475. Later that year the agency changed and A.A. Feldman, with a garage on Main Street and Second Avenue Southeast, obtained the agency for Ford cars and trucks.

As a result of the interest being shown in the automobile, it was not long before businesses catering to the motoring public should establish themselves in Dauphin. An early garage was located on the corner of Main Street and Third Avenue Northwest on property owned by Dr. Harrington. The garage opened under the management of J.R. Eagle in December of 1918. J.R. Eagle had previously operated a Dodge agency on Front Street from April, 1917.

In June 1916, Dauphinites were reading newspaper ads for Ramsay & Copeland, Dauphin's newest department store. By August it was announced that Cameron & Heap, wholesale grocers, would open a branch warehouse on the railway siding east of Main Street to supply northern Manitoba's needs for fruit and groceries. A new creamery was to be built at Gladys Street and First Avenue Southwest. The contract for the new telephone exchange building had been let to Sam Brown of Winnipeg. The timing was fortunate, for in December of 1916 the telephone exchange building then in use, was gutted by fire.

Another major business move in Dauphin occurred in April, 1917 when the town's two newspapers, the *Dauphin Herald* and the *Dauphin Press*, amalgamated to become *The Dauphin Herald and Press*. The move was necessitated because of the wartime depletion of staff, making it difficult for each newspaper to operate efficiently and also for the need, in wartime, to conserve materials. At any rate, the merger proved successful. The newspaper served and still serves Dauphin very well. It has been honoured on several occasions for the quality of its producct. Its early life was guided by the father and son team of George King and W.D. King and later by W.D.'s brother-in-law, W.S. Marsh and his children, Bill, Jim and Helen Marsh. A *Herald* subscription in 1917 was $1.50 per year.

It was in 1917, too, when a young Irish immigrant, having completed his apprenticeship as a tailor and having worked for a few years in Winnipeg, arrived in Dauphin. He had been attracted to Dauphin by a letter written by J.N. McFadden to the Tailor's Union in Winnipeg, extolling the opportunities for a tailor in Dauphin. John Gardner soon opened a Ladies' and Gents' Tailor Shop on the south side of Burrows Avenue near the post office next to Bill McCormick's store. He stayed in that shop until 1926 when he enlarged his business by buying out E.J. Wallwin and moving to a shop on Main Street North, just north of the Malcolm block. A year later he moved into the Malcolm block. His business grew and thrived throughout most of the years and still serves the community through his son, Bob, and his grandson Bob Jr. John Gardener played a stellar role in Dauphin through his business interests and his sporting interests — particularly in golf and soccer. In the political life of the area he was a staunch Conservative and, finally, he served with great distinction in the provision of quality health care in Dauphin. He was a long-time member of the Dauphin Hospital Board and a strong worker for the Manitoba Hospital Association. He was one of several Dauphin citizens who devoted many years of voluntary effort to the cause of hospitals in Manitoba. Among other early contributors were Harry Macneill and Robert Hawkins.

Other tailors set up shop in Dauphin. Steve Voychesin Sr. advertised as a merchant tailor with his shop next to Cort's grocery store on Main and Third Avenue Southwest, later occupied by V.W. Jackson. The Dauphin Tailoring Company, with Sam Solomon as manager, opened a shop on the Front Street side of the Grandview Hotel. This shop continued in business, through several moves and including the Tip Top agency, for many years. Sam Solomon became a major force in municipal government in Dauphin and was, at one time, its longest serving alderman (1930-37, 1939-48).

In mid-February of 1918 a major fire, which tested the town's fire-fighting capacity to the limit, occurred in the Malcolm block of that day. It caused extensive damage to Ed Wallwin's men's clothing store and to H.C. Purdy's ladies' wear store. Purdy decided to sell out his business, which was bought by W.G. White of Souris. When W.G. White moved to his new store, John Gardner moved into his old location.

Almost coincidental with the announcement of the armistice to end World War I was the annoucement from E.A. Ramsay of Ramsay & Copeland that he had purchased property on the northeast corner of Main Street and Third Avenue North. This gave him a 141 ft. frontage on Main Street on which he proposed to build a large department store of the most modern kind. Shares were to be offered to the public to finance the venture. In fact, the sale of shares went very well and the Ramsay-Wright building became a reality in the 1920s.

The agricultural aspect of the town's affairs is recognized by the many efforts toward better methods of farming and of animal husbandry. At the beginning of 1914 a dairy industry was evident in the existence of the Excelsior Dairy which had recently been bought by Frank Harvey from John McKee, and in Mr. Patterson's Roslyn Dairy which was said to be doing a brisk business. This, in spite of the fact that many households in town had their own cows to supply their own needs and to sell to others. Butter was selling at 25¢ a pound and eggs at 20¢ a dozen in March 1914. There was said to be twenty racehorses training in Dauphin, presumably many of them belonging to the Playfords or the Chutes, who were ardent promoters of the sport. Billy McLernon brought in five pedigreed carrier pigeons. For some time the pigeon racers had meeting rooms in the basement of the Hamilton Hotel. Two standard-bred stallions, Dr. Gift and Spanish Jack, stood at stud that season in Dauphin. In 1915 Royal Astoria, a champion Clydesdale stood at stud at William Blair's farm at Ochre River. Horse auctions, particularly those called by Dan Hamilton, were very popular and well-attended. Dan Hamilton is said to have sold 23 horses in the space of 80 minutes at one of his auctions in 1917. Art Boughen brought in a pure Holstein bull for service in an attempt to improve herd quality. Adam Justice offered egg settings from prized white leghorns.

Wheat farmers were concentrating, in the main, on growing the new Marquis wheat, developed by Dr. Charles Saunders, at the Ottawa experimental farm. The quick ripening and the high quality of this wheat was particularly suited to the short prairie growing season. The new elevators were built in 1918, one by the Dauphin Milling Company and one by the McLaughlin Elevator Company. The first was built on the railway siding at the Dauphin Millingsite on Mackenzie and Vermilion while the second was east of Main Street on the south side of the tracks. Some of the farmers growing grain to fill those elevators, and whose names became well-known over many years in Dauphin were Esplen, McQuay, Buchannon, Boughen, Cruise, Strang, Durston, Ritchie, Miller, Gorby, Armstrong, Nicholson, Birss, McCorvie, Fisher, Spillett and Lee.

Relaxation from the day's activities and diversion from the

cares of the war were to be found in many activities in the area. Cottages at Dauphin Beach were put to good use and "the lake" was a popular summer area. Cottages with names like "Lafalot", "Dunworkin", "What's It To You", "Kumonin", "Osolazy", and "Uneeda Rest" became well-known to beach fans. Townspeople were able to enjoy lake cruises on the "Norma Rae", a local boat owned by T.T. Malcolm. Contracts were let for the building of a large pier at Dauphin Lake in June of 1915. That pier was to have a chequered history.

The Gay Theatre was showing such stars as Lillian Gish, William S. Hart, Douglas Fairbanks, Charlie Chaplin and Tom Mix. In 1917 the Chatauqua show visited Dauphin for the first time and was enjoyed by many.

There were six tennis courts in Dauphin. They were the town courts, the C.N.R. courts, the Epworth League courts, the hospital courts, the Baptist Young People's courts and the Southend Club courts. A garden club, an auto club, a horticultural society, a temperance society, a children's aid society, a soccer league, a baseball club and literary groups were active during those years.

The crops were good, one farmer reporting 72 bushels of wheat per acre. Land values were rising, costs for food and shelter were on the increase. Shoppers were buying such articles as Zam Buck, Fruitatives, Chamberlain's liniment, Beecham's Pills, Lydia Pinkham's Vegetable Compound and Dr. Williams Pink Pills (for pale people). Fifty students were enrolled in the Normal School while at the same time it was said that 20 percent of children in Canada between the ages of 7-14 years did not attend school. Mr. Harding had resigned his position as principal of the High School at the end of the school year and Mr. Spenceley had been named in his place. Mark Cardiff became secretary of the school board to replace William Smith-Jackson who died a short time later, after having served his community with distinction in the area of education.

The new telephone exchange, the new courthouse, Joe Clarke's new business and apartment block, a new creamery and many new houses and barns were being built in Dauphin. A new pavilion had been proposed for Dauphin Beach. The first issue of the high school paper *The Echo* was published in January, 1918.

Coal was in short supply. John Gardner reported that cloth to make suits and overcoats was difficult to obtain. In September, 1916 the first rat reported in the farming district was killed on a local farm. Towards the end of the decade union members of the staff of the Canadian Northern Railway struck in sympathy with their brothers of the Winnipeg Strike of 1919. The strike lasted from late May until late June of that year. Bootleggers were busy during prohibition days. Teachers' salaries were $1400 to $2000 dollars for principals and $750 to $900 for teachers. A curfew was in effect in Dauphin which imposed a 9:00 p.m. deadline on those under eighteen years. The powerhouse whistle blew to announce the time.

In June, 1919, the Canadian Northern Town Properties Company Ltd. placed on the market part of the old Company Farm along the east bank of the Verilion river beyond the northern boundary of the town proper (north of present day River Ave.). The lots sold for $250 - $600 dollars; one-half was to be paid in cash and the balance in 12-18 months. Judge Bonnycastle bought four lots on which he built his home and raised his family. Others bought eagerly and a new and future subdivision began in Dauphin.

In July, 1919 it was announced that Captain Ernest Hoy, a former Dauphin boy, would attempt a trans-mountain flight from Calgary to Vancouver. In August the flight was successfully completed, the first air flight over the Canadian Rockies.

And finally, Dauphin continued to lose some of its early pioneers. Thomas Gorby, who had come to Dauphin in 1890 with his family, died in 1915, as did Mrs. William Buchannon. Matt Lee of the Gartmore district, who had come to the Dauphin area in 1889, died in 1919. Andrew Malcolm, the farmer and cheesemaker, who had crossed the mountain from Minnedosa in 1887 died as 1919 moved into 1920.

Chapter 6 — The Great War
Books and Reports:
Canada in the Great World War: Toronto: United Publishers of Canada, 1919.
Cosgrove, Edmund. *Canada's Fighting Pilots.* Toronto: Clark, Irwin Company Ltd., 1965.
Jones, H.A. *The War in the Air.* London: Oxford at the Clarendon Press, 1937.
MacIntyre, Lt. Col. D.E. *Canada at Vimy.* Toronto: Peter Martin Associates Ltd., 1967.
Newspapers:
The Dauphin Herald, January 1914 to December 1918.
The Dauphin Press, January 1914 to December 1917.

GREATER LOVE HATH NO MAN THAN THIS

These Dauphin men gave up their lives in the 1914-1918 war

J. Adams	A.E. Arnold	W.E. Arnold
L.H. Barnard	H.C. Batty	W.J. Bawdon
S. Blough	J.R. Brown	G.W. Buchan
J. Calder	L.A. Campbell	R.A. Chard
W.J. Chesire	G.B. Clarey	J. Clark
F.W. Clarke	J.C. Clarke	W.A. Cleland
W.W. Code	R.O. Crowe	R. Cruise
C. Curtis	H. Curtis	F.J. Dagg
R. Dewar	B. Dilworth	R.R. Elliott
E. Engebretson	H.S. Ferguson	L.M. Fleming
H.W. Gardiner	W.J. Gardner	C.W. Gray
S. Hesson	R.J. Hewey	W.H. Hicks
G.H. Hills	H.C. Hunter	J. Hutson
F. Jauncey	W.A. Johns	J. Kerr
H. Knight	J. Kuryk	L. Lane
T. Latta	B. Law	W. Lee
D.B. Leigh	C. McKee	D. McLellan
J.H. McMillan	H. Murphy	H. Nicodemus
M. Olson	A. Paul	H.L. Pearson
G. Phare	F. Pike	R.W. Pitts
D. Pollard	A.B. Reid	J.E. Reinhart
J.B. Richards	J. Rollings	J. Ross
J.A. Secord.	R.H. Secord	C.W. Shaw
H. Silverstein	C.W. Skinner	G.E.T. Smith
C.C. Stacey	D.V. Stelck	G. Stewart
C.H. Storey	H. Tomlin	A. Tverdun
H. White	H. Whitmore	A.H. Whittaker
S.R. Widmeyer	F.L. Younghusband	

7

THE SPORTING TWENTIES

As 1920 dawned on Dauphin, the country and the world were still in the process of readjustment after the war. On the international scene the League of Nations was formed without the membership of the country which proposed the idea. Woodrow Wilson won the Nobel Peace prize although he never took part in any of the deliberations of the League of Nations after 1920 when the American Senate voted against joining. Mahatma Ghandi was emerging as India's leader in her fight for independence which, at the time, lay a long way in the future. Adolf Hitler, a relatively unknown and disgruntled German corporal held the floor in a beer hall in Munich on February 24, 1920, to announce his 25-point program to a small group of the German Workers' Party. No one thought that this small seed from the first world conflict would produce the foul fruit of World War II.

In science, Herman Rorshach devised his ink-blot test and a retired army officer, John T. Thompson, developed a submachine gun, to be known in future as the "Tommy Gun". Ernest Shackleton published in "South" the story of his great Antarctic adventure of 1914-17. Sir William Osler, having brought great distinction to Canadian medicine through his work in Montreal, Philadelphia, Baltimore and Oxford, died in 1919; while his future biographer, Harvey Cushing, was developing new techniques in brain surgery.

On the national scene, Canada mourned the death of Sir Wilfred Laurier but hailed Mackenzie King, who had become national leader of the Liberal party and, in 1921, Prime Minister of Canada. The Winnipeg general strike was over but the trials of the chief activists in 1920 kept the issues alive for some time and were responsible for an upsurge of political unrest in the west which never really disappeared.

The difficult period of the pioneer years, when life was a continuum of back-breaking labour, of struggles with the vagaries of nature in spring floods, winter blizzards, summer mosquitoes and black flies and the depleting loneliness of homestead life, had eased somewhat after the coming of the railway. Truly, the work was still difficult and the workday long, but time could then be given over, in some degree, to the few pleasures that church, school and community provided in those days before radio. The automobile, the church, books, journals and letters from home provided most of the pleasures of those early days.

Many of these pleasures were short-lived, however, as 1914 brought a call which many answered and most supported. The anxieties of those at home and the carnage of the Western Front, for those overseas, created a post-war psychology which had never existed in Canada previously. There was a sense of independence and a new confidence in a nation which had faced its first foreign battles and had acquitted itself well. There was a disillusionment with existing political structures and a desire to fashion a government which would fairly express the yearnings of a majority of Canadians and which would not be based on class lines. There was the sweet taste of victory and the happiness, for those who survived, of a reunion with family and friends.

These feelings resulted in a subconscious desire to enjoy life, to celebrate victory and to be optimistic that now, as the war to end all wars came to a close, life would be rewarding, progressive and, most of all, fun. As Jerome Kern wrote in 1920, we must "look for the silver lining". As couples danced to his tune they were, whether they knew it or not, determined to do just that.

The 1920s have been referred to as the "roaring" twenties, the "ballyhoo" years and by many other sobriquets. In Dauphin they might well have been called "the sporting years", for a review of affairs in the period from 1920 to the fall of the stockmarket in the autumn of 1929, reveals a remarkable string of achievements by individuals and teams in the field of sport.

The background to the surge of interest in sports was a

worldwide phenomenon, aided in no small way by an American craze for sport and the concurrent development of radio broadcasts, following Marconi's remarkable accomplishments in that field. It was 1920, after all, when Marconi opened the first public broadcasting station in Britain at Writtle. It was also in 1920 when the Boston Red Sox sold Babe Ruth to the New York Yankees for the then, very large sum of $125,000. Bill Tilden won the Wimbledon lawn tennis championship in 1920 and dominated tennis until 1925, causing a major resurgence of tennis all over North America. Man O' War was retired to stud in 1920 after winning 20 of his 21 races.

Olympic games were held in Antwerp in 1920 after an eight-year hiatus due to the war. The games introduced the great Paavo Nurmi of Finland to the world's sporting fans. Australia first won "the Ashes" in London to spur great interest in cricket. The first regular broadcasting station in America was established in Pittsburgh. This opened the airwaves to sports broadcasting so that the world began to feel that it could "be there" at the great sporting events.

A sporting revolution took place around the world. Knowledge of sport increased. Sporting heroes were made and emulated by young people in every city and town of the country. Dauphin proved no exception and added its share to the ever-growing pool of fine young athletes in Canada.

The greatest individual accomplishment of the 1920s in Dauphin in the field of sport was, undoubtedly, that of Jimmy Ball, a track and field star in the middle distance runs. Jim Ball was one of a moderately large family, raised in Dauphin before and after World War I, having been born there in 1903. His parents were both good athletes so that he came by his abilities not only through his genes but by dint of hard training. His mother, a good track and field competitor, was known in her hometown as the "Hartney Flash". His father, who came to Dauphin to open a tailoring shop, was a native Ontarian who had come west at the invitation of a sports club to play lacrosse; he was considered to be one of the best at the game in Manitoba.

Jim Ball's childhood and youth were spent in Dauphin. By the time the soldiers were returning home he was a tall and gangly boy of fifteen. He is remembered as being a boy in a hurry, for he ran everywhere. He took part, usually successfully, in sports events at picnics and sports days. He recalls joining with his brother, Don, and other boys in the neighbourhood, to run races around the streets of Dauphin. He and Don Ball had that special spark which made good competitive athletes and they revelled in the fun of their sport. Another brother, Jack, is said to have been equally capable as a runner but, perhaps, not as competitive by nature.

After high school, Jim apprenticed in Dauphin to become a pharmacist and, following his apprenticeship with Otto Heaslip, he left Dauphin in 1925 to enter the University of Manitoba. Up to this time he had received no professional coaching of any kind. At university he entered competitions, usually in the 100, 220 and 440-yard sprints. He made great improvements under the guidance of more expert coaching. During his first year at university it was noted that he had done well on the track team. By 1926 he began to establish a solid reputation as a runner when he won the individual honours by winning all three of the 100, 220 and 440-yard races at the university track meet and again at the Western Canada Universities' track meet. In 1927 he entered the Olympic trials at River Park in Winnipeg where he repeated his good showing. His best event in that trial was the 440-yard race. Following his success in the Olympic trials in Winnipeg he ran at Varsity Stadium in Toronto where he won the 440-yard event and anchored the four-man relay team, which won its class.

All of these successes were a build-up to the selection of Canada's team for the 1928 Olympics, to be held in Amsterdam. The formal trials before the selection committee were held in the early part of August, 1928, in Hamilton, Ontario. The day was hot and muggy, just the type of day that brings on rapid fatigue in athletes. In spite of the day, Jim Ball broke the 440-yard record twice within the space of an hour, winning the semi-final in a time of 49.4 seconds and the final in 48.6 seconds. A few weeks later, in Amsterdam, he became the first Canadian runner to run the 440 yards in less than 48 seconds. Even then, he had to settle for a silver medal.

There were some who felt that he was a better runner than Ray Barbutti of the U.S.A., the gold medallist. Most placed the responsibility for his second place finish on his inexperience in running

Victoria Daily Times, August 3, 1928.

Jimmy Ball of Dauphin was regarded as one of the greatest quartermilers the world has ever produced. c.1928.

the lanes. An official description of the race says:

> Ball finished second but it was admitted that he was the best man in the race and only his inexperience in running lanes deprived him of victory. He drew the fifth lane, and because he caught the man in the sixth in the first thirty yards, he thought he was setting the pace up the back stretch, when it appeared he was running under restraint. Rounding into the home stretch he was surprised to find himself in fourth place, five yards behind the leader, who was Barbutti. In spite of this tremendous lead, the American just managed to finish a scant inch or two in front of Ball, collapsing at the finish while Ball had plenty in reserve. Ball's race down the stretch was an amazing effort and brought the huge crowd up in wild acclaim. In my opinion Ball is one of the greatest quarter-milers the world has ever produced, and only his inability to compete internationally the past two or three years has prevented him from establishing this fact.

Jim Ball also won a bronze medal at Amsterdam as anchorman in the 1600-metre relay. Following the games, before returning to Canada, he won the 440-yard races in Glasgow. He broke records at the Tailteann Games in Ireland and won the Queen Tailteann Trophy by winning gold medals in each of the 220 and 440-yard races and anchoring the 1600-metre relay team.

His return to Dauphin following his successes in Amsterdam and in the United Kingdom had the hallmarks of a celebration for a returning hero. On a lovely September day, hundreds of Dauphinites turned out to greet him as he returned on the afternoon train from Winnipeg. As the band played "Happy Days Are Here Again", the procession flowed to the steps of the town hall, opposite the railway station, where the mayor extended the congratulations and gratitude to the town's now-famous and favourite son. It was a day for all young people to remember and from which many took their inspiration to excel in sport.

Jim Ball went on to win other races and trophies, including a bronze medal in the 1932 Olympics in Los Angeles. He won the Norton H. Crowe Memorial Trophy as Canada's outstanding athlete of the year in 1933. He was inducted into the Canadian Hall of Fame in 1959, the A.A.U. Hall of Fame in 1973 and the

Manitoba Sports Hall of Fame in 1980.

Another unique and individual record, in the field of sports in Dauphin, was the accomplishment of Sadie Delmage in tennis. Tennis had flourished in Dauphin before and during World War I. At one time there were six clubs operating in Dauphin. Very soon after the end of the war, the Dauphin Tennis Club searched for a new and larger site for their courts. It obtained several lots in "Company Farm" at the north end of Vermilion Street. Here, the club built a small clubhouse and four tennis courts. The club thrived to a greater extent than others and became, easily, the most active club in town. One of its most ardent members was Sadie Delmage, the wife of John (Jiggers) Delmage who had come to Dauphin from Ochre River as a teacher. He subsequently was principal of the Smith-Jackson school for many years.

Sadie Delmage went on to make an indelible mark in provincial and interprovincial tennis circles. She won the ladies' singles provincial championship for twelve consecutive years and in 1926, 1927 and 1928 she not only won singles honours but was also part of the championship teams in the ladies' doubles and mixed doubles events. She continued her successes well into the 1930s. For many years she was "Mrs. Tennis" in Manitoba on both grass and clay courts.

Hockey, of course, was a major interest for both old and young in Dauphin. These were the days of open-air rinks, shinny games on every sheet of ice that one could find and pick-up games under the streetlights in the evenings, with a frozen ball of horse manure as a puck. Choosing sides, with young and older on each team, was the order of the day and, oh, how sweet it was to be on the same line as one of your older heroes.

Ice rinks in Dauphin until this time had been uncovered, except for one rink on First Avenue Southwest which was a combination of curling rink (2 sheets) and a skating rink which had a canvas roof. This rink had been built in 1897 and lasted until 1900, when a second rink, also a combined curling and skating rink, was built at the corner of Third Avenue Northeast and First Street East (where the present telephone building stands). In 1920 a proposal was made for a new skating rink, since the old rink had been declared unfit for use. For two winters A.J. Rawson, the photographer, operated an open-air skating rink with the McMurray orchestra supplying music on weekends. During the two winters that Rawson's rink operated, a committee considered plans for building a more adequate rink for hockey and skating. In 1922 the lumber companies in town donated the lumber for a new rink in return for the mortgage on the building. A contract was let that year for the new rink at $11,750. In November of 1922 Bob McAllister began to build. The arena was to be on the corner of Second Avenue Southwest and Vermilion Street. It opened on December 18, 1922.

Very soon after the opening of the rink, Dauphin began to make its mark in provincial hockey with a team which, by and large, remained together through junior and intermediate leagues. That team with some few changes won many championships. Many of its players would, today, be standouts in professional hockey. Among the players were George (Troque) Heard and his brother Burns (Squee) Heard, the Leech brothers, (Gar and Herb), Mickey McMaster, Tom Scrase, Ernie Bennett, Metro (Rats) Slobodzian and, later, such players as "Butch" Craig, Norm Nantais, Bill Cowtun, George Love, Gordon Churchill and "Mindy" Bjornsson. This was truly a hometown club and was almost continuously a serious contender for provincial honours.

Radio had, of course, popularized the game by its broadcasts of "Hockey Night in Canada" with Foster Hewitt on Saturday evenings. Murray Westgate was the voice of Imperial Oil, its sponsors. The voices of Elmer Ferguson, Baldy Cotton and others became familiar through the "Hot Stove League". Those who were unable to hear the broadcasts in their homes could hear it outside Robson's drug store on Main Street North where an external speaker had been installed for the public's convenience. Since the stores were open until at least 10:00 p.m. on Saturdays, there was always a large group of people parked in cars along Main Street or shopping the stores. Those broadcasts brought the names of Howie Morenz, Aurel Joliat, King Clancy, Eddie Shore, Red Horner, George Hainsworth, the Cook brothers, Charlie Gardner, Sweeney Schreiner and many others, into the homes of Dauphin where everyone came to know of them. It was the heyday of professional ice hockey, played as a sport of finesse.

The success of the new skating rink was short-lived since, soon after it opened, the roof collapsed following a severe spring snowstorm, early in 1923. Undaunted, the people of Dauphin dug deep into their pockets to assist a new rink company to find a site and to issue bonds for the financing of the new building. Some legal entanglements slowed progress but by the fall of 1927 a larger rink, with bleacher seats along each side of the rink, decent waiting rooms for ladies and for gentlemen, a speaker system for music and dressing rooms with showers for both the home and visiting teams, was opened just next to the powerhouse at the west end of Front Street. Initially, the Elks Lodge took over the management of the rink and Hugh McAllister was selected as the on-site manager. This rink hosted many exciting hockey games, fun-filled Travellers' Carnivals, garden shows, flower shows and was a major stimulus to the development of minor hockey and ice skating.

In the fall of 1920 an interest was evident among many Dauphin residents in the game of golf. At that time Bobby Jones was a major name to those interested in the "royal and ancient game". His exploits were to boost the game into public imagination with great force. A site for a golf course was determined on when it became possible to purchase land near Dauphin Beach in the municipality of Ochre River. Fifty shares were sold at $50 each, although the club was capitalized for 400 such shares. During that winter and the spring of 1921 further organizational meetings and the efforts of many in "work bees" on the site, made it possible for golf enthusiasts to begin play on July 21, 1921. The course was a picturesque, well-treed nine holes with sand greens and a rough rough! It was without a clubhouse until 1928 when the Dauphin Country Club, as it was called, built a small clubhouse and pro shop.

The ten-mile distance from town to the golf course site at Dauphin Beach made it difficult for many to partake in the game and the Dauphin Country Club was not, in reality, a community club, for that reason. Since there were others who wished for a club closer to hand, a drive for funds was begun and, as a result, land was obtained in 1925 on the northeast edge of town, along Mountain Road, which became the Dauphin Community Club. Both clubs thrived initially. There were interclub competitions for the Sam Solomon Cup. When Johnny Lawrence, later and for many years the golf pro at Wasagaming Golf Club in the Riding Mountain National Park, came to Dauphin in 1928, he came to serve as a golf professional at both the Dauphin Country Club and the Dauphin Community Club.

The Dauphin Country Club survived the Depression and is still the sole active course at Dauphin. Unfortunately, the Dauphin Community Club fell on hard economic times during the early 1930s and is now defunct. The greater ease of travel and improved roads soon made the trip to the Dauphin Country Club an easy one.

Curling, in the twenties was a growing and active sport, as well. The game had been played since David McIntosh had been elected first president of a curling club in 1897. His brother, Will McIntosh, had the first pair of granite curling stones in Dauphin. The games took place in the first curling rink, which was in the combined skating and curling rink with the canvas roof, on Mackenzie Avenue Southwest.

When the second rink was built on Third Avenue Northeast, the curlers moved into it and remained there until 1928. After the collapse of the roof of the new skating rink, the curling club negotiated with the town for the use of that property for a new curling rink. The negotiations were successful and resulted in a new four-sheet curling rink, with a kitchen and some spectator space on two floors at one end of the rink. All of these curling rinks had natural ice. Artificial ice was not seen for many years in Dauphin. The curling club stayed at the Second Avenue South site until 1947 when it moved to the Dauphin Memorial and Community Centre grounds.

Many of Dauphin's curlers made good impressions at the great Winnipeg bonspiels during those early years. Among the most enthusiastic curlers were David and Will McIntosh, David Sutherland, Alex Eagle, Wilfred Robson, Joe Barker, Otto Heaslip, Jimmy Oliphant, Dr. Trimble, J.J. Crowe, Dr. Harrington, J.L. Bowman, Ed Wallwin, Bill Strang, Tom Pollon, Archie Chute, Bill Esplen, Tom Pollon, Jr., Bill Cruise, Dr. Bishop, Bob Brown, Roger Watson and countless others. J.L. Bowman and Otto Heaslip were together on a team representing Canada, in the 1932 Olympics. On several occasions Dauphin curlers — Dr. Harrington in 1921, Otto Heaslip in 1926 and 1950, Wilfred Robson in 1926 and J.L. Bowman in 1950 — were represented on teams touring Scotland for international competition. The realization of the dream for a Brier champion had to await a much later date.

During all these years, from 1910 onwards, the ladies of Dauphin were active curlers as well. Foremost amongst them, in the early years was Mrs. Sadie Delmage who skipped a rink consisting of Alma Cox, Olive Cruise, Min Williams and herself, to a provincial championship in 1951. She had on another occasion in 1928, won the grand aggregate honours in the Winnipeg bonspiel. She was, in curling as in tennis, a serious and aggressive contender.

Soccer was popular throughout the twenties. A Northwest District Soccer League began its first season in 1921, with Gilbert Plains, Grandview, Ochre River and Dauphin as participants. John Gardner was Dauphin's goalkeeper. Joe Barker and H.N. Miles were referees for local games. By the late 1920s Dauphin was fielding teams that contended for provincial honours and in 1928 the Dauphin Rangers won the provincial crown. The team consisted of Frank Baird, Jack Crowe, Tom Scrase, Stan Brickman, Wilf Cardiff, Earl Hamilton, Jim McMaster, Gar and Herb Leech, Gordon Churchill and Alf Buckwold.

Dog racing proved exciting winter entertainment for some in the 1920s. In the winter of 1921, an annual dog race was initiated by the Elks and was run regularly throughout the 20s and early 30s. In 1922 a Dauphin-to-Winnipeg dog race was held in February. Pigeon racing continued its popularity. A lawn bowling green was built at the west end of the C.N.R. station grounds and was actively used for many years.

Fishermen were complaining again about the level of Lake Dauphin, especially in 1926. In that year a 45-pound jackfish was pulled from Lake Dauphin by A. Coombs, a record to that time. The Elks organized a summer beach sports day on Labour Day in 1922 and this event occurred annually for many years.

The professional circles in Dauphin in the twenties saw the New Year's Honours list name F.E. Simpson as King's Counsel in 1920 and J.L. Bowman in 1924. In Manitoba, to that date, lawyers earned their call to the bar by reading law, in an apprentice mode, in a local law office and then writing the examinations of the Law Society of Manitoba. There was no law school in Manitoba until, in 1921, the lawyers of Manitoba met to discuss the formation of such a school at the University of Manitoba. There was divided opinion as to whether or not compulsory attendance at the school should be a prerequisite to the practice of law, since it was felt that many would lose the opportunity to join the profession, if attendance was compulsory. Secondly, the legal profession found the articling students of value in the day-to-day research necessary in criminal and civil cases. Some did not wish to lose their services.

George Tritschler, a Dauphin boy who read law with Simpson, McGirr & Katz, convocated in 1923. He was to have a distinguished career in law, culminating in an appointment to the bench in the higher courts in Manitoba. Isaac Johnston and Thomas Little were also reading law with local firms and both had passed their second year exams in 1923. Isaac Johnston later took a job with the Land Titles office when he passed his final exams in 1924.

Heap, Arsenych and Waryniuk opened a law office in the Ramsay-Wright building in 1924. The firm did not last long and only T. Waryniuk remained to practise for years in Dauphin as Tommy Warnock. Arsenych was to return to Dauphin many years later as Judge Arsenych of the County Court. In 1928, for a short time, Joseph Dyck practised law in Dauphin, in the Stelck block.

In 1923 it is noted that C.S.A. Rogers had opened a law office in town with a Mr. Masterman. That law firm, Rogers & Masterman, did not survive long after Rogers became Crown Prosecutor and Masterman left town. Richard C. Smith practised law for a short time in the mid-twenties. In 1923, Mark Cardiff became the County Court clerk. In 1922, John Watson, the first sheriff, died and was succeeded by H.V. Smith, who had recently owned the Dauphin Steam Laundry.

Finally, it was in 1928 that Frank Simpson, by that time one of the senior lawyers in the northern area of Manitoba, was appointed a judge of the County Courts, a responsibility he acquitted with distinction. His old firm became McGirr & Katz.

Most of the action in the daily courts centred around charges for the manufacture of illicit spirits. During prohibition there were

REX BOUGHEN

The Dauphinolians, c.1928. Front row: Dorland Palmer, Jack McMurray, Bill Cox and Nina Boughen. Middle row: Claude Williams, Alf Harpham. Back row: Hamilton McKee, Jack Burton.   RUTH BREKKE

J.L. Bowman, Dr. Trimble and Dr. Walter Bell, after a successful hunting expedition. c.1926.

many stills around the country. Following prohibition they continued to thrive because of what was considered to be exorbitant costs for liquor in government stores, much of which, as today, consisted of taxes on the liquor. Many of the other cases involved family altercations, assaults, drunkenness and motor vehicle transgressions. Each year's assize court might produce one or two murder trials.

In medical circles, 1920 was ushered in by the return of the influenza epidemic which had been so devastating in 1918-19. Fortunately, the return was short-lived, lasting only during January and February. An increase in venereal diseases, possibly the indirect consequence of the war, was responsible for a free V.D. clinic run by Dr. Bottomley. An increase was also noted in the incidence of diseases "due to stress following in the great rush of life in a hectic world". There was an outbreak of diphtheria in the Ukrainian settlements at Keld and at Sifton. Typhoid fever was still prevalent.

Amongst the dentists, the year 1920 produced some changes. Dr. Walker was joined in practice by Dr. Wilbur Weir and then left Dauphin for the west coast, within a few months. Dr. Weir and Dr. Walter Bell then joined forces to form the Dauphin Dental Clinic. The clinic lasted only a short time, closing when Dr. Bell moved into the Burrows block. Dr. Weir continued practice until 1923 when he relinquished his practice to Dr. Walker who had returned to Dauphin. For a very short time Dr. Harold Trotter practised with Dr. Bell in 1923. He later joined the provincial health services to provide dental care to the mental institutions of the province.

Chiropractic was also an active profession in Dauphin's early days. Originally, A.J. Sherwood opened an office for the practice of chiropractic in June of 1914. He was joined by Dr. Cornell in May of 1917. They had offices in the Pollon Block. In 1919 Sherwood left Dauphin and a brother of Dr. Cornell joined in the practice of Cornell & Cornell. This partnership was short-lived; in 1920 one of the brothers went to Windsor, Ontario and, in 1921, his brother joined him. In 1920, Agatha Justice (née Hamm), a graduate nurse of the Dauphin General hospital of 1910, returned from a year's training in Iowa to begin the practice of chiropractic. Her husband, Adam, then studied chiropractic and joined her in practice until she left for Los Angeles in 1923. F.C. Hill began a chiropractic practice in the Ramsay-Wright building in 1924 which sold out to M.J. Oscar in 1928. Oscar stayed only a short time. In 1926, W.F. Skinner opened an office in the McDonald-Voigt building but sold out the next year to D.L. McPhail who subsequently moved his office to the second floor of the Stelck block. McPhail was a popular hockey referee during his stay in Dauphin.

In 1921 Dr. A.J. Tripp opened a medical practice above Heaslip's drug store and subsequently moved to a house on Second Avenue Southwest. He remained in town until 1931. Dr. N.G. Trimble, who had been in the Dauphin Medical Clinic, left in 1928 to practise in The Pas. His place was filled by Dr. R.E. Dicks who moved from Kelwood to Dauphin where he practised for the remainder of his days.

While all these changes were taking place, the Dauphin General Hospital survived only by dint of public donations, rigid expenditures and the devotion of its Lady Superintendents and its boards of directors. The Swan River hospital closed in 1921 and many in Dauphin wondered whether the same fate was in store for the Dauphin hospital. In 1923, the Sisters of Providence offered to take over the hospital but the offer was declined. There was a determination to maintain the hospital as a community institution and, although support seemed fragile at times, there was little doubt that a majority of the citizens wanted a continuation of the services being provided.

Annual reports at this time, however, showed a declining use of the hospital except in the case of maternity care. As early as 1922, a delegation went to Winnipeg to solicit support for a new maternity home. In the event, an annex was opened in a home at the southeast corner of Fifth Avenue Southwest and Hospital Street, just a block from the hospital. It was to close again in 1925. Not all births took place in the hospital. This was shown to be so, most publicly, when a mother gave birth to a baby boy while on board a C.N.R. train going to Swan River. The child was named Charles Newell Roscoe in honour of Charles, the brakeman of the train; Newell, the conductor and Roscoe, the name of the station passed through while the baby was being born. The whole initials of the baby honoured the railway system on which the baby had been born.

While the hospital was appealing for funds to remain operative, the doctors of the district were organizing a Northern Manitoba Medical Society as one of the district societies of the Manitoba Medical Association. Dr. T.C. Routley, secretary of the Canadian Medical Association and Dr. Gordon Fahrni of the Manitoba Medical Association, arrived in Dauphin in late October, 1923 for the organizational meeting. Dr. Fahrni said, "Our meeting in Dauphin was a great success and, in this happy atmosphere, our first rural district medical society was born, including old-timers like Harrington in Dauphin and Bob Orack and Pete Robinson, all the way from The Pas. Even some physicians from the neighbouring towns in Saskatchewan attended". By this time Dauphin had six doctors, Gunne, Bottomley, Rogers, Harrington, Trimble and Tripp. Dr. Medd was in Winnipegosis and Dr. Shortreed in Grandview. The society arranged annual meetings and, later, semi-annual meetings.

On the public health scene, Dauphin enjoyed the services of several excellent public health nurses during the twenties. Miss Street became public health nurse for the town in 1919. She was succeeded by Miss Stothard in 1925. She, in turn, left in 1928 and her work was continued by Miss Broadfoot in 1929. All three established excellent rapport with the community and did valuable work.

A great deal of the public health activity in the twenties centred around the problems of tuberculosis. Early in the decade, travelling teams of specialists, led by Dr. D.A. Stewart of Ninette, came to Dauphin to see new cases, review former patients and to deliver medical and public lectures about the prevention and current treatment of the disease, which was then a prevalent and often fatal disease. Typhoid fever, although still present, had diminished in frequency, although as late as 1929 one of the hospital's nurses died from the disease.

In 1922 the Dauphin hospital admitted 1037 patients. There were 157 births and 494 operations were performed. By 1927 the admissions had dropped to 652, the births to 39, and 458 operations were done. Two years later, in 1929, the admissions had returned to a level of 1034 but births still lagged at 62. In spite of these figures, or perhaps because of them, a move was made to increase the size of the hospital. The town fathers and the rural council supported this venture and in 1928 a new hospital wing of 24 beds was opened, doubling the hospital's bed capacity to 48 beds. The hospital wing was built by James Chisholm & Sons of Winnipeg at a cost of $50,000. It was in this year that Dr. Trimble left Dauphin, while Dr. R.E. Dicks and Dr. Michael Potoski came to Dauphin to practise. Dr. Potoski had come to Manitoba as a nine-month old baby when his parents, Paul and Katherina, crossed the Atlantic in very rough seas in 1897, on the first leg of their trip to Sifton, Manitoba. They were amongst the earliest of the Ukrainian pioneers in that area. One other son, Peter, practised in Yorkton, Saskatchewan while a third son, John, became a household name as a reeve in the rural municipality of Dauphin. All of them furthered the proud Ukrainian heritage handed to them by their parents.

In 1928, Miss Cotter resigned as Lady Superintendent of the hospital. She had come in 1919 to succeed Miss Foyer. She, herself, was succeeded for one year only by Miss Morris. Following Miss Morris came Miss Kettles who was to make a solid mark on the medical life of the community. Another important change in hospital administration was the appointment of Miss Winnifred Miller as full-time secretary of the hospital. Until that time the work of the secretary had been done on a part-time, voluntary basis by Mr. Tritschler. Winnifred Miller continued in this capacity over the next twenty years. She served the hospital very faithfully. During the 1920s there were twenty graduates in nursing from the Dauphin General Hospital.

In 1923 a major change in the drug businesses of Dauphin came about when Bruce Goodhand bought out the drugstore business of Fred Wright of the Ramsay-Wright store. Bruce Goodhand came to Dauphin as a youth when his father, Thomas Goodhand, started a draying business in town. After completing his high school courses, Bruce Goodhand apprenticed with Wilfred Robson and T.T. Malcolm. He worked afterward in the drug department of E.A. Ramsay's new store which was managed by Fred Wright. After taking over this business, Bruce Goodhand moved to the Franklin block on Main Street North, abutting the south side of the lane between Front Street and Burrows Avenue.

It was on the second floor of this building that Michael Potoski had his office for many years.

The political ferment in Manitoba did not miss Dauphin. The Dominion Labor party was organizing and F.J. Dixon, an early socialist enthusiast, came to Dauphin to promote his party in the early part of 1920. The United Farmers of Manitoba was also active. In the provincial election of 1920 their nominee, George Palmer, defeated the incumbent, Dr. W.J. Harrington, to win the seat which he held until 1922. In 1925 and 1926 he was mayor of Dauphin.

There was a tendency, after World War I for people of specific interests, to join together in single-interest groups, to push on the political front, for their interests. To some this was a step away from the independent action by each elector for what he thought best for the country. Arthur Meighen expressed this feeling, well ahead of his time, in the 1920 election campaign when he said, "The period we are passing through now is something of an enigma, but this can be said about it, that there is a greater tendency to class consciousness, to a belief in class interest and to a reliance on class organization than in any previous age. . . . The tendency is general. Indeed we are becoming organized and inter-organized until such a thing as individuality is well-nigh forgotten and the air is thick with assertions of class rights. I wish we had today more plain Canadians, men and women who depended for success on themselves, on the excellence of their work, on individual courage and enterprise and thoroughness and who reasoned out their convictions on public questions in the good old way and not as members of any class or group". As the poet, William Wordsworth might say, Meighen "thou should'st be living at this hour"!

Mackenzie King and Prime Minister Arthur Meighen, bitter political rivals, spoke in Dauphin during the 1921 election campaign. J.L. Bowman was the Conservative nominee: W.J. Ward as the nominee for the Progressive Party, was entering politics for the first time, and Robert Cruise was the Liberal nominee. The result of the election on December 6, 1921 showed that the Liberals had won 117 seats, the Progressives 66 seats, including the Dauphin seat, and the Conservatives took 50 seats. The Liberals had no clear majority and needed some support from the Progressives, led by Thomas Crerar. The Progressives, in practice if not in fact, held the balance of power. This condition held until Mackenzie King called an election for October, 1925. In Dauphin, J.L. Bowman had to return early from a vacation trip to Europe to accept the Conservative nomination. W.J. "Billy" Ward was again the Progressive nominee. There was considerable confusion in the Liberal party as to their course of action. Archie Bennett was to be their nominee but, after further deliberations, the Liberals threw in their lot with the Progressives, so that Billy Ward became a Liberal-Progressive candidate. During the election campaign Baron Byng of Vimy visited Dauphin as Governor-General of Canada.

"Arthur Meighen campaigned hard" is the way the *Dauphin Herald* described the situation when Meighen campaigned in Dauphin. He did remarkably well for the Conservatives, increasing their strength in parliament from 50 seats to 116 seats. King had 101 seats and was able to form a government with the support of 25 Progressives, amongst whom was Bill Ward of Dauphin. Then followed the Byng-Meighen crisis of 1926 which ended in political crisis and the dissolution of parliament, to be followed by an election which the Liberals won handily. Throughout the decade from 1922 to 1930 Billy Ward was the member from Dauphin. He was never a brilliant star in the parliamentary firmament but objective observers agree that he was a diligent member who served his constituents well. He was never a favourite of Mackenzie King.

Elections seem to have been the order of the day in Manitoba in the 20s. In early 1922 the Norris government was defeated in the legislature on a vote of confidence concerning the abolition of the Public Utilities Commission. Active in opposition to the government in that house was A.E. Smith, the former minister of Grace Methodist church in Dauphin. An election was called for July 18, 1922. In that election Dauphin chose the Liberal candidate, Archie Esplen, who remained the member until 1927. It was in the election of 1922 that the first major disagreements between the United Farmers of Manitoba and the Labor Party became evident. The One Big Union group was also quarrelling with other groups, probably a residuum of the Winnipeg strike. There was, however, evidence at this time, of the formation of a socialist party which came into being because of the early work of Dixon, Woodsworth,

Heap, Queen and others.

John Bracken, then president of the Manitoba Agricultural College, was asked to lead the government in 1922, in a house which had 28 members representing the United Farmers of Manitoba, 7 Liberals, including Archie Esplen of Dauphin; 6 Conservatives; 6 Labour members and 8 Independents.

It was on October 25, 1926 that Theodore Burrows, the pioneer lumberman from Dauphin, was appointed Lieutenant-Governor of Manitoba. He served in that position until his death on January 25, 1929.

In the 1927 provincial election, Bracken's Liberals retained control of the government although Dauphin returned Robert G. Ferguson, their Conservative candidate. Whether this was the result of Bracken's withdrawal of prohibition by the passing of the Moderation Act of 1923, is doubtful, as support for that withdrawal was evident in the 33,000 majority which the liquor referendum obtained. This contrasted with the large majority of "Drys" in October of 1920. The new act certainly tapped a rich source of income for the government then and for the future. Liquor was to be dispensed by government liquor stores. The first manager of Dauphin's liquor store was Fred Wright who took the position in 1923, selling out his interest in the drug store to Bruce Goodhand who continued in the business until his son, Cameron Goodhand, took over in the late 1950s. Bruce Goodhand served Dauphin, not only by way of his reliability as a pharmacist, but also, for many years through support of the Dauphin Agricultural Society. He was an avid horseman. By his interest and support of the acquisition and breeding of good saddle horses, and of harness racing in Manitoba, he made a major contribution to these activities on a provincial scale. For many years, Dauphinites were accustomed to see him returning home from his early morning rides, astride a fine Kentucky saddle horse, with his Dalmations alongside.

At the local level, several matters of concern were settled in the decade of the twenties. After many meetings and considerable debate, a war memorial was unveiled on a rainy day in mid-June of 1924. Sir James Aikens, Lieutenant-Governor of Manitoba and John Bracken, Premier of Manitoba, attended the unveiling of a beautiful memorial column, topped by a nine-foot figure of Miss

The Cenotaph, Dauphin. c.1930.

Bruce Goodhand on Leon Gaines, with his sons Cameron (centre) and Tom. c.1935.

RUTH JUDSON

Canada and inscribed on two sides with the names of 82 Dauphin and District men who had fallen in the 1914-18 war. The inscription read "There Is No Wealth But Life — These Gave Their All". The memorial was paid for by public subscription and was contracted to Guinn and Simpson of Portage la Prairie, at a cost of $5500.

Soon after the railroad came through Dauphin it was found that one access road across the tracks at Main Street was frequently blocked by trains stopping at the station or by freight trains being made up or passing through town. Both road traffic and pedestrian traffic could be held up for long intervals. Gladys Street, at that time, was closed just south of the railway tracks and had no connection with Front Street West. As a result, the town council, and through it the railway, agreed to build a pedestrian subway on the west side of Main Street between First Avenue South and First Avenue North which was completed late in 1921.

Main St. was made more attractive by the construction of boulevards on both sides from Fourth Avenue North to the courthouse. Agreement was reached in March, 1926, with the rural municipality, for the maintenance of Riverside cemetery, one mile south of town on the east bank of the Vermilion River. The level of Lake Dauphin was, again, the subject of debate. Some efforts were made, unsuccessfully, to borrow money from the provincial government to build a major drainage system to control the lake level.

Dauphin celebrated its 25th. anniversary of incorporation as a town in 1926.

The Governor-General and Lady Willingdon visited Dauphin in 1928. The same year a new postage rate, two cents to any location in the British Empire, was announced.

The period following World War I was a difficult period, economically. Shortly after the war it was evident that many were suffering. The unemployed group grew, the listing of properties for tax sale increased. Work camps were established in the Riding Mountain Reserve where the unemployed could find some work, for pitiful wages, cutting wood. The price of #1 Northern wheat dropped from $1.87 in 1920 to $1.36 in 1925.

Out of these difficulties, and especially as a result of the increased awareness of the geography and resources of the Riding Mountain, came a drive, spearheaded by a group of business and professional men from the communities surrounding the mountains, for consideration of the site as a location for a national park. In Dauphin, J.N. McFadden led the group in interest, and in effort, toward such an end. He and D.D. McDonald are credited by some as conceiving the idea for the park. Jack McFadden became the permanent secretary of the Riding Mountain Association. D.D. McDonald was its first president.

Against opposition from those who favoured the Whiteshell area of southeastern Manitoba and those who feared loss of timber and hunting rights or who disliked entrance fees and permits, the committee set about to solicit support for their idea and to acquaint politicians and the public with the beauties and resources of the Riding Mountain area. That they were successful was evidenced by the visit of the Minister of the Interior, the Hon. Charles Stewart, in August of 1928 and was proven by the announcement in 1930 that a national park would, indeed, be established in the area. About the official opening of the Riding Mountain National Park on July 26, 1933, Emma Ringstrom comments sharply in her book *Riding Mountain — Yesterday and Today* on the fact that "not one single member of the Riding Mountain Association was on that historic platform, not one member was an invited guest and not one word of acknowledgement from that official platform of the dedicated service of the twelve men who spent three years in achieving the important goal". So much for politicians.

Locally, "Clue" Smith succeeded Mr. Everett as police chief in 1926. H.W. Sumpter became caretaker of the cemetery which, by this time, had become a beautifully treed area bordering the Vermilion River south of town. R.J. Malcolm was appointed census commissioner in 1921. The road from Dauphin to Swan River was completed in the same year. Fifty men were employed to spread gravel on district roads in that year. Without the gravel, many roads were impassable for much of the year.

During the 1920s Dauphin was served by several of its citizens as mayors. R.J. Malcolm was mayor in 1920 and 1921, H.V. Smith in 1922, Bob Fagen in 1923 and 1924, George Palmer in 1925 and 1926, J.W. Skinner in 1927 and 1928 and in 1929 W.E. (Hungry

Bill) Robson began his four-year term as mayor.

The 1920s brought to Dauphin the annual Rose Ball, a New Year's extravaganza by local standards. The first Rose Ball, sponsored by the Widmeyer chapter of the Imperial Order, Daughters of the Empire, to usher in 1920, was a resounding success. For years this success continued. The Rose Ball was one of the few formal or semi-formal balls to be held in Dauphin. An invitation to attend was coveted. The town hall was always tastefully decorated. Wilfred Caldwell was, for years, at the entrance doors to take tickets. Dance programs were duly marked and often autographed. Gaiety abounded until early morning, often to be followed by a "light repast", until the last waltz when you danced "with the one who brung you". The Rose Ball continued for years as the highlight of the New Year's activities, although its formality gradually diminished over the years. McMurray's orchestra was popular in the dance circles of the early twenties.

A new pier at Dauphin Beach had been constructed by the federal government in 1924. A few months later it was largely destroyed when the ice moved out in the spring of 1925. It was rebuilt and stood for many years, although commercial fishing boats on Lake Dauphin were decreasing in number and most of these moved toward Winnipegosis. The level of Lake Dauphin was a thorny problem again in 1929 when the town requested $100,000 from the federal government to help in the control of the problem. Tenders were called for an addition to Dauphin's post office which had become one of the busiest of the rural post offices in Manitoba. As the decade ended, #5 highway to Roblin was officially opened in the summer of 1929.

In the field of education in Dauphin, the outstanding event of the 1920's was, without doubt, the burning of the Mackenzie school on the early morning of December 12, 1926. This was a 12-room, solid brick school which had been built in 1909 to replace the first Mackenzie school which, also, was lost by fire. In 1926 the school was totally destroyed and no definite cause was determined. Temporary classrooms were soon established in various locations, the Great War Veterans' Association hall, the courthouse, the Ramsay-Wright building and the Burrows block. Classes were re-arranged to accommodate a full schedule in the mornings and a full schedule in the afternoons. There were few, if any, disagreements about the necessity of accommodation on everyone's part. No complaints were heard from parents about early or late classes. Students did not complain, since they were fortunate to have any classrooms at all and, besides, they were out of school for half the day. Teachers took on the extra load willingly and without looking for additional recompense. The school board met with the crisis firmly and by February of 1927 plans were completed for a larger, divided 16-room school with an auditorium. The collegiate institute was to have eight rooms and the auditorium while the elementary school was to have the remaining eight rooms. Excavation started on May 27 and by October of 1927 the building was progressing well. On November 10, 1927, Lieutenant-Governor Burrows laid the cornerstone of the new school which was officially opened on December 22, 1927, almost exactly a year after the fire on December 12, 1926, a remarkable feat.

It was also in the early 1920s that a new 8-room school was originally proposed to house the collegiate institute. It was built on Main Street South between Seventh and Eighth Avenues, on the east side of Main Street. By mid-1920 the building was well started. Debentures for its financing had all been sold. It was determined that the school would bear the name of Smith-Jackson, honouring the first chairman of Dauphin's school board and later its secretary-treasurer, a man who dedicated his public voluntary efforts to Dauphin's schools. The Smith-Jackson school was opened on November 10, 1921. It never became the collegiate institute but, instead, served as an elementary school for children of the south end of town.

In the early 1920s there were some 200-225 students in the collegiate. W.N. Ball became principal in the fall of 1921. There were 20-25 student teachers in the Normal school in the early years, with about 50 students in the latter part of the decade. There were 800-900 students in the elementary schools. In addition, 41 students attended a business school which opened in Dauphin in January, 1920 as a branch of the Success Business College of Winnipeg. By 1921, a teachers' federation was being promoted. It had started in the major cities of Manitoba, two years previously, and was now soliciting support from the rural areas and small towns. Its main concern, in those days, was for the upgrading of qualifications in teaching and the maintenance of standards.

Joseph Wicklund was hired for the collegiate staff in June of 1923 and began teaching in the fall. Mary Clay, an elementary school teacher, came to Dauphin to teach in 1924. Both of them stayed many years in the Dauphin school system. Mary Clay was active in the formation of the public library. In 1927, Inspector E.H. Walker, who had served the Dauphin schools for twenty years, died suddenly. His place was filled by R.M. Stevenson, an able administrator and educator. Both men had also served as principals of the Dauphin Normal School. Mr. Stevenson was a co-author, with R.D. Barager, of the standard geography text for Manitoba schools.

W.N. Ball's tenure as principal of the collegiate institute was marked by a high standard of excellence in academic pursuits. He gathered around him an excellent staff who established, with the help of Mr. Ball's insistence on fair but demanding discipline, a quality of teaching that produced some outstanding students and put Dauphin in the ranks of the better school districts of Manitoba. One of the teachers of that era, Hugh Saunderson, went on to become a respected university chemistry professor and then, president of the University of Manitoba.

J.T. Jonasson succeeded W.N. Ball as principal of the Dauphin Collegiate in 1926. He was in that position only a short two years when he was replaced by Gordon Minto Churchill who had come to the teaching staff in 1927 and became principal in 1928. Throughout the years he was principal of the Dauphin Collegiate, Gordon Churchill built on the solid reputation left by W.N. Ball, as he established an enviable record as an educator and administrator and acted as a model for his students. His intellectual interests were broad and he was an excellent athlete. He went on from Dauphin, in later years, turning his attentions to politics; in the end, taking a leading role, as a minister of the crown, in the Diefenbaker cabinets of the fifties and sixties.

In 1929, Mr. Churchill brought "Jake" Lysecki and A.S. Moore on staff. Later, Leonard Caners, Harold Robson, Isobel Stewart (Mrs. Ray Dicks) and Beth Crowe were on the same staff. The school flourished under Churchill's leadership and was given

THE SPORTING TWENTIES 171

further impetus by the election, in 1928, of J.N. McFadden to head the school board. Under these two men education in Dauphin took a quality step forward.

A Literary Society was started in the Collegiate in the twenties, while home economics extension courses and "Scientific Temperance Schools" were held from time to time.

In 1925 the Success Business College of Winnipeg was again advertising for students. By September of 1927, Dauphin had its own business college when Thomas Little opened his school in the Ramsay-Wright building. Thomas Little came to Dauphin in 1917 as a court reporter when the new judicial district was formed. After his emigration from Scotland to Canada, he had worked in Winnipeg for a number of years before coming to Dauphin. In Dauphin he carried on his work as a court reporter during the hours that court was in session and then read law with Simpson, McGirr and Katz in the afternoons and evenings, passing his law examinations in 1924. His abilities as a shorthand reporter had, by this time, become widely known. He was often invited to report on major cases outside of Dauphin, and as far away, on one occasion, as Montreal. In 1925 he was invited to join the Hansard staff in the House of Commons. He stayed on that staff for one session until the end of February, 1926, when he determined that his future and his family's future, were likely to be more fruitful in Dauphin than in Ottawa. In order to prepare for the university studies of his children and to earn the additional income needed for those studies, he came upon the idea that to put his own talents to the best use and to satisfy a need in the community, he should establish Dauphin's first home-grown business school.

Mr. Little taught shorthand and business English, Bob Fagen was employed to teach bookkeeping and Miss Lily Christie had the responsibility to teach typing. The school was successful from the beginning, subsequently employing Miss Vina Hunt in Miss Christie's place. Vina Hunt remained an employee with Little's Business College until Mr. Little's death in 1959, after which she assumed ownership and management. Through the years, 30-50 students attended each year except for a few slim years during the thirties. Early students will remember the annual dances, when the town hall was decorated in lavender, black and coral and almost

Thomas Little, Dauphin's first court reporter.

PROVINCIAL ARCHIVES OF MANITOBA

The Court House, 1946.

three hundred guests danced the quadrilles and minuets, the waltzes and the fox trots. Unfortunately, the Depression put a stop to this revelry but the business college carried on, taking cash, poultry, meat, wood, eggs or anything of some value, in exchange for the education. Many young people received their educations whether or not they could afford to pay.

In 1929 Thomas Little joined with other book lovers to discuss the possibility of starting a public library. There had been some commercial lending libraries which had short lives: The Bookworm in the Dauphin Theatre block, and earlier, a lending library in the Manby & Company store. There had also been a hope for a Carnegie library during 1909, which never came to fruition. As a result of the enthusiasm of Mrs. Madge McFadden, Mary Clay, Thomas Little, Harry Macneill, Mr. & Mrs. H.J. Everall, Joe Wicklund, Roy Watt, R.M. Stevenson, the Rev. A. Lochead, Emma Whitmore and several others, a library was started which was first housed, for a few weeks, in Thomas Little's residence on Fifth Avenue Southwest. It was then moved to Little's Business College where, after 4:00 p.m. on Tuesdays and Thursdays and for one hour in the evenings of Monday, Wednesday and Friday, borrowers had access to the books.

The business climate in Dauphin during the twenties hit high and low spots. To a great extent prosperity depended on the success or failure of the crops. In 1920 heavy hail damaged crops in the northeast section of the municipality. In 1921 there was a heavy infestation of grasshoppers. In 1922 the crop was good but harvesters were in short supply. In 1923 and 1927 rust damaged the wheat. Wheat prices fell slightly over the first half of the decade. There were long lists of land available at tax sales.

In town, the establishment of new businesses, or the transfer to new owners of already established businesses, continued. Bowman & Manning opened a wholesale fruit outlet in Dauphin in 1920. The firm of Bay & Katz sold out to the three Bay brothers, Eli, Aaron and Abraham who, in 1922, sold the entire business to Eli. Thus began Eli Bay Company Ltd., a name associated with men's styles for the next sixty years.

Mrs. I.C. Montgomery & Son opened a shop at Main Street and Third Avenue Northwest where Lepper's bakery was later and

P.A.M.

The Dauphin Creamery, c.1920

R. GARDNER

Dauphin Park, c.1920.

where Gardner & Son are now. A.A. Brewer sold his poolroom to Dan Hamilton and purchased a grocery store on Sixth Avenue Southwest and Vermilion Street, which he operated until his death. There are many memories of the jawbreakers and licorice sticks and Jones "Cremola" toffee sold to the students of the Whitmore school at recess and after four.

The Dauphin Milling and Creamery Company sold the creamery portion of their business to Crescent Dairies of Winnipeg and the mill was sold to A. Reznoski. E.A. Ramsay was selling debentures for his department store and hiring staff to man it. A.H. Lepper came to Dauphin to take charge of the bakery department but left, later, to enter business on his own. William Weir opened a tailor shop in 1921 at 216 Main Street North where J.A. Ball had operated. He later moved to Burrows Avenue. The Christie-Grant store opened opposite the Mackenzie school on Second Avenue Northeast but soon moved to the Blue Store on Burrows Avenue West. The Great War Veterans' Association announced in 1921 that a site had been chosen on Main Street North between Third and Fourth Avenues for the erection of their new hall. J.W. Skinner, Warren Wright, Cyril Bates, Doug Kitney, Ed Batty, Walter Percy and Harry Oliphant were amongst those active in the original building program.

The Ramsay-Wright store opened in March of 1921. The staff included E.A. Ramsay as president, F.T. (Fred) Wright as vice-president and general manager, Robert McPherson as secretary-treasurer, Harold Lepper (groceries, bakery and hardware), Bruce Goodhand (drugs, stationery and sundries), R.I. Steen (dry goods), R.M. Hunter (Gent's furnishings) and Robert Argue (building & plant). By 1923 H.R. Hopwood had replaced Fred Wright as general manager when the latter took the position as manager of the new liquor store. The store beame known as the Dauphin Mercantile Company and by the next year, just Hopwood's. In 1928 A.N. Doupe bought out Hopwood and the business changed its name again to A.N. Doupe, Ltd.

W.G. White bought the Jordan block on Main Street and Third Avenue Northeast which he proceeded to renovate and enlarge into his fine dry goods and ladies' wear shop. Working for him for years and eventually managing the store was Wilfred

Caldwell, a son of H.F. Caldwell who was Dauphin's mayor in 1911-13 and had been a partner with A. Reznoski in a general store. Wilfred took a great interest in his church and was often a soloist in the choir of the Dauphin United church.

Another change in Dauphin's business circles was the sale of Eagle's Machine Shop on Front Street East to Stanley Beetham. The Eagle Scrub Cutter, which was a very efficient machine for clearing scrub trees up to 4" in diameter, in a swath of 7', was the chief claim to fame of its inventor, Alex Eagle. Unfortunately for him, motor power became available and popular about the same time so that he was unable to profit from his invention, which would have been a marvellous benefit to the early settlers of the district. Stan Beetham, apart from his business, was a man interested in music. He played an important role in Dauphin's musical life for the few years he lived in Dauphin.

H.M. Park, who had come to Dauphin in 1897, chose to close his jewellery business in 1922. He put his stock up for auction in the fall of the year. It is not clear how successful his auction was, since he stayed in business another year and then sold out to E.F. Fox in December of 1923. In turn, H.M. Park then bought W.S. Marsh's confectionery and fruit business when Mr. Marsh went with the town and then the *Dauphin Herald*.

It was noted in 1922 that Canada's economy was down. There had been some inkling of a recession even as early as the immediate post-war years but this economic downturn was most acute during the 1921-24 years. By 1924 grain prices had started up again and business began to pick up. The recession in Dauphin was not so marked as in other parts of the province. The generally heavy crops and the continuing influx of new settlers did much to counter the effects of the recession.

The railway was still an integral part of Dauphin's life, in spite of the almost constant criticisms of its service. The consolidation of the Canadian National Railway System in 1917, raised the hopes of farmers and merchants that improvements in service would soon be forthcoming. All of this seemed possible when, in 1922, the railway announced that a new freight shed would be built on Main Street at Front Street East. The contract was let to Carter-Halls-Aldinger of Winnipeg in October, 1922. The old freight shed was pulled down and the new freight sheds opened in December, 1923, at a total cost of $25,000. Within a few months another decision was made by the railway authorities to enlarge the east yards to allow for greater freight traffic and to ease the congestion that existed at that time.

John Bryce sold out his business, excepting the bakery, in the late months of 1922. Sutherland & Stelck celebrated their 25th anniversary in 1923. Five years later, David Sutherland left the partnership and Dauphin, to open a hardware business in Macgregor, Manitoba. This brought to an end thirty years of devoted service to his business; to the town, for which he served on the original town council in 1898; and to his church, St. James Presbyterian. He was remembered for many years by the host of friends he left behind him.

In the early 1920s, radio was rapidly becoming a feature of life in Dauphin. The first broadcast to be received in Dauphin was heard on June 22, 1922. The receiving aerial was 52' high and 150' long. From that time on the sale of radios was brisk. An added impetus was provided to advertisers and, as a consequence, broadcasting for entertainment, especially in sport, became intensely popular.

Two signs of the darker side of things revealed themselves in the early years of the twenties. In 1923 the Home Bank collapsed. It had become so active in farm mortgages that in the recession of the early twenties it found it impossible to remain solvent. The Dauphin branch, which was housed in the McDonald & Voigt block, closed at the end of August, 1923. The forewarnings were evident in the long lists of farmlands advertised for tax sale, together with low grain prices, grasshoppers and rust. Prices at this time showed eggs selling at 30 cents per dozen; butter, 30 cents per pound and chickens, 20 cents per pound.

Liquor ads were abundant following the vote to end prohibition. There were also ads supporting greater moral responsibility in the conduct of business. There was a feeling that some of the merchants and professional men were dealing unfairly with some, in particular some of the ethnic minorities.

The Style Shoppe, operated by Mrs. Gertie Wright, opened its doors in the Malcolm block, in 1925. It remained an important part of ladies' shopping for another twenty years until it was taken over by the Mary-Jayne shop. Captain Scrase and his son, Bert, started a family butcher shop on Main Street South in 1925. T.T. Malcolm bought the pavilion at Dauphin Beach, planning that his son, Frank, who was then a medical student, would manage it in the summer months. Swift-Canadian took over the Dominion Creamery plant at the corner of Vermilion Street and Second Avenue Southwest. J. Symons came to Dauphin to manage this plant. Thomas J. Clark bought the garage previously operated as Feldman's Garage opposite the Hamilton Hotel. He and Felix Geiler were the pioneers in establishing bus transportation in and out of Dauphin in 1929. Clark's operation was called the Clark Transportation Service while Geiler operated the Manitoba Motor Transit Co.

Business changes also occurred as the decade was closing. Safeway opened a new store on Main Street North next to the Burrows block at a cost of $15,000. The T. Eaton Company took a lease on the Ramsay-Wright building, causing A.N. Doupe to sell out, and opened their Dauphin branch store on November 22, 1929. McBean's, a new store in Dauphin, opened on Burrows Avenue, just off Main Street in the Burrows block, for the sale of dry goods, millinery and ladies' ready-to-wear. Cameron & Heap, wholesale grocers, sold out to Western Grocers.

A new hotel, the Brierley, was planned for the east side of Main Street next to the Wallace Block. This was owned by Walter Brierley and, later, named the "Hotel Dauphin". It was built in 1926. The Ellis Cash and Carry Store opened on Main Street South between First and Second Avenues Southeast. It continued into the 1930s when it became Slobodzian's Second Hand Store. It stood north of the old Orange Hall, which, in the interval, had become a service garage operated in the thirties by Jack Bowman. In 1929 the Burrows Lumber Company was sold to the Monarch Lumber Company after Theodore Burrows' death. The Victory Café opened next to the Brierley Hotel in 1928, and was operated by Toy Sing, a favourite of his many patrons for years.

Car dealerships became a lucrative and competitive business enterprise. Stan Phillips, on Burrows Avenue had the Durant and, later, the Studebaker agency. Felix Geiler was the Chrysler agent;

the Hall Motor Co. sold Chandler cars and Gary Peebles sold Hudson and Essex cars.

Kelly's barn, in the laneway between Burrows Avenue and Third Avenue Northeast burned in a spectacular fire in November of 1928. The Crescent Creamery sold out to the Manitoba Co-Operative Creamery in 1929. The town transferred land to the Imperial Oil Company for $1298, to allow the building of an $18,000 service station which, in August of 1929, opened as Allard's Garage.

Just as sport became the symbol of the twenties, so dancing took its place as another symbol of the times. The change in the style of dancing, away from the classical European dances like the polka, the schottische and the Viennese waltz, to the newer steps of the foxtrot, the modern waltz, the tango and the rhumba, created a dance enthusiasm which swept the country. In postwar Canada the craze seemed to suit the mood of the people, just as it did in the rest of North America, where dancing became a favourite pastime in many circles.

In Dauphin, dances were frequently sponsored by sporting or social clubs as a means of raising funds for other purposes. The fraternal organizations were alive to the appeal of dancing and sponsored some of the more "glittering" affairs in town. The Rose Ball, the Military Ball, the Bachelors' Balls, the Hospital Benefit Balls and the Hogmanay Balls were among some of the annual and successful dance parties. A weekend never went by without a dance, or several dances, in nearby schools, community halls or dance parlours. The Orange Hall, the Elks' Hall, the Town Hall and the Roseland Dance Garden were the venues for most of the dances in town. Clubs of all kinds abounded. The C.N.R. social and athletic club, the cadet corps, musical and literary clubs and the Dramatic Society; tennis, snowshoe, soccer, curling, hockey, golf and baseball clubs were all active and raised some of their funds by the sponsorship of dances or other recreational pursuits.

Theatres boomed in the twenties. In the early years of the decade, patrons were viewing *Huckleberry Finn* at the Gay Theatre or following the movies with Rudolf Valentino, George Arliss or Harold Lloyd. The Dauphin Theatre, which opened on October 14, 1921, soon had Marie Dressler, Wallace Beery, Jackie Cooper and Our Gang comedies to entertain the moviegoers. All of the films were silent films until 1929, when, in July, it was announced that "talking movies" would soon arrive in Dauphin. Tom Mix, Mary Pickford, Charlie Chaplin, Lillian Gish, Norma Shearer, Dolores del Rio and Warren Baxter, along with many, many others, thrilled the movie fan in Dauphin in those days.

The church remained an important part of the town's life throughout the twenties. As early as 1921 the Y.M.C.A. organized the Tuxis and Trail Ranger groups which remained active until the World War II. The Tuxis mock parliament in Winnipeg during the Christmas break, was the highlight of the year for the lucky representative from Dauphin. During most of these years the groups were associated with, but not adherents of, the Presbyterian church.

In the Presbyterian church, the Rev. Philip Duncan succeeded the Rev. Cormie in 1920, and remained in Dauphin until 1926 when he was succeeded by the Rev. H.M. Lyons, in September of that year. In the Methodist church, the Rev. Haw left in 1921 and was succeeded by the Rev. T. Neville who stayed until 1925 when he was succeeded, in turn, by the very popular Rev. F.C. Middleton. He, in turn, accepted a call to Roland, Manitoba in 1929.

During the years of the twenties church union between the Methodists, Presbyterians and Congregationalists reached a conclusion, in June of 1925, when these churches officially agreed to union. In Dauphin, however, although there had been joint services in the summer months, union did not actually occur until 1929. The day chosen as the actual day of union was July 1, 1929. For this union the Rev. David Fleming was the first minister, succeeded shortly by the Rev. L. Lochead. The body of the two churches moved to the building of Grace Methodist church, which then became the Dauphin First United Church. The old St. James Presbyterian church building became a church hall to house the activities of the various church groups, until it was sold to the Jehovah's Witnesses. It, later, burned to the ground.

The congregation of St. Viator's Catholic Church made plans in 1922 for a new church building. In November of that year the new church was consecrated by the Msgr. A.A. Sinnott, archbishop of Winnipeg. The new pastor was Father William Holloway who, with the exception of one year, served the church until 1941.

In 1923 the Rev. Harry Barrett of St. Paul's Church, left Dauphin after five year's service. He was succeeded by Canon A.E. Cousins who remained in Dauphin until 1930. He was in charge when the Diocese of Brandon was divided off from the Diocese of Rupertsland. The Rev. Duncan Ritchie served the Baptist congretation from 1919 to 1925. He was succeeded by the Revs. Church, Broughton and Julian.

The Ukrainian Catholic church, which had been officially opened in 1917, in the building which had served as an Anglican church in early Dauphin, was first served by Father Olenchuk and then by Fathers Krakiwski, Andruchowich and Pasichnyk. The Ukrainian Orthodox church was just in the process of organizing a Dauphin church, as the decade ended.

On the farms there was continuous activity in the 1920-30 period. The desire to upgrade stock continued after a wartime delay. A poultry show in 1920 was the first annual poultry show. A sale of prize Aberdeen Angus cattle by J.D. McGregor of Brandon was very successful. Jake Buckwold and McKinstry & Chute were selling Percheron and Clydesdale horses. A Shorthorn Club was started in early 1922. Wolf pelts were sold under bounty. One farmer collected $450 for twenty-one pelts. In 1921 the first annual sale of purebred Aberdeen Angus cattle was held. Grasshoppers were bad in 1921. An early harvest was expected and, in fact, the first cars of barley and wheat were delivered by August 20, in that year.

Following the war, a decade of political action engaged the energies of the farmers. In 1921 the United Farmers of Manitoba was organized for political action. It was only one of the forces which weakened the party system of government in Manitoba, for at least a generation. To help finance its activities, the U.F.M. held an old-timers ball in 1922. It was in the period 1921-22 that grain prices collapsed. In September, 1921, #1 hard wheat sold for $2.85 per bushel on the Winnipeg exchange. By November, 1921 it was $1.78 and by November, 1922 it was $1.02. The following year rust was a major problem. Prices remained low for grains. Many farmers supplemented their earnings by cutting and selling firewood. On a winter's Saturday afternoon, wood could be purchased from any number of farmers, around the livery stables in Dauphin where they would rest and feed their teams, before striking out for the return trip to their homes. In 1924, wood prices showed tamarac at $7 per cord, poplar at $5 per cord and oak wood at $7 per cord. A million dollar crop was expected in 1924 and when the harvest came, yields were reported as follows: wheat 38-40 bushels per acre, oats 50 bushels per acre, and barley 57 bushels per acre.

Among the farmers winning plaudits for their livestock achievements were R.H. Brown, Art Boughen and the Lytle brothers for their Percherons; Blair and Hamilton of Ochre River for their Clydesdales. Parker and Crowe of Gilbert Plains were always prominent in heavy horse shows. George Cornwall, in 1925, had the Manitoba champion milk producer, a Guernsey, which produced 9000 pounds of milk, which was made into 467 pounds of butter in one year. This amounted to more than one and a quarter pounds of butter each and every day of the year! Still, at 30 cents a pound for butter, her gross earnings would have been only 38 cents a day, a small return for the labour and costs in producing the milk, even from a champion.

By 1925, wheat prices had started to rise again. Manitoba Pool Elevators determined to build an elevator at a cost of $15,000 with an additional $5,000 for the machinery. One man died in a fall during the building of this elevator. In 1929, the experimental farm at Indian Head, Saskatchewan put on a drive for seeds from the Manitoba maple trees. The children of Dauphin, literally, stripped the trees that year and sent a ton of seeds to Indian Head for distribution to many western points. There were those who wondered why anyone would want to grow the Manitoba maple, especially during years when they were infested with the small, green worms that hung by threads over the heads of pedestrians.

Throughout the early twenties, Dauphinites were like onlookers during a series of bank robberies, rum-running escapades and stolen car importations, mainly along the U.S. border with the prairie provinces. Nothing of that kind took place in Dauphin but its relative isolation was greatly disturbed for a week in mid-June, 1927 when Earle Nelson, the legendary "Strangler", was on the loose, somewhere in Manitoba. The natural fear, particularly of the women who bolted their doors and refused to answer calls, was whipped into panic by the news media and by Nelson's escape after his arrest near Wakopa, Saskatchewan. The fear dissipated quickly, however, with his second arrest at Killarney and his subsequent execution at Winnipeg in January, 1928. In one day he had raped and murdered two women.

By the end of the decade, Dauphin had seen the passing of more old-timers. James McKillop who had come in 1895, died in 1920. Emma Whitmore who had come with her husband, William, in 1886 and Henry Cardiff who arrived in the district in 1892, both died in 1921. Mrs. Thomas Gorby who had come with her husband and sons in 1891 and John Watson who had been in Dauphin since 1896 and had been its first sherriff, died in 1922. In 1923 J.A. Fisher who had resided in the Dauphin area since 1900, died. William Blackadar who had come to Dauphin in 1898 with the Burrows Lumber Company and had developed Dauphin's first greenhouse nursery, died in 1924; as did George King, who had become editor of the *Dauphin Press* in 1898 and who was Dauphin's first mayor. Mrs. Tom Pollon who had come over the mountain from Strathclair with her husband in 1889 and Mrs. Mary McArthur, a resident since 1894, both died in 1925, the latter being 100 years old. Mrs. Charlotte Spillett who had farmed with her husband, Isaac, eight miles south of town at the foot of the Riding Mountain, died in 1926. The next year Dauphin lost Inspector Walker, a man responsible for the high standards of the Normal School. He came in 1906 as a district inspector of schools and became principal of the Normal school when it was established in Dauphin. The year 1927 saw the deaths of Henry F. Caldwell, a prominent businessman since 1900 and a former mayor of the town; Mrs. Bessie Whitmore who, with her husband Harry, was truly a pioneer, having been in the Dauphin area since 1884, and Mrs. William Hall who had come to Dauphin in 1894. Already the ranks of the earliest settlers were being thinned. In 1928 Isaac Silverwood drowned when a car went through the ice of Lake Dauphin near the mouth of the Valley River. Arthur French who had developed one of Dauphin's finest farms and who had supported the movement for upgrading the quality of farm stock by breeding Guernsey cows and heavy draft horses on his farm, died in 1928, as did Mary McDonald, a school teacher since 1900, and James Gardner, an early farm implement dealer who came to Dauphin in 1897 when the railway opened up the country.

One of the greatest losses of all, in terms of pioneers, came in 1929 when John Edwards, who first was attracted in 1883 by the beauty of his creek and his land, died in Sidney, B.C. in his 95th year. Thus came the break with the first settler, forty-six years after his arrival. Tom Pollon who came in 1887 and Gavin Strang Sr. who came in 1895, both died in 1929.

The decade closed with a cold snap in December, 1929. Temperatures of −40 degrees F. being frequent in the closing weeks.

The ten years had their peaks and valleys. Economically, the recession which had ushered in the twenties gave way to relatively good times after 1924, but ended with the apprehensions resulting from the disruption of the stock market crash in October of 1929. Throughout it all, the times were effervescent and the social and sporting life of Dauphin was very active. Politically, there was a new air of self-confidence tempered with an anxiety about the distinctive problems of Western Canada and western agriculture. The United Farmers of Manitoba withdrew from political action in 1929 and its strength waned from that time.

At the end of the twenties a new movement had begun towards northern Manitoba where the provincial government had renewed its efforts on the building of the Hudson's Bay railroad. Flin Flon appealed as a place for regular employment. The lure of the north attracted many workers as Flin Flon became a new northern frontier as Dauphin had once been.

Notes to Chapter 7

Books and Reports:

Hodgetts & Burns, Thos. *Decisive Decades.* Don Mills: Nelson & Sons, 1973.
Gray, James H. *The Roar of the Twenties.* Toronto: Macmillan of Canada, 1974.

Newspapers:

The Dauphin Herald & Press, 1920 to 1929.

Letters:

Ball, Jim & Don, 1985. Collection of A. Little.

8
THE DEPRESSION YEARS

The years of the Depression in Dauphin will be remembered as being a continuum of hot, dry and lazy days. The heat waves over the grainfields in August, the cloudless skies and the humdrum pace of life, were an outward reflection of the effects of a prolonged continental drought and a worldwide economic recession. When clouds did appear they were often "Just empties goin' back!", as Anne Marriott described them. After the stock market crash in October of 1929, economic reports showed a decline in the sales of automobiles, radios, jewellery and other luxury items. Slowly but surely, the declining business activity resulted, at first in pay cuts, and then in lay-offs. Industrial construction and new home building slowed or was postponed, and soon carpenters, plumbers and bricklayers were out of work. As income decreased, the wealthy sold their second cars, the middle income group sold their summer cottages and the low income young moved in with their parents or took to the rails. They roamed Canada in search of work or food. Initially, they were driven from the trains, but as their numbers increased the railway police, at least in Dauphin, found it impossible to handle them, so they rode in relative peace. In Dauphin they usually left the trains just west of the railway bridge over the Vermilion river and proceeded into the bordering bush which became the "bums' jungle". There, around a campfire, they would spin yarns, debate a political point or sing a little, especially if one of them had a guitar. They "bummed" their meals from the townsfolk or for free in exchange for a little work. Out of this group came many of our liberal or socialist philosophers and leaders.

America passed the high-tariff Smoot-Hawley Act which

made it more difficult to export to the U.S.A. Since Canada's economy was largely export-dependent, that Act had serious effects. America also curtailed loans to foreign countries who, in turn, believing that their own industries must be protected, responded by imposing high import duties on foreign goods coming into their countries. This increased the difficulties for Canada and aggravated the suffering already being felt. The suffering was most marked in western Canada because it was dependent on a few primary resource industries, in contrast to the more diversified industries of central Canada. In addition, the most important of Canada's industries, farming, was suffering from the worst drought to strike the west since its settlement.

Not only did crop yields decrease markedly but world prices for grains slumped to their lowest recorded levels to that time. By 1932 wheat was selling at 40 cents a bushel; yet the world's surplus reached 700 million bushels in spite of poverty and starvation in many parts of the world. Canada's revenue from external trade dropped from $1400 million in 1929 to less than $475 million in 1933, a fall of 67 percent in just three years. In Saskatchewan, provincial income fell by 90 percent within two years, while 65 percent of the rural population went on the relief rolls. At the same time, while incomes dropped, prices dropped even faster. The standard of living for those who kept their jobs or had other income improved, while the unemployed, the farmers, small businessmen and the young bore the brunt of the Depression.

Social consequences followed. Marriages were postponed, birth rates dropped, suicides rose and marital problems resulting from living with parents and in-laws increased. Idleness and boredom in young adults took hold, while worry and anxiety in the adult group increased by leaps and bounds. Many were denied the opportunity for further education; many chose work not to their liking but just to get a job. Many young men found themselves in the Unemployed Relief Camps run by the Department of Defense. These camps provided construction jobs in the woods, for which the men were paid twenty cents per day. One such camp was established in the Riding Mountain area to provide labour to build the roads into the new Riding Mountain National Park.

The extreme conditions of the drought were not felt in the

Dauphin area, since it was blessed with a more adequate rainfall than much of the rest of western Canada. Any dust storms experienced in Dauphin, and there were some, were usually the result of high winds carrying Saskatchewan soil across that part of Manitoba. Even so, they were sufficient to cause the dust to seep in under windows and doors in Dauphin's homes. Although crop yields did decline they were still acceptable as compared with other parts of the province. The effects of the economic slump, however, were felt in Dauphin as elsewhere. The lists of lands and properties for tax sale gradually lengthened, the Dominion land office in Dauphin closed, municipal tax rates declined and prices of land fell. Money was just not available for activities which, to that time, had thrived. Several Dauphin boys who left to play hockey with Yorkton, returned when Yorkton found it impossible to finance the team. Town council lowered the mill rate but still there were pages of appeals against the new assessment rates. Salaries of town employees were cut. Dances were held to raise money for families on relief.

Most stock and grain speculators suffered losses of much of their capital. Although this did not involve a great number of Dauphin's citizens, it did involve some of the business and professional group and some farmers. More serious was the mounting unemployment and the decreasing income amongst the workers and farmers in the Dauphin area.

The town council, in early January of 1930, erected "wood camps" in the Riding Mountain to give employment to the idle workers and to assure a plentiful supply of fuel for the electric power plant. It was often an issue as to which workers obtained work in this way and whether or not any favouritism was shown in the allocation of jobs. The council had to show great care that the work was allocated fairly. Poplar wood cost the town $2.50 a cord, which included the falling, sawing and delivery to the town woodlot beside the powerhouse.

The unemployment and economic hardship continued through the early and mid-thirties. It was not until shortly before the onset of World War II that anything resembling economic recovery took place. The stringent economic times had caused some to lose their homes or farms. They were the unfortunate victims of events beyond their control. The more fortunate, but not more deserving, increased their property holdings at bargain prices. In the course of events their wealth was further increased when airfields opened in Dauphin in the early years of the war when the income from the rental of the houses proved very profitable, especially for some who took advantage of the times, to charge excessive rents.

By 1934 the return fare from Dauphin to Winnipeg by train was $3.50. Eli Bay was selling men's Hartt shoes for $7.00 and calf or kid boots for $2.95 to $5.00. Eaton's had men's "fancy neckties" for 25 cents, women's spring hats at $1.00 and flannelette sheets were $1.15 for double bed size. Children's cotton pullover sweaters sold for 29 cents and women's tailored wool skirts sold for $2.95. John Gardner advertised men's suits with one pair of pants for $18.50 and for $22.50 with two pairs of pants. A custom tailored suit sold for $35.00 and men's topcoats for $10.00 to $22.50. Prentice's Taxi would go anywhere in town for 25 cents.

The Citizen's Welfare Association pleaded for clothing for pre-school and school children. There was usually a generous response from the community. Theatre admissions were 35 cents for adults and 15 cents for children in 1935. An "Unemployed Association" was formed in the mid-thirties to provide a base for some self-help for those out of work. Sponsored dances raised funds for acute needs, while meetings to discuss mutual problems provided a morale boost for many. It was necessary in early 1936, for the town council to raise money by debenture, part of which was to meet the escalating costs of relief from the privations of the Depression.

Even when memberships in the public library cost only a dollar a year, the Dauphin Public Library found itself in financial difficulties with diminishing memberships. It entertained hopes for some municipal help. The Rotary Club held an "Apple Day" in the fall of 1936 which garnered the sum of only $70.02.

The difficulties for farmers with lighter crops, low wheat prices and relative drought, were compounded in 1937 and 1938 by epidemics of encephalitis in horses. In 1938 the *Winnipeg Free Press* estimated that 150 horses had died in the Dauphin area and a further 1000 in Western Manitoba. It was not until the fall of 1938, when crops began to show heavier yields and wheat was pegged at 80 cents a bushel that economic prospects took a turn upwards. It should be noted that the 80 cent price for wheat was f.o.b. Fort William.

By July of 1934 lack of rain caused an acute shortage of water in the town reservoir. Water restrictions were placed on the use of water in gardening. Farmers were being paid 8-10 cents a pound for live chickens at the Swift Canadian plant. The Dauphin General Hospital reported a per diem cost of $1.79 per patient day for 1935 and, in that year, showed a deficit of $44.00 on operating costs. Little's Business College offered a ten-month tuition for $125.00. Much of the payment was made in barter. Wheat crops in 1936 averaged about 20 bushels to the acre, while in the 1920s it was common to see 40-45 bushels to the acre. Threshing gangs were being paid one dollar a day, in contrast to four dollars a day in much of the 1920s.

The worries and economic concerns of the people needed an outlet to relieve the tensions of the times. As in so many other prairie towns, sports provided much of the opportunity for relaxation in an anxious population, in a depressed economy.

Intermediate, juvenile and midget hockey, in particular, thrived in the early part of the decade. It was in March, 1930 when Dauphin hockey fans were treated to an outstanding display of hockey when the local midgets played host to a Poplar Point team which numbered amongst its members, Bryan Hextall, who was to go on to a brilliant career in the National Hockey League. Even in 1930 one could discern the great ability of this athlete. Bobby Bend, later M.L.A. and Lorne Fidler were also standouts in that game. Playing for Dauphin were Jack Gardner, Bonar Whaley, Jack Murray, Bill Cowtun, Dan Craig, Ross Wilkinson, Fred Young and Bill Porter. The following year the same two teams met in the provincial juvenile final, with Poplar Point winning with a 3-2 score.

George (Troque) Heard was signed by the New York Ranger organization to play for their Springfield farm team and his brother "Squee" Heard went to play for Saskatoon in the old Western Canada Professional Hockey league. They were the first native boys to be recruited by professional leagues, although many were

Dauphin Juniors 1926-27. L to R, back row: Captain Scrase, O.E. Heaslip, Not identified, Herb Leech, Metro Slobodzian, Les Weir (?), Tom Scrase, Doug Houston, George "Troque" Heard, Ernie Bennett, Not identified. Front row: "Squee" Heard, Duncan "Mickey" McMaster, Roy Hamilton, "Gar" Leech.

The Dauphin Midget Hockey Team c. 1929. Left to Right: A. Walker, J. Kells, J. Marsh, J. Armstrong, J. Little, E. Derrick, R. Mulligan, J. Symons, R. Eastman. Coach and Manager E. Chase.

Troque Heard, signed to play with the New York Rangers. c.1927.

to follow later.

Throughout the early thirties Dauphinites enjoyed the luxury of hockey which was competitively played by a team of locals several of whom were exceptional in their craft and sportsmanlike in their behaviour. Enough thanks could not be given to the likes of Mickey McMaster, Norm Nantais and Chuck Willis in goal; Tom Scrase, Ernie Bennett, Butch Craig and Herb Leech on defence; Gar Leech, "Squee" Heard, Bill Cowtun, Mindy Bjornsson, George Love, "Feechy" Andrykiw, Gordon Churchill, G. Harritt and others, for the countless evenings of thrilling entertainment provided by them against such rivals as Glenboro, Souris, Treherne, Portage la Prairie, Winnipeg Falcons, Winnipeg Canadian National Recreation Association and other teams throughout the dirty thirties. They provided Dauphin with the opportunity of seeing such stars as Walter Monson, "Duke" Campbell, Romeo and Gus Rivers, Monty Muckle, Harry Neil, "Turk" Broda, Norm Yellowlees and Norm Malloy.

The juvenile teams continued to have success during the years of the Depression. The Signallers' hockey team, with Jimmy Wilson, Jim (Sonny) Watson, Irwin Vasbinder, Ross Wilkinson, Gus Hjalmerson, Norm Delmage, Merv Weir, Gordon Bulloch and Archie Wilson played good hockey in 1933 and by 1934 the juvenile team reached the provincial finals, which they lost in overtime in the second game. Playing then were Jimmy Wilson and Jack Little in goal, Roy Alf, Sonny Watson and Gordon Nicholson on defence. Forwards were Feechy Andrykiw, Tom Klym, A. Gadzosa, Cecil Patterson, Stan Bladon and Trigger Love.

The success of these teams brought great interest to Dauphin hockey and, eventually, paved the way for better coaching, with improved individual skills and better teams in the years that followed. The result was that within a few years Stan Bladon was starring with the Portage la Prairie Terriers and the Regina Aces, Pete Slobodzian was with Brandon and then Regina, Sam Love and Merv Weir with Emerson, Feechy Andrykiw with the Flin Flon Bombers and Bill Klym with the Kenora Thistles. About this time a "Dollar-a-Month" club was started to fund minor hockey. Open-air rinks at the Collegiate grounds and at the Smith-Jackson school grounds did much to promote hockey in the thirties. Every few weeks, on Saturday mornings, the thrill was playing in the big rink on Front Street.

In athletics, Joe Grant gained a reputation locally for his ability in track and field. He was a sprinter in 100-yard and 200-yard dashes and represented Manitoba in a track and field meet, sponsored by the Canadian National Railway in Montreal. Mrs. Sadie Delmage and her daughter, Marion, swept the provincial tennis championships by winning the senior ladies' and the junior ladies' singles events and the ladies' double events. The Dauphin Rangers reached the provincial soccer finals in 1930, only to be defeated by the Winnipeg Wanderers.

Several miniature golf courses were opened in Dauphin in the 1930s. Alf Buckwold ran one course behind the Clarke Block on Second Avenue Northeast. Another, sponsored by the Dauphin Women's Hospital Aid opened "on waste land by the river" on Third Avenue Northwest. It was owned by Gary Peebles and Mike Zworon. In 1930 the old Gay Theatre was refurbished as an indoor golf course under the management of Johnny Lawrence, the Dauphin Country Club professional.

On the track, Jimmy Ball was still very active. In July, 1932 he broke the Canadian record for the 200-metre distance. He represented Canada again in the 1932 Olympic games, gaining a bronze medal in the relay event. In 1933 he was awarded the Norton H. Crowe Memorial Trophy as the outstanding Canadian amateur athlete of the year.

Sport was not the sole preserve of the male population of the time. Girls' hockey thrived in the early thirties with players such as Rita Young, Peggy Sheridan, Isobel Hoy, Dorothy Caldwell, Flora Rawson, Vi and Norma Weir, Helen Marsh, Myrtle Porter and Renee Winters. In 1934 the Dauphin Girls' hockey team lost 1-0 in a one-game provincial final in the Olympic rink in Winnipeg, to a team representing Eaton's.

Great skill was also shown by a group of girls who played in the 1930s and provided an exciting brand of softball. Among them were Norma and Vi Weir, Vivian Thompson, Flora Rawson, Rose Koshey, Thelma Shand, Laura Brickman, Rita Young, Helen Magalos, Ann Tabak, Alice Presunka, Jennie Koshey and Barbara Thompson.

It was in 1932 that J.L. Bowman and Otto Heaslip, along with Errick Willis of Winnipeg and W. Poive from Port Arthur, represented Canada at the Olympic Games where curling was a demonstration sport. The Brown rink, composed of Bob and Ernie Brown, Gerald Harrington and Sam Dunstan, fared very well in the Winnipeg bonspiel of 1933. J.L. Bowman, an active sportsman, was also a mainstay of the Dauphin Country Club which, in the 1930s managed well financially and gradually improved its nine hole course as the years went by. Golf enthusiasts of the day included Dr. Harrington, Dr. Walker, John Gardner, I. Vasbinder, Wilfred Robson, Roger Watson, R.I. Steen, W.G. White, Otto Heaslip, R.E. Dicks, Tommy Warnock, Dr. Rogers and many others.

The eclipse of the sun which occurred on April 24, 1930 may have presaged the eclipse of the Liberal government of Mackenzie King, particularly as it was only a partial eclipse, occurring in Dauphin in the early afternoon. At any rate, in the federal election of late July, 1930, J.L. Bowman, who had been the Conservative candidate several times before, defeated W.J. Ward by 684 votes. This marked the beginning of a successful term of office for Mr. Bowman, as he later became Speaker of the House of Commons. The tenure of the government was short-lived, however, as the Bennett government, suffering the political fall-out of the Depression, was defeated in 1935. Billy Ward regained the seat for the Liberals.

The hazard of fire was present in Dauphin from the very beginning of its life. The work of the members of the volunteer fire brigade was meritorius but the existence of frame buildings, many of them housing animals and dry hay, the frequency of overheating in the winter months, the occurrence of "spontaneous combustion" on hot summer days, all conspired against the prevention of fires or the minimization of their severity. This was never better exemplified than in the 1930s when, in the early months of the decade, fires destroyed a barn and icehouse behind the King's Hotel, Drewry's warehouse and Porter's barn on Main Street South. Within a year a spectacular blaze brought to the ground the elevator of the Dauphin Milling Company. For months the smell of burned and smoldering grain and feed gave the air a "burned porridge" odour. Plans for a new mill were announced shortly after.

The blaze that most Dauphinites of the time will remember clearly, is the early morning fire of a very cold December 10, 1932, when the oldest landmark in Dauphin, the Grandview Hotel, burned to the ground. The hotel had been built in 1896, in preparation for the coming of the railroad with the consequent influx of settlers and merchants. In the morning, firemen were seen to be sheeted in ice, in spite of the heat of the fire, so cold was the weather. With the destruction of that hotel, a very large part of the early history of Dauphin became a memory of the past. For several years after 1896 the life of the business community and of the travelling public had revolved, to a great extent, around the "Grandview".

Another memorable fire of the 1930s was the one that destroyed the Western Grocers' (formerly Cameron & Heap) warehouse on the south side of the railway right-of-way, east of Main Street. There, the stocks of canned goods exploded sporadically in the heat of the fire while the flames from the burning building leaped towards the clouds of smoke issuing from the burning mass. The result was not only a visible exhibition of fire and smoke, but an audible concert of exploding containers. There were many onlookers at that fire, as there were at many fires, for as the alarm was sounded at the town hall, a whistle would also indicate the ward in which the fire was located. The result was that many citizens found their way to the fire, some out of genuine concern, others out of pure curiosity. In 1934, the Blue Store on Burrows Avenue, also a landmark building, was destroyed by fire and displaced the business premises of Frank Bumstead, the Singer Sewing Machine Company and James Richardson & Sons, grain brokers.

The major effort of several of Dauphin's businessmen to obtain a national park in the Riding Mountains was successful in 1931, although the park did not open until 1933. It resulted in the construction of a road over the mountain from Dauphin to Clear Lake, for which construction camps were established as a winter work project in the winter of 1930. While that road was being built, travellers reached Clear Lake by way of the Norgate entrance to the park. Soon the work camps organized athletic teams for the entertainment of the men who were living in relative isolation. It was one of these teams that played the Dauphin Intermediates in the winter of 1932-33 in the provincial playdowns. On that Clear Lake team was a young goal tender by the name of "Turk" Broda. The success of the venture which resulted in the park has always been evident in the popularity and the growth, from its inception, of the resort at Clear Lake. Some years later, in 1981, another Dauphin resident, Mrs. Emma Ringstrom, described the history of the National Park in her book, *Riding Mountain — Yesterday and Today*.

Before the Depression had taken a firm foothold in Dauphin several new businesses started. In 1931, Gerald Porter sold his drug business in Bowsman to return to Dauphin where he operated a very successful drugstore in the Burrows Block for years. In the same year Wilfred Robson opened a second drugstore in the space vacated by Otto Heaslip in the south end of town. This store did not have a very long life and was taken over by Max Bay, who operated his drugstore just north of Bryce's bakery, in a building owned by Jake Buckwold. A Red and White store, originally operated in 1930 by H.J. Hjalmarson, was housed in the Malcolm block. It was sold two years later to Mr. A. Waldo. Western Grocers, in 1934, bought the land along the C.N.R. right-of-way, south of the tracks, bordering the west side of Main Street. It had been occupied by a vacated United Grain Growers' elevator, which was demolished to make room for the new warehouse.

In 1930, the Imperial Oil Company built storage tanks and a distributing centre beside the C.N.R. right-of-way on Front Street East. Stelck's began the construction of a new and modern store with room for a variety store (Woolworth's), a shoe repair shop (Crest's), a barber shop (Johnston's) and a tailor shop (Solomon's). Eaton's took over the basement floor of the Ramsay-Wright building in 1936, in an expansion program, displacing the local liquor store which then moved to the Edgar Block on Main Street North between Burrows and Third Avenue North.

"Dinky" Farrell and Nick Hryhorchuk opened a law office in the Stelck block in 1936. It remained active until the early war year when enlistment caused its closure. In 1937, Bill Cruise installed the first milk pasteurization plant in Dauphin in his dairy operation at Vermilion Street and Second Avenue Southwest. Bruce Goodhand moved his drugstore from the Franklin block to space in the McDonald & Voigt block which had been vacated by the Royal Bank of Canada when its branch was closed. Another business closed when Max Goffman sold his business to a group which carried on as The Model Shoppe. In the following year, 1938, A.F. Farrell, for a long time Dauphin's leading undertaker, sold his business to W.L. Bullmore who later became a very active player in municipal politics.

Much has been said about the prices of goods during the Depression. As we have noted, Harrt shoes were selling at $7.00 and men's suits for $18.50 to $22.50. Some other prices in 1934 were:

Wabasso sheets	$1.19
Flannelette sheets	$1.15
Cotton Pullovers	.29
Spring Hats	$1.00
Fancy Neckties	.25
Lettuce (2 heads)	.17
Apples (3 lbs.)	.23
Sunkist Oranges (doz.)	.33
Butter (3 lbs.)	.85
Bananas (2 lbs)	.23

In May, 1934, an 8-piece oak dining room suite with buffet, table and six chairs, was advertised for $29.50.

Prices continued downwards and by 1936 some of the advertised prices were:

Grapefruit (6)	.25
Coffee (1 lb.)	.39
Cheddar Cheese (1 lb)	.30
Beef Sausages (3 lbs)	.25
Work shirts	$1.15
Angora Wool (per ball)	.50
Shirts & Sweaters	$1.49
Ladies' Hats	.95
Afternoon dresses	$1.95
Hudson Seal Coats	$210.00

On the international political front, the news of the decade was dominated in the early years by the economic conditions around the world and the collapse of the world's markets. Towards the middle of the decade, the death of King George V on January 26, 1936 and the troubled reign of Edward VIII, culminating in his abdication on December 11, 1936, held the spotlight. Edward's "At long last" speech dominated conversations and debates for a considerable time and changed many attitudes toward the monarchy but many more toward the person, himself. Interspersed with this news and continuing at an increasing rate, in the latter part of the decade, were news items from the capitals of Europe concerning the activities and intrigues of the Nazi regime in Germany and of its leader, Adolf Hitler.

In early 1937, the editor of the *Dauphin Herald* wrote with concern about the actions of Stalin, Hitler and Mussolini. Germany had already occupied the Rhineland and had started the construction of the Siegfried Line, Mussolini had invaded Abyssinia and he and Hitler had initiated the Rome-Berlin axis. Stalin was busy in Russia with a purge of communist and non-communist "dissidents". Europe was in political turmoil, while Britain fiddled with constitutional problems created by its romantic king. Truly the stage setting seemed to indicate a coming power struggle. This was the concern of the editor and of others who spoke about the international tensions of the day, among them Gordon Churchill, J.L. Bowman and Alex Katz.

In Manitoba, 1930 was a signal year, being the province's sixtieth anniversary. Dauphin celebrated in several ways. The public raised funds, and with great help from the Imperial Order of the Daughters of the Empire, dedicated Memorial Gates at the entrance to Riverside cemetery. The town council supplied funds for the completion of a tourist camp in Vermilion Park, a project that proved very successful. The citizens joined in the celebration for the linking of Manitoba highway #5 with Saskatchewan highway #10, just west of Roblin. Unfortunately, the picnic ended in a shooting with a resultant charge against a Royal Canadian Mounted Police Officer, who received a 10-year sentence for manslaughter.

The continuing problem with the Dauphin Lake level, reared its head again in the early 1930s. The Board of Trade expressed its concerns about too low levels. Still, the farmers, whose lands bordered the lake, expressed the opposite view. In December 1931, the discussions resulted in the approval by the provincial government, of the construction of a dam on the Mossey river. The dam was to be built in the summer of 1932. It would make it possible to more accurately control the level of the lake in all seasons and in all years. By May of 1937, the argument flared again. It seemed that the Dauphin Lake level was a cross which would be, perpetually, heavy on the shoulders of all concerned. It did seem an example of the inability of those concerned, to tolerate an opposing view or to make accommodation between differing legitimate interests.

As the Depression continued, people searched for political solutions to their problems. In 1934 alone, J.L. Bowman called for an inquiry into the price of farm machinery, Robert Hawkins proposed a Ministry of Health and Hospitals in the provincial government and Judge Simpson spoke to the Rotary Club about "too much government". He stressed the need to get government out of many of its activities. People, he felt, were being hampered by too much bureaucracy.

Robert Hawkins won his seat in the provincial legislature, against E.E. McGirr and J.W. Wickes, in 1932, necessitating his resignation as police magistrate after seventeen years in office. He was succeeded by Thomas Little who was not long in the position when he had an urgent call from the Attorney-General of Manitoba, requesting his help in discovering the circumstances of a charge against two persons at Winnipegosis who had taken off with a boat belonging to another fisherman. It seems that when the complaint was laid with the Justice of the Peace, he searched the Criminal Code for a suitable charge. Thinking that a simple charge of theft was inadequate, he opted for the more serious charge of "Piracy on the high seas". That may be the only time that such a charge has been laid in the middle of the continent. Suffice it to say that the charge, which was punishable by death, was withdrawn and the men were charged with theft of the boat.

Robert Hawkins won his provincial seat again in 1936 when he defeated E.E. McGirr of the Conservative party and Ronald Moore of the C.C.F. When the house convened in September of that year, Robert Hawkins became its Speaker.

THE DEPRESSION YEARS

Churches struggled with their budgets during the thirties and, except for the building of the Greek Orthodox church on Main Street South, little new building occurred. Canon Cousins of St. Paul's left to return to Bristol. The Rev. W. Brailsford succeeded Canon Cousins and remained until 1935 when he, in turn, was succeeded by the Rev. H.E. Bridgett, who remained until 1950. In the United Church, the pulpit was relinquished by the Rev. Lochead in 1931 when the Rev. Douglas Telfer arrived. He stayed the usual five years and was followed by the Rev. D.K. Burns. In 1937, the Baptist congregation, and Dauphinites generally, were pleased to hear that a former pastor, the Rev. J.C. Bowen, had been appointed Lieutenant-Governor of Alberta. It was during the thirties that evangelistic meetings came to Dauphin through the Pentecostal Mission. Their first church was on the north side of Third Avenue Southwest between Main and Vermilion Street. It began services in 1929 but became much more active in the 1930s. It was this congregation that bought St. James' Presbyterian church building on Main Street North in 1940 and used it as their place of worship until it was destroyed by fire. The sale of their land to the federal government for the site of a new post office building, allowed them to move to their present site at Main Street and Fifth Avenue North.

A significant event in the life of the community occurred in June of 1938, when Harry Macneill retired from his position as Registrar of the Land Titles office. He was succeeded by Jack Ramsden who left the firm of Bowman, McFadden & Ramsden to take the position. Harry Macneill was a true pioneer of the district and a major source of its history, during his lifetime. He came to the area with his father, Peter Macneill, in 1889. He farmed with his family until 1903 on section 3-6-20 W. For a short time he was involved in business in Dauphin operating a retail store. He also served as a justice of the peace in Dauphin, before reading law with J.G. Harvey. In December, 1908, he passed his final law examinations and for a short time practised with Mr. E. Bawdon in Dauphin. He left that firm in the spring of 1910 to practise in Kindersley, Saskatchewan. By August of the same year he was back in Dauphin where he entered practice with Campbell & Simpson. He sayed with Campbell & Simpson for five years, until he accepted the position as Registrar of the new land titles office, when it opened in 1915. He never married. During his years in Dauphin he gave unstintingly of his time and efforts to his church, to sports, to the educational interests of the town and province, to the Dauphin Agricultural Society and the Children's Aid Society. Lastly, but perhaps chiefly, he supported the Dauphin General Hospital, which he served continuously from its inception until his death. He was one of Dauphin's greatest citizens.

In the mid-thirties Harry Macneill resigned from the local school board, having served twenty-five years as a trustee, several of them as chairman of the board. He was to miss most of the action precipitated in educational circles in the latter part of the decade. At the beginning of the thirties, Dauphin schools enjoyed an enviable reputation in educational circles in Manitoba. The elementary schools were managed well and local children were provided with a solid basic education. The Collegiate Institute, having had a high standard laid down by principals such as W.N. Ball and Gordon Churchill in particular, and having been blessed with excellent teachers for a number of years, was well commended by the authorities for the success which Dauphin students enjoyed in the provincial examinations and when pursuing university studies.

Several factors, however, were to appear which disturbed the equanimity of those in the system and of the townspeople. The first factor was the economic situation. The difficulty of raising taxes during the Depression, or of collecting the taxes already levied, necessitated careful budgetting for salaries and other costs. Teachers, having only recently formed an association to further their own interests, felt that their pay scales had remained low for too long. They had already suffered salary cuts in 1932. In addition, the hiring and firing of school teachers seemed, to them at least, to rest, often, on the whim or fancy of only a few members of the school board, or even just the chairman himself. The case of the dismissal of Dorothy Caldwell from the high school staff, without any explanation, seemed a case in point. The teachers longed for some kind of tenure system after a certain period of employment. Their pressures did not sit well with those who called for a "frugal" administration.

The second factor was created as the result of the debate,

principally between urban and rural trustees, about the desirability of the "large school area" of administration. Some argued that savings would be made and that a broader curriculum could be provided to more students, if the small rural schools were closed in favour of a larger "composite school", especially in the higher grades.

A third factor, especially for those who wished to pursue university studies, was that in 1932, the chairman of the board of governors of the University of Manitoba, who was also its bursar, was found to have embezzled almost a million dollars of University funds. The result was a doubling of university fees from one year to the next. Many citizens, often those with the greatest interest in education, were therefore reluctant to see further increases in local costs.

The final factor was an apparent incompatibility, probably based on political philosophy, between some members of the school board, including the chairman, of traditional bent, and a second group of trustees, espousing a philosophy of a more socialist nature. The result was that in 1938, the pro-C.C.F. faction won a vote which resulted in the "slashing" of teachers' salaries. A major row resulted in which many citizens, as well as teachers and school board members, participated. The chairman of the board, J.N. McFadden, along with two of his supporters, resigned from the board. Gordon Churchill resigned his principalship and was joined by his associates, A.S. Moore and Miss Ethel Cadman. Miss Cadman had come to the school staff in 1902. After 31 years with the Dauphin Schools she was asked to take a pay cut to $1150 per annum. The shock waves from this row were felt throughout the system and there were some who felt that the schools never really recovered from it. A.E. Reid became principal of the high school in 1938.

During the turmoil of the 1930s few noted the demolition of the building which had housed Dauphin's first single-room school, in order to make room for a filling station. The building had been moved to the southeast corner of Main Street and First Avenue South. It had originally been built on Main Street between Third Avenue and Fourth Avenue North where it served as a temporary schoolroom while Central School was being built. The first floor was a carpenter's shop while the classroom was on the second floor.

The medical community in the decade of the thirties was active in many respects. Infectious diseases had changed their nature to some extent. While typhoid fever and smallpox decreased in frequency, meningitis, poliomyelitis, scarlet fever and tuberculosis continued to ravage the community from time to time. Rheumatic fever with "St. Vitus' dance" and heart disease were common. An understanding of pernicious anemia and iron deficiency was still incomplete. Blaud's pills for iron deficiency and Sippy powders for peptic ulcers were commonly prescribed. Angina sufferers broke their vials of amyl nitrate to get relief of pain. Crude digitalis compounds for heart failure and "Southey tubes" inserted under the skin of the legs, to allow drainage of "dropsy" fluid, were common remedies. Lobar pneumonia, with its seventh-day crisis, was a major killer. Often the doctor sat up all night with the patient, administering Scotch whiskey, to give the heart enough energy to last through the crisis. There were times when the public wondered if the doctor or the patient benefitted more from the whiskey.

In 1931, Dr. Rogers became president of the Manitoba Medical Association, the first Dauphin doctor to be so honoured. He, and the other doctors in town, had begun a drive to upgrade medical services to the community. Dr. Frank Malcolm, son of T.T. Malcolm, returned to town to join the Dauphin Medical Clinic. Dr. W.H. Thorliefson opened an office in the Stelck block but remained in Dauphin only a year, before leaving for further study. Dr. R.E. Dicks began urological surgery in the hospital in 1934, after having studied the techniques of the surgery at the Mayo Clinic in Rochester. The same year D.L. McPhail sold his chiropractic practice to Les and Ethel Pascoe.

Dr. Frank King came to Dauphin in 1931 to practise dentistry for a few years. The sudden death of Dr. W.I. Bell in 1932 created a void in the dental group which was filled when Dr. A.D. McKee came to Dauphin to take over the practice in the Burrows block. He moved later with the Dauphin Medical Clinic, when it moved to Third Avenue Northeast in 1951. Dr. C.S. (Scotty) Robertson came to Dauphin to practise dentistry in 1938, taking over the practice of Dr. G.C.J. Walker. His office was in the Malcolm block for many years, until he moved to Third Avenue

Northwest when Dr. Adam Little and Dr. Marvin Brandt built medical offices next to the old Harrington house.

The Dauphin General Hospital board in April, 1935, announced plans for the construction of a new wing to be added to the hospital which would bring the bed capacity to 100 beds. The nurses' home was to be torn down. The cost of the new wing was estimated at $35,000. In order to house the nurses, the home at the corner of Fourth Avenue and Hospital Street, which had been built by Robert Lilly, was purchased for a nurses' residence. The new wing of the hospital was officially opened on October 28, 1935, six months after being announced. Six months later, an isolation wing was built behind the old hospital. It contained a full basement for the storage of fresh vegetables. It housed ten patients and was built at a cost of $6000.

For light entertainment, "500" card parties were popular, some being organized by the Daughters of England. Jitney dances were also well attended. The cost was designed for the times at three tickets for twenty-five cents. The Dauphin Theatre was the scene of much of the daily entertainment, showing such classics in 1930 as Al Jolson in *Mammy,* John Barrymore in *Moby Dick,* Will Rogers in *A Connecticut Yankee,* and the popular Western hero, Buck Jones, in *The Texas Ranger.* The Gay Theatre had become a victim of the recession and remained closed for several years.

It was during all these years that the Married Couples Club began their series of dances in various meeting places, the Great War Veterans' Association hall and the Elks' hall included amongst them. The club continued throughout the thirties into the postwar period, providing a much-needed, inexpensive social outlet for younger married couples in depressed times.

Towards the end of 1940, the public library was a functioning reality. Several fund-raising events, including a benefit performance by the Little Theatre group, made the work of the executive easier. Merle Armstrong was the first secretary-librarian. Mrs. Middleton became the librarian in 1938 but was soon succeeded by Mrs. H.J. Everall, in September of that year. Initially there were few books, about 200, and fewer members, about 65. Memberships were $2.00 annually or $1.25 for six months. By 1934 there were

Dauphin Collegiate Orchestra c.1934. Back row: A. Lafontaine, G. Bumstead, H. Buckwold, G. Penman, N. McIntosh, V. Watson, C. Weir, L. Stelek, A. Rampton. Middle: W. Miller, N.I., N.I., N.I., N.I., Bill Syme, R. Smith, J. Watt, J. Voight. Front: A. Arnold, B. Hjalmarson, Helen Gray, N.I., H. Wardwry, L. Caners, N.I., H. Melnyk, H. Alf, N.I., J. Montpetit.

The Dauphin Hospital. c.1950.

1181 books and 175 members. In 1932, the library moved from Little's Business College to Porter's drugstore where it remained until 1934, when it was given space in the council chambers in the Town Hall. In 1949 it moved again, this time to the Great War Veterans' Association hall, where it stayed until the Lion's Club provided new and individual accommodation at the corner of Main Street and Fifth Avenue Northeast in 1958. It is now 58 years since a small group met to give impetus to a library which is now expanding further to provide a modern and well-stocked regional library for the Dauphin area.

In the summer months, the annual agricultural exhibition and fair was the centre of fun and excitement for many. The marvellous heavy horse teams, the massive bulls, the attractive Jersey and Guernsey cows, the sulky races, the grandstand show and the Conklin Brothers midway, were highlights of the event. The Exhibition Hall, with its displays of fruits, vegetables, flowers, preserves, baked goods and crafts, revealed the great bounty of the area and the skill of its gardeners and homemakers.

Chatauqua, too, was a great attraction for people who had infrequent opportunities to see live entertainment from outside the area. *Peg O' My Heart* brought tears to many eyes, under the shade of the big tent erected just west of J.L. Bowman's home, on the old Canadian Northern Land Company Farm land.

The Depression spelled an end to the annual musical festivals which had been a highlight in Dauphin's entertainment calendar for years. The appearance, on stage, of excited girls and reluctant boys, filled the morning and afternoon programs while, in the evenings, adults from all around the district, singly or in groups, vied for the adjudicator's praise as they performed "to their best level". While the musical festival died away, other musical groups formed. Johnny Johnston's Music Makes Orchestra, following upon the successes of the Dauphinolians of the twenties became Dauphin's premier dance band. Amongst its members were Jack McMurray, Vernon Watson, Al Lafontaine, Leonard Stelck, Beulah Knowles and Johnny Johnston. Additionally, the Dauphin Collegiate Orchestra, under the leadership of Leonard Caners, was gaining a fine reputation for its music.

The Dauphin Commercial Girls' Club sponsored children's

playgrounds. They opened the first one in May, 1938 on Vermilion Street and Third Avenue Northwest, the present site of the United Church. In 1934 a Coffee Club was formed. It consisted of the business bosses and lawyers, in the main, for in those days the employees did not have a coffee break.

An item of considerable interest was that in January, 1935, an alleged 80-million year old skull was taken from a well near the foot of the Riding Mountain. In 1938, the *Winnipeg Free Press* commented on the discovery of an Indian grave near Dauphin, in which were found bangles stamped "Montreal".

Air mail service began in Canada in 1938. It was announced that a letter mailed in Vancouver at 10:00 a.m. on Tuesday would reach Dauphin at 6:00 p.m. on Wednesday! All this for six cents postage. The new Bank of Canada opened in 1934 with Graham Towers at its head. Boxing Day became a statutory holiday in 1934 and the "eight-hour day" legislation passed the federal house in 1935. Sally Rand offered to come to Dauphin to entertain the locals for $1000 per day. Unfortunately, the offer was declined.

The town council was busy keeping its utilities in order. A decision was made to construct a water filtration plant and a new dam at Edwards Lake. The wisdom of the decision became apparent very soon when in June, 1935, the dam gave way to the pressure of the spring run-off causing Dauphin's worst flooding since 1912. The power plant and the town park were flooded and water reached the level of some of the connecting streets. In the following year, the town erected a 150-foot smoke stack at the powerhouse. The town council, in 1932, asked for the resignation of its police chief when he was found to have been in cahoots with the thief in a puzzling robbery of Zworon's poolroom.

The Depression was a difficult time for many individuals. It was also a difficult time for members of the various town councils. They had to maintain the institutions and utilities of the community and the added burden of relief costs. A measure of their success and a tribute to the work of all of Dauphin's councils, was to be found in the report of a Toronto bonding agent who, in September, 1938, said, "I should like to point out that, in my opinion, the credit of the Town of Dauphin is better than any western province or almost any city in the west."

Many of the citizens who had made such a statement possible, passed away during the 1930s. The pioneers who came to the Dauphin Lake area before the railway and even those who had come to town when the railway came, had, by the mid-1930s, added thirty-five to forty years to their lives. For them, time and the ravages of the hardships which they had endured throughout their lives, began to show in the obituaries of the thirties. Amongst the earliest of the pioneers were Harry Whitmore and Charles N. McDonald, both of whom came in 1884 and both of whom died in 1938. Andrew Malcolm, who had crossed the mountain in 1888, died in early January, 1930. Thomas and James Shaw, who had brought Dauphin its first grist mill, at Valley River, and its first major lumber business, also died in the 1930s; the former in 1931 and the latter in 1937. Archie Esplen and H.P. Nicholson, who had both come in the late 1880s, both died in 1933, one a successful farmer and Liberal member of the Manitoba legislature, the other a successful businessman.

Dr. J.R. Gunne, who had come with his family in 1893 and went on to become the spirit and leader of the early medical profession, died in 1935, to the great sorrow of the community. William R. Buchannon, who had come in 1899 and was a leading agriculturalist of his time, who represented Dauphin in the Manitoba legislature during World War I, died in 1930. Robert Cruise, another very successful farmer who served in the House of Commons for ten years from 1911 to 1921, and who had come to Dauphin from Quebec in 1891, died in 1932. His wife died in 1937. Gavin Strang, Sr. who came from the Touchwood Hills in Saskatchewan to seek better land in 1894, died in 1935; as did Annabelle (Mrs. Dan) McKillop who had come in 1897 when the McKillops and the Gillies reached the Wilson River area. John Daniel, a bachelor pioneer who came to the area in 1886, died fifty years later, in 1936. Duncan Dickson, who gave his name to the Dickson area and school, died in 1933, as did several other pioneers including Mrs. John Boyd, Edward McMartin, Jake Porter, John Hassard, Mrs. Jack Sinclair, William Gorby and Charlie Black. W.R. Alguire, Thomas Secord and Merritt Spillett, and Thomas Playford, all early members of the community, died in 1936, 1938 and 1939 respectively.

Amongst the list of townspeople and businessmen who were

lost to Dauphin in that decade, included John Bryce, who ran the International Inn at Gartmore before the railway came and who then moved into Dauphin to start his bakery and confectionery shop in 1897; W.D. King who had established a firm reputation for the *Dauphin Herald*, during his years as editor; Ed Batty who was an early fire chief; James Wait who established his jewellery shop in 1898; Mark Cardiff, an early tinsmith and country court clerk; Adolph Reznoski, a leading merchant and, later, the operator of the Dauphin Milling Company and the Green and White store; A.A. Brewer, a grocer and town councillor; Fred Race, who barbered in Dauphin for almost forty continuous years; Archie Hoy, a blacksmith, firefighter and town councillor; Dan Hamilton, the flamboyant hotelier and auctioneer; Eli Bay, who started his business in Dauphin in 1909; "Chappie" Chapman, the caretaker of the town hall for many years and a faithful member of the Salvation Army; J.E. Hedderley, a mayor in 1905 and 1906 and a prime mover in the early days of the Dauphin General hospital; W.H. Wallace, the jeweller who built Dauphin's first brick business block; Wilfred Robson, one of the early pharmacists; T.T. Malcolm, a successful pharmacist, optometrist and businessman and Dr. W.I. Bell, one of Dauphin's dentists.

It was a decade of great loss for Dauphin.

Books and Reports:
Broadfoot, Barry. *Ten Lost Years.* Toronto: Doubleday Canada Limited, 1973.

Hodgetts & Burns, Thos. *Decisive Decades.* Don Mills: Nelson & Sons, 1973.

Horn, Michael. *The Dirty Thirties.* Mississauga: Copp Clark Publishing Company, 1972.

Ringstrom, Emma. *Riding Mountain, Yesterday and Today.* Winnipeg: Prairie Publishing Comapny, 1981.

Newspapes:
The Dauphin Herald & Press, 1930 to 1938.

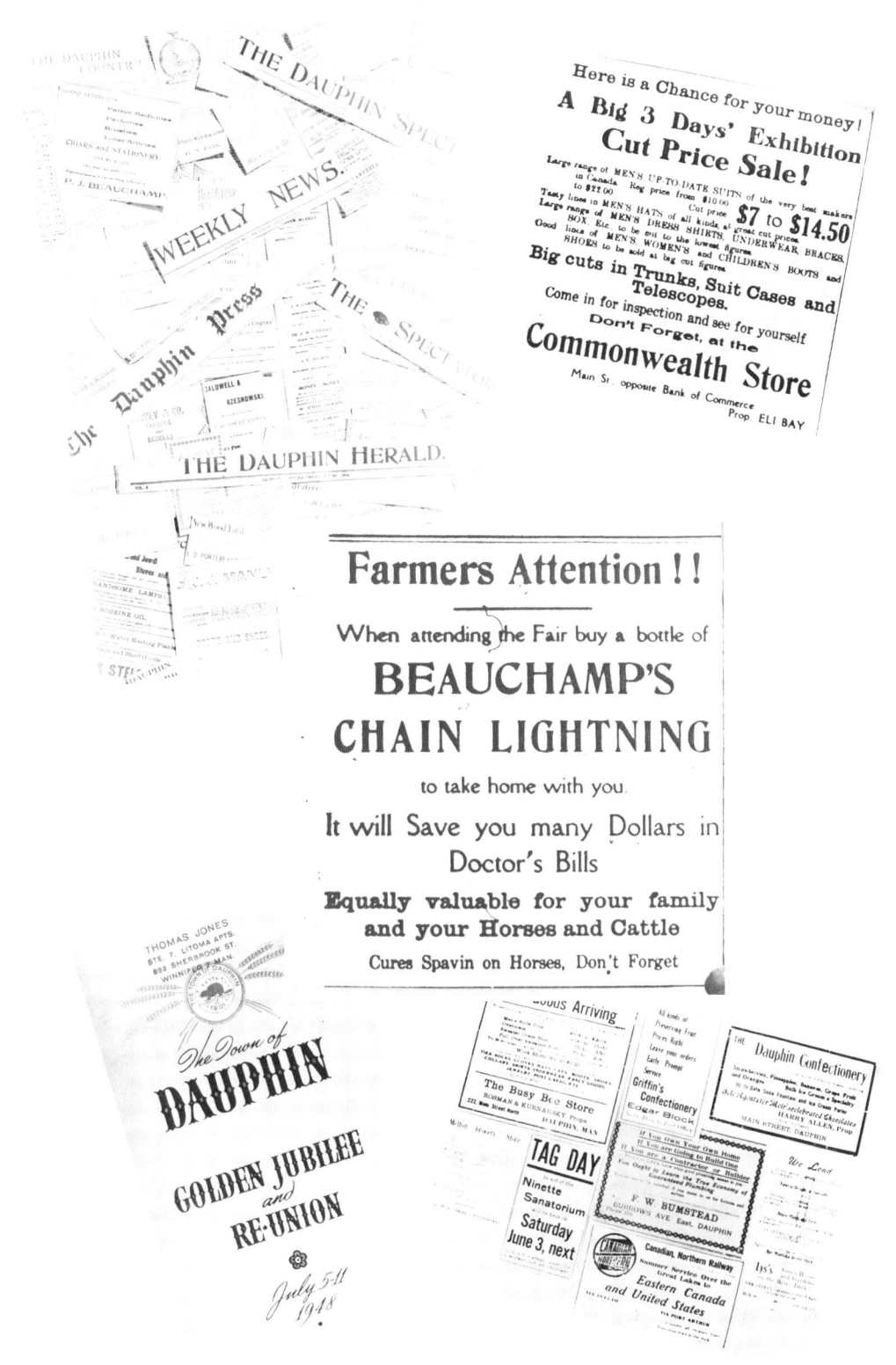

Newspaper banners, advertisements and brochure cover.

9

THE SECOND WORLD WAR

It has been noted that the young community of Dauphin, at the time of World War I, received the news of the beginning of that war without having much foreknowledge of the events leading to it or of its imminence. In great part, this was due to its relative isolation from major centres and to the lack of sophistication in the communications systems of the day. Such was not the case when war was declared in 1939. Throughout the 1930s, the news from Europe documented the progress of Germany's economic and social change under the Nazi regime. From 1933, when Hitler became Germany's chancellor, through the events of the Reichstag fire, the book burnings of 1933, the Roehm massacre of 1934, "Kristallnacht" in 1938, the "rape of Austria" and the annexation of Czechoslovakia, politicians — especially Winston Churchill — and newsmen — especially William Shirer — warned of the imminent danger of war if Hitler and his Nazi followers were not stopped. The world seemed strangely unreceptive to these warnings. Perhaps the memories of the tragedy of World War I, perhaps the lack of vision to see or the courage to resist, perhaps the duplicity and greed of the world's leaders were all responsible, in some degree, for the inertia of the world powers in facing what Churchill so aptly described as "the gathering storm".

In Dauphin, itself, the international situation was discussed on many occasions. During 1934, Alex Katz, speaking at public meetings, refuted the Nazi claims about Germany's Jewish community and criticized the Nazi treatment of Jews as a group. *Collier's* magazine spoke about the "moral isolation" of Germany. In 1936, following the Berlin Olympic games, Gordon Churchill, the principal of Dauphin's high school returned with the news that Germany's military units were much in evidence. In 1937, Gordon Churchill spoke again, to the Rotary Club, on "Is War Inevitable?". Local newspapers carried editorials about the activities of Stalin, Hitler and Mussolini. Bruce and Douglas Middleton, former Dauphinites, were with the Royal Air Force. Bonar Whaley, one of Dauphin's favourite sons and a promising athlete, lost his life while training with the Royal Air Force in 1938. J.L. Bowman, prominent in politics, and W.S. Marsh, editor of the *Dauphin Herald,* in the same year, wondered publicly about the imminence of war.

Thus, when Britain and France declared war on September 3, 1939, after the Nazi blitzkrieg in Poland, there should have been no surprise. Strangely, however, Canada did not follow suit until a week later when, on September 10, 1939, Mackenzie King's government signalled its willingness to support Britain's war effort. Many, at that time, wondered about the delay but, as the war continued, it became clearer to many that not everyone in Canada was enthusiastic about becoming a party to the war. In addition to Quebec's hesitancy about the war, there were pockets of resistance in the churches, in the C.C.F., particularly in British Columbia and amongst many of non-British stock throughout Canada.

In spite of the hesitancy there had been signs of activity very early in the year. A royal visit in May of 1939 was followed closely by Canadians and was arranged, to a great extent, by the need to excite the flames of patriotism, in the event that war did come. The R.A.F. had stepped up its recruitment of Canadians. In late August of 1939, federal government officials were studying the Dauphin area for possible airfield sites. On the day of England's declaration of war, Dr. Owen McGuirk and Bill Easterbrook, reserve officers of the Fort Garry Horse unit in Dauphin, were summoned to Winnipeg for orders concerning the war effort.

Within two weeks, thirty-five recruits left Dauphin to join the Fort Garry Horse. The townspeople settled to a life devoted to the war effort, during a war which many believed, at the start, would be a short war. Representations were made by the town council that Dauphin should be considered as a desirable location for an air training field.

Reorganization of a branch of the Canadian Red Cross occurred swiftly. J.N. McFadden was named to the Manitoba Central Red Cross committee for the duration of the war. Recruiting continued, but at a relatively slow pace, in spite of reports reaching Canada of heavy casualties in the European fighting. In December, 1939 the first Canadian Division began to arrive in Britain. It was on the same day as the signing of the British Commonwealth Air Training Agreement, an agreement which was to change the face of Dauphin for years to come.

The war went badly, initially. As the months went on the might of the German forces and the deficiencies of the Allied forces became apparent. Civilian morale fluctuated between depression and optimism, depending on the news of the day. It picked up considerably when Winston Churchill became Prime Minister of Great Britain and offered nothing "but blood, toil, tears and sweat" in May of 1940.

Recruitment continued at a moderate rate. A "Home Guard" was formed for para-military service in Canada. Most of its members, veterans of World War I, served as guards at the prisoner-of-war camp in the Riding Mountain, a camp which housed German prisoners, in the main. Announcements had been made in April and May of 1940, that Dauphin would have a Service Flying Training School three miles south of town and a Bombing and Gunnery School ten miles east of town near Paulson Siding on the Canadian National Railway. The latter would have the use of large parts of Dauphin Lake, as a practice bombing range. Work was rushed on both sites. Hundreds of men came to Dauphin seeking work on the construction of the runways and buildings. The Service Flying Training School was to open in February of 1941 but delays resulted in its opening on April 15, 1941. On June 23, 1941 training operations began at #7 B. & G. school. From that time forward, Dauphinites accustomed themselves to the high whine of the Harvard training planes, to a housing shortage, to airforce blue on the streets, in the movies and at the dances. Airforce wives and children used whatever accommodation was available to them in rooms, basements, apartments and summer cottages. Throughout the war they had to accustom themselves, also, to the tragedy of air accidents in their own skies and to the news of casualties amongst their own husbands, brothers, fathers, neighbours and friends in other parts of the world.

The personal nature of war touched Dauphin early in 1940 when it was learned that a son of a former Methodist minister was missing in action. Don Middleton was later known to be a prisoner of war, having been shot down over Norway. War came home to Dauphin in the early fall of 1941 when Dan Craig lost his life in the sinking of a Canadian corvette. His was the first reported death of a native-born Dauphinite in World War II. From that time onwards, hardly a week went by without reports of death, woundings, missing in action, prisoners of war or presumed dead. At Dieppe, during the Italian campaign and after the Normandy landing, casualties were noticeably higher. In one month in the summer of 1944, Dauphin received news of ten men killed, five wounded and one missing. People dreaded having the C.N.R. telegraph's delivery girl, Miss Meredith, coming to their home. She usually brought bad news in those days.

For some families the personal burden of war was particularly heavy. One woman who had seen seven members of her family serve in World War I, had five grandchildren in the second war. The Cathcart family had nine members in the service. The Thomas Little family sent six members of its family into active service and one other was attached to Sir William Stephenson's intelligence group headquarters in New York. Many families had their only son or all of their sons in active service. This necessitated a much greater involvement by women in the business and commerce of the country, as well as in the services where they rendered important support, in Canada and overseas. More than 21000 women served in the Canadian Women's Army Corps before the war was over. In the labour force there was a great increase in the ranks of women workers. The separation from mothers, fathers, sons, wives and husbands took a heavy toll on many families. This resulted in many family and marital problems, which continued into the post-war period.

On the home front, strictures were placed upon Canadians which persisted throughout the war. In Dauphin, the Wartime Prices and Trades Board established an office on Main Street North, next to the King's Hotel. Wages and prices were fairly strictly controlled by them. In June, 1940 the government asked for voluntary contributions of field glasses to aid in the war effort and for musical instruments to help build a band at the south airport. Many materials such as paper, clothing, scrap iron and rubber were recycled where possible and other goods and materials were rationed. A "salvage corps" was organized to encourage collection. Gas rationing, which was, at first, voluntary, became compulsory in July of 1941. Ration books soon became available with the new car licences. Automobile tires and tubes and retreading came under strict control. Rubber inner tubes were replaced with synthetic rubber tubes. This may have been beneficial for the war effort but it certainly proved a major inconvenience in Dauphin, especially in cold weather, when the synthetic tubes would leak, it seemed, in direct relationship to the drop in temperature.

In July, 1942 rent controls came into effect and within a month tea, coffee, butter, sugar, and liquor were all rationed and gas rationing became more severe. By January, 1943 the butter ration was also decreased by one-third from one-half pound per week per person. By May of 1943 meat rationing began. Canned salmon was rationed as a meat exchange. Meat allowance was two pounds per person per week. Meatless Tuesdays were instituted. Rationing was applied to canning sugar which resulted in an annual allowance of twelve pounds per person for rural residents and ten pounds per person for urban residents. During the summer of 1943, jams, marmalades, honey and jellies were put on the ration list. The liquor ration in December of 1943 was twenty-six ounces of hard liquor per person per month, three bottles of wine per person per month and one dozen bottles of beer per person per month. In March, 1944 the butter ration had fallen to eight ounces per month per person temporarily, while some other goods were more freely available. Beer rations increased to one case per day per person. Meat rationing and meatless Tuesdays were suspended in March, 1944 and, of course, by the summer of 1945 most of the wartime controls were relaxed.

"Victory gardens" were promoted to supply the home front and the military establishments with fresh vegetables and to have preserves for the winter. Most of the homes in Dauphin had a good productive garden plot. Many of Dauphin's avid gardeners kept a garden or two on vacant lots, as well as their own home garden. People were encouraged to send vegetable seeds in their packages to Britain. Old fur coats were donated to make fur jackets for sailors in the northern seas. A "buckshee" fund was established to provide cigarettes for overseas forces. In March, 1944 there was a request for sportsmen to turn in their old golf balls so that "rebuilt" golf balls could be made with synthetic rubber covers. Waste paper was urgently needed and diligently collected.

The *Dauphin Herald* began a column devoted to the goings-on at the two airports. The column was called "Wings Over Dauphin". It served as a useful line of communication between the townspeople and the military establishments. A much greater interchange occurred after the establishment of "The Hostess Club", which opened in the Mayo building on Burrows Avenue in April, 1942. The club was a project of the War Services Committe, headed by J.N. McFadden and created to oversee and co-ordinate various activities related to the welfare of the service men in town and to the war effort, generally. Grace Peebles was very active in it and she eventually relieved Mr. McFadden of his responsibility for it. The work of Grace Fagen and Alice Greig was particularly notable, as they acted as official "hostesses" for the duration of its life. The Hostess Club provided a meeting and entertainment site for men and women away from home. It was well used and greatly appreciated, until its closure in June, 1945.

Initially, recruitment was on a voluntary basis. Beginning in August, 1940 there was a national registration of men over sixteen years of age but no strong pressure for these men to join up, although many, of course, did so. Within six months, questions were being raised about voluntary enlistment. On the one hand the war was going badly. German advances and victories in battle were reported almost daily; men and materiel were being lost in the shipping lanes by heavy U-Boat activity; Holland and Belgium had fallen; 340,000 men had been evacuated from Dunkirk; France had given only token resistance until her fall in June, 1940 and Britain was left to carry on, largely alone, for a time. On the other hand Mackenzie King, whose political base depended, to a great extent, on support from Quebec, stood firm in supporting a doctrine, first enunciated by R.J. Manion, leader of the Conservative party, of "no conscription for overseas duties". There was a call-up system, however, presumably for service in Canada only, but the call was frequently ignored. Courts were constantly hearing cases of "draft dodgers", even as late as mid-1941. In July of that year, the Hon. J.L. Ralston, minister of defence in the federal cabinet, issued a call to arms to encourage enlistment. This was successful only to a moderate degree. The need for more and more men remained and, as a result, King was forced to a referendum on the question of conscription. The support for conscription won the day across Canada by a majority of 64%, although a breakdown of the vote showed a range of 38% in Quebec to 81% in Manitoba. Still no conscripts were sent overseas until 1944. In the meantime the "zombies", as they were called, were enlisted for service within North America.

Morale during the war, at least on the home front in Dauphin, was tremendously aided by several speeches by Winston Churchill. What might have happened had not the world heard, "we shall not flag or fail" on June 4, 1940 or on June 18, 1940 "Let us therefore brace ourselves to our duty and so bear ourselves that if the British Commonwealth and Empire lasts for a thousand years, men will still say 'This was their finest hour' ", or, in tribute to the men who had fought in the skies in the Battle of Britain, "Never in the field of human conflict was so much owed by so many to so few?" Even as the war went on, supported by American lend-lease agreements, Churchill's courage under intense danger and the enormous political pressures of wartime, made him the centre of the whole war effort. His plea to Roosevelt and to America in February 1941 to "Give us the tools and we will finish the job" and his "some chicken, some neck" speech before the Canadian parliament on December 30, 1941 served as inspirations which, literally, raised the spirits and determinations of thousands, even millions, of Canadians to continue the sacrifice and the effort needed to win the war.

As the war continued there were increasingly heavy casualties. This increase was reflected in Dauphin homes, as in homes across the country. It was a heart-wrenching time for many families, during which they had the warmest sympathies of their neighbours who had already borne the same sadness or might bear it in the near future.

THE SECOND WORLD WAR   217

Victory in Europe on May 8, 1945 and victory over Japan on August 15, 1945 were celebrated in many ways by Dauphinites. Parties, parades, services of thanksgiving, quiet meditation and deep despair were the range of reactions to the end of a world disaster. As had happened so many times in the pioneer life of so many of their forebears, people accepted their fates, bolstered up their resourcefulness and planned for the days ahead.

During the war and afterwards, the people of Dauphin began to hear the stories of courage and sacrifice of its many sons and daughters. The cenotaph, which had honoured the war dead of the first world war, would now honour the eighty Dauphin and district men who gave their lives in World War II. Many others returned from prisoner-of-war camps in Europe and Asia or from hospitals around the world. At least five others were decorated for their bravery in action. Some had had miraculous escapes from enemy custody. Hershell Smith, on being promoted to Lieutenant-Colonel, was one of the youngest Canadian officers ever to receive this rank.

During the war years, of course, the day-to-day business of the town continued, making adjustments as required by the political and war situation and by the availability of labour.

In November, 1939, men's suits with two pairs of trousers were being sold by John Gardner for thirty dollars. Suits could be dry-cleaned and pressed for one dollar. McIntosh apples, fancy wrapped, sold for one dollar and five cents a case. Veal was fourteen cents a pound, butter three pounds for eighty-two cents, an 8 oz. tin of Campbell's soup cost eight cents while fresh pickerel fillets were nineteen cents a pound.

Several improvements were supported by the town council and were accomplished. The storm sewer system was extended to the south end of town in 1940, having been completed in the north end a year earlier. No longer would Dauphin lack the capacity to handle excess storm water with the consequent flooding of the streets. The provincial government began the paving of highway #5 from Neepawa to Yorkton. A long-time public servant, Walter Wickes, retired in 1939 after twelve years as reeve of the rural municipality of Dauphin, to be succeeded by Michael Szewczyk. Frank Bumstead became fire chief in January, 1940. In 1939 Dauphin's links with the outside improved by the opening of a highway to The Pas and by the stringing of more long-distance telephone lines to Neepawa.

The summer of 1940 was a very hot summer in Dauphin. Temperatures in the 90 degrees F. and higher were common. Some concern was expressed for the available water supply, as dry, hot weather continued. The housing conditions became very tight with the influx of airforce families. Local citizens were encouraged to rent rooms or suites and to invest in new housing, if possible. Dauphin was also a distribution centre for children being sent from Britain for the duration of the war. In September, 1940 the first two children arrived to spend the rest of the war period with Mr. and Mrs. Darwin Chase. The town council tried to regulate dance halls, which sprang up in many places, by restricting the halls to those over seventeen years of age and insisting on managers of "good character". The halls were to have "distinct" dressing rooms and adequate toilets. Not always were these requirements met, a condition that kept the military police and the Royal Canadian Mounted Police busy on many nights.

Victory loan drives were scheduled with regularity in order to produce the funds to drive the war effort. In Dauphin these drives were invariably successful throughout the war. Some kind of carrot was usually offered to guarantee success. In 1941 a new corvette was commissioned by the Canadian Navy, to be known as *H.M.C.S. Dauphin*. On another occasion the town was "occupied" by mock Nazi forces. The senior officials were jailed to give the town a taste of what might be, if the war effort failed.

In mid-1941 the local police attachment suspended when the town reached agreement with the Royal Canadian Mounted Police to take over the policing functions. Water and sewer lines were extended toward the southern extremity of the town. Garages were closed after 7:00 p.m. and on weekends, partly as a result of gas rationing but partly, also, because of a shortage of labour. A.E. Iredale retired as postmaster after thirty-four years in the position, to be succeeded by Dave Justice. The customs office closed permanently. Dauphin citizens voted to sell their electric powerhouse and join the Manitoba Hydro System. This was a necessary step in the rural electrification plans for Manitoba. It was not long before farm houses were lit by electrical power and the appearance of the night landscape was changed by bright yard lights, dotted across the countryside at mile or half-mile intervals.

Shortly after the beginning of the war, Mr. Duplessis of Quebec called an election in his province which many saw as an attempt to declare Quebec's neutrality in the war. A bitter fight ensued during the campaign, which resulted in the defeat of Duplessis. Shortly after that, Mitchell Hepburn of Ontario put a resolution through the legislature, condemning the government's war plans as being too weak. Faced with this challenge and worried about the conscription issue, King called an election in 1940. In Dauphin, W.J. Ward won the seat for the Liberals over J.L. Bowman for the Conservatives and Ronald Moore of the C.C.F. Ward's majority was only 69 votes and required a recount. Across Canada, the Liberals swept in with a big majority, including all the seats in Quebec.

Provincially, Robert Hawkins was returned to the legislature by acclamation in April, 1941. No further elections were held during the war. In the federal election of 1945, Fred Zaplitny of the C.C.F. won the seat from Ward by 717 votes. George Dowler represented the Conservatives. Later in the same year, Robert Hawkins was re-elected in the landslide win of the Garson government.

The dispute about teachers' salaries which had raged in the late 1930s in Dauphin and which resulted in the resignation of at least two of Dauphin's well-respected teachers, G.M. Churchill and A.S. Moore, continued in other matters relating to broader issues in education. J.N. McFadden was said to have delivered a "slashing attack" on the administration and financing of schools in Manitoba. He was one who believed that better education at smaller cost per pupil could only be attained by the organization of larger school adminstrative areas. His opponents felt that his plans were too expensive. The editor of the *Dauphin Herald* remarked that the "fight in education in Dauphin seems to be between idealists who may have been careless of money and pragmatists who wondered where the money was to come from". Whatever the merits of the debate, there is no doubt that the efforts of J.N. McFadden had great effect on the discussions which followed and eventually led to the formation of the Dauphin Ochre River school district, the first of Manitoba's large school administrative areas.

Mr. McFadden also championed the formation of a parent-teacher or Home and School Associaton. In June of 1943 a signal event occurred when Miss Ethel Cadman retired from the school staff. She first came to the Dauphin schools in the fall of 1902 and except for a five year break to study music, she taught in Dauphin since that time. Little else of note occurred in educational circles during the war years. Soon after the war, however, the subject of a composite high school and a large school administrative area, had resurfaced.

During the first year of the war, the Dauphin General Hospital celebrated its fortieth anniversary. In that time it had grown from a few beds in Dr. Bottomley's home to a one hundred bed regional hospital. A new hospital had opened in Ste. Rose du Lac in 1939, relieving some of the pressure on the beds in the Dauphin hospital. The nursing school thrived under the direction of successive Lady Superintendents, who protected the quality of nursing with great fervour. A great deal of credit must go to them and to the various doctors who carried the load of teaching, over the years. About ten nurses graduated each year, a marked increase from the classes of one or two when the school first opened. The responsibility of looking after a community of approximately twenty thousand persons and educating nurses to their profession put a fairly heavy load on the staff of five doctors, Dicks, Potoski, Malcolm, Peacock and Peacock. Within two years the two Doctors Elaine and Kenneth Peacock left Dauphin leaving three doctors to carry the load. As the population increased with the coming of airforce families, the load became extreme. By early 1943 an appeal was made by the doctors for people to give serious thought before using medical resources needlessly. At the time, in the Dauphin area, there was one doctor for every three thousand of population. The Canadian average was 1:1261 and the Manitoba average was 1:1408. Some suggestion was made to have the military doctors help out in some areas, including Dauphin, but the suggestion never bore fruit. In April of that year, Dr. Adam Little arrived to work with Dr. Dicks and Dr. Malcolm. For the rest of the war period the four doctors met the demands for medical care in the community. Changes occurred as result of the war. A blood donor service was opened in December of 1943. Such was the co-operation of the Lady Superintendent of the day that those in charge of the clinic were obliged to enter the hospital by way of the back door.

At about this time, the first reports of the efficacy of penicillin and of its availabiltiy, reached Dauphin. This drug was to bring a major change in the treatment of infections and some infectious diseases, some of the major killers of the time. There were plans for a public health unit in the area and by May of 1944, a board was established for that purpose. By January, 1945, plans for a diagnostic unit were announced by the provincial government. In retrospect, one sees the early beginnings of the national health plan to come, since both were strongly influenced by Dr. F.W. Jackson, the deputy minister of health for Manitoba and, later, an architect of the national health plan.

In the legal profession, the war years were marked by the acquisition of a K.C. by two of its members, J.N. McFadden in 1939 and Alex Katz in 1943. Frank Simpson was appointed County Court judge in the Dauphin Judicial district in January of 1942. E.W. Hawkins returned to his home town to practise law as did Helen Bowman. J.N. McFadden became district governor of Rotary International in 1943.

Sports and recreation played a major part in removing the tensions of military life and the stresses of wartime civilian activity. Movies in the early part of the war tended towards propaganda. *Mein Kampf — My Crimes,* a title badly translated was, nevertheless, shown as a revelation of Hitler's plans. The airmen at #10 Service Flying Training School and at #7 Bombing and Gunnery School presented *Southfield Follies* and *Paulson on Parade* to appreciative audiences in October of 1941. *Gone With the Wind* was the rave show of the year in 1940. A new bowling alley was opened in the basement of the Edgar block, run by the Youngs, and became an overnight success.

In hockey circles, Pinkie Davie was selected to coach in Dauphin and the hockey interests in Dauphin prospered as a result. The Dauphin Intermediates won the provincial crown in March, 1941 with a team composed of Bob Gardner, Roy Alf, Pinkie Davie, Bill McCulloch, Vic Love, Tom Love, Tom Klym, Andy Kerr, Bill Porter and W. Carrol.

The Dauphin Country Club went through the war years with a small membership, looking forward to the postwar years for possible development of grass greens for their golf course. Helen Bowman won the ladies' golf tourney at Clear Lake in 1944. In May, 1945, the Dauphin Lions' Club produced a minstrel show, under the guidance of Grace Peebles, which was well received by the community.

Some major changes occurred in the businesses of Dauphin towards the end of the war years. D.D. McDonald retired from the partnership of McDonald & Oliphant, leaving a business he had founded some forty years earlier. Mrs. Gertie Wright sold her ladies' wear shop to Mary and Jay Slobodzian, who renamed it the Mary-Jayne Shoppe. For years it was *the* fashion store for Dauphin's women. The Lodge Funeral Home became Sneath's Funeral Parlours. J.J. Crowe retired from the lumber business after forty-one years, selling his interests to Beaver Lumber Company. The Craig brothers, Dan and Gavin, sold out to the Dauphin Furniture Manufacturing Company after being in business in Dauphin since 1906. Throughout that time they established an enviable record for high quality workmanship. Lastly, Ray Dicks, who had served in the town office for many years, became a partner with Joe Allard in the Ford agency to be known as Allard & Dicks.

The Dauphin Pioneers' Association, which had been meeting annually since 1926, celebrated its 25th anniversary in 1941. The lists of its members and of the old-timers in the area, at that time and during the rest of the war years, showed great losses in the number of surviving pioneers. In the years from 1939 to 1945 the following oldtimers had gone: Alexander Birss, who had come to the Gartmore area as a bachelor in 1887, subsequently marrying Cynthia, the daughter of Neil McDonald, one of Dauphin's earliest pioneers; Albert Durston, who had come with his family in 1889 to the Mountview district, and Alton Nicholson, who had also come in 1889 as a small boy, all died in 1940. In 1941 two oldtimers who would be missed by the community died. They were Isaac Spillett, who had come in 1891 and Dr. W.J. Harrington, who had served his community so well as a doctor, politician and sportsman since his arrival in 1901. In 1942, Mrs. Dora (Alguire) Winers, a pioneer of 1892, died. In 1943, Dauphin lost its very early pharmacist and "Doctor", Philip Beauchamp. He had come to the Mayflower area in 1886. His work in the early community, in his church and for the aid of the sick, were vital to the welfare of the growing district. Another early settler, Henry Esplen, died in 1944. He had come to Dauphin in 1886 with his family, from Minnedosa by the old Lake Audy trail. Dr. G.C.J. Walker, Dauphin's first full-time dentist, who had first come to town in 1901, Mr. H.E. Lys, the florist and gardener, who came in 1890, and William Buchannon who came in 1892 and became one of Dauphin's most prominent farmers and an M.L.A., all died in 1944. In 1945, Dauphin lost Dr. H.E. Bewell, who had started a dental practice in Dauphin in 1904 and contributed greatly to the educational system in Dauphin. Also prominent in education and who died in 1945 was W.J. Henderson, who came to Dauphin from Gilbert Plains during World War I and stayed to become principal of the Whitmore school for many years. One of Dauphin's newer schools honoured him by adopting his name. Mrs. E. Widmeyer, who came in 1898 when her husband took over the Grandview Hotel and Jack Buckwold, the fuel and implement dealer who came first in 1898, both died in 1940.

As the war ended in the summer of 1945, people individually and in groups, realized that many changes were in store. The wartime economy would give way to a peacetime economy for which a great deal of planning would be necessary. Men and women would return to positions in business for which there had been some guarantees when they left. Some would choose to change their life careers. Some would choose to use their service benefits to acquire further education and to move further afield. Unfortunately, many sons who were to take over family farms or businesses never returned and families were forced to make alternate plans. Governments had been preparing programs to provide veterans with opportunities to acquire land, homes and education, to ease the transition back to "civy street". Many took advantage of those plans. In addition, there were clear indications that comprehensive plans were afoot for the provision of public social programs in much greater variety and degree than had been known before. A national hospital plan followed by a national medical care plan, an enlarged unemployment insurance program, universal old age pensions and many other items of social welfare were much more than idealistic dreaming. Much had already been accomplished.

Dauphin's job was to see that the postwar years would be years of solid planning, sound financing and sound accomplishment. Until the end of the second war, excepting the nine years of the Great Depression, it had moved steadily forward from a small and scattered pioneer settlement, isolated from the outside world, to a major marketing, farming and railroad centre. It was the major population centre north of the Riding Mountain escarpment in Manitoba. Could it now pick up the pieces and forge ahead again?

Notes on Chapter 9

Books and Reports:

Broadfoot, Barry. *Six Years War.* Toronto: Doubleday Canada Limited, 1974.

Shirer, Wm. L. *The Nightmare Years.* Toronto: Little, Brown and Co., 1984.

Shirer, Wm. L. *The Rise and Fall of the Third Reich.* New York: Simon & Schuster, 1960.

Newspapers:

The Dauphin Herald & Press, 1939 to 1945.

"THEY SHALL NOT GROW OLD AS WE THAT ARE LEFT"
These Dauphin men sacrificed all — 1939-1945

J.W. Arthurs	C.H. Baxter	D. McBaxter
J.S. Bladon	L.C. Burr	G.W. Carruthers
D. Chalmers	S.V. Chambers	R. Chartier
D.A. Craig	W.G. Crawford	K. Crawford
B.D. Davis	G.H. Durston	V.D. Ferris
H.A. Fisher	V.R. Folkerson	R. Fulton
E.T. Garlinski	A.L. Gibb	F. Gidilevich
H.R. Graham	R.J. Gurr	J.F. Harrington
W.D. Harrison	A. Hawrysh	R. Justice Sr.
R. Justice Jr.	D.V. Jackson	T.J. Karaim
M. Korney	W. Kormarnisky	J. Kustra
S. Lintick	T.B. Little	E.E. Locke
J.H. Love	M.R. Maksymetz	A.J. Marsh
F.M. Myers	J.A. McFadden	T. Negrich
M.J. Neill	C.C. Patterson	T. Pearson
F.G. Peebles	J.D. Pilote	O.R. Pipe
E.S. Pollon	K.F. Ray	J.W. Richardson
H. Roussin	B. Rudkawich	C.E. Saunderson
W. Schykulski	D.H. Scott	M. Senchuk
H.A. Shewfelt	I. Schwetz	A.R. Skinner
W.T. Skinner	A.G. Skwarok	J. Slyzuk
W.C. Smith	W.G. Smith	C.W. Snyder
F.B. Snyder	J. Sosnowski	S. Tkachuk
H.K. Veal	J. Wakula	C.R. Ward
B.R. Whaley	G.S. Whitmore	A.F. Wickes
D. Williamson Sr.	D. Williamson Jr.	S.T. Willis
J. Yurkiw	J. Zinchyshyn	

10

THE RECONSTRUCTION

Towards the end of World War II, when it seemed apparent to governments in the allied cause, that the winning of the war was only a matter of time, national, provincial and municipal governments began to make plans for the post-war years. The world depression and the war had forced postponements of the projects which were desired by many but enjoyed by only a few. Dauphin had not yet enjoyed the luxury of relatively dust-free streets, of sewer and water services to all areas, or of a clean and safe water supply. The boom economy of the war years was the first experienced by many. Most had not experienced the boom of the early part of the century, when the area was filling with settlers coming by the new railway. The boom of the twenties had been a short one, petering out with the drought years and the worldwide economic slump which resulted in falling prices for Canadian grain.

Although a few of Dauphin's people had benefitted in the economy of the twenties, the conditions of the 1930s abbreviated the benefits. This is not to say that Dauphin suffered as much as many parts of the prairies during the drought years. Rainfall in the area, while less than average, was a good deal heavier than in the southern part of the province, in Saskatchewan or in Alberta. Also, the land was, generally, well treed, although less so than in the earlier days. There was, consequently, less damage done by wind. Any dust storms in Dauphin in the thirties were the result of Saskatchewan dust being carried in, rather than the result of local damage. Local wits remarked that this was the only change of real estate from which the lawyers didn't take a cut. By the time the drought ended in 1937-38, the war was close upon us.

THE RECONSTRUCTION

Any profits made in the wartime days, and there were many, were generally invested in the war effort. Still, they became available for use in the post-war period. In addition, income taxes had been levied at fairly high levels, for those days, and in the post-war period, although taxes were reduced, they never returned to pre-war levels. Governments, therefore, found themselves in a position of relative affluence after the war and were able to proceed with plans for many public projects.

Among the projects which Dauphin hoped to forward, as early as possible, were those outlined in a council meeting of January, 1944, together with projected costs:

Water and Sewer extension	$35000
Municipal Office Building	$100000
Filtration Plant	$65000
Fire Hall and Police Station	$20000
Auditorium, Library and Rest Room	$50000
Curbs, Gutters and Boulevards	$75000
Hard Surface Streets	$150000
Parks Improvements	$50000

Some of these programs were initiated as planned. By August of 1947, the paving of Main Street was almost completed. Final completion was delayed until the summer of 1948. This paving program, together with the installation of curbs and gutters, to improve the drainage of the streets, was supervised by the town engineer of that time, Ron Everall. The town purchased a one-million gallon reserve water tank, in June 1946, to ensure an adequate and clean supply of water at all times. Water and sewer extensions were begun but the bulk of this work had to await the extensions of the town limits and the increased influx of residents in the 1950s. The paving of the remaining streets in Dauphin had, also, to await the late fifties before completion.

Housing took a major thrust forward after the war. There had been some building of "wartime" housing during the war, especially in the southeast quarter of the town. After the war, new families looking for housing when the veterans returned from the war, used their wartime credits and the favourable terms of mortgages under the Veterans' Land Act to erect homes on small holdings or on vacant property in town. Small districts of such homes sprang up on land in the northwest part of town on what had previously been farm lands. That area and the Winnipegosis highway were filling up quickly after the war's end.

Progress on the provision of a new firehall and police station was dependent on the removal of the town offices from the town hall. This, in turn, was dependent on the plans for a new federal post office in Dauphin. The plan was for the town to take over the old post office on Burrows Avenue and refurbish the building to accommodate the growing municipal responsibilities. Such a move was not possible, however, until a suitable, central site could be found for the post office. The site was found when the Pentecostal church, the old St. James Presbyterian church, burned to the ground in April, 1949. A new post office went ahead later on this site, the town moved its offices to the renovated old post office and, eventually, the police and the fire brigade obtained enlarged premises in the now "old" town hall. The remainder of the town hall building came to be used by the arts and crafts community and at a future date was dedicated to the memory of Dr. Vernon Watson who, in his lifetime, made a very signal contribution to the arts, especially music and painting, in Dauphin. That dedication seemed a fitting tribute, as well, to a building which, for so many years, had been the structural centre of Dauphin's cultural life.

Dauphin had always been blessed, in the main, with very stable municipal government. Reference has already been made to its high standing with the credit agencies of the country. This was never better exemplified than in the years, 1938-1955, when the town councils of those years served under only three mayors. Jack Ramsden was a very effective mayor from 1938 to 1943 inclusive; Isaac Johnston filled the office with distinction in 1944 and 1945; Bill Bullmore was so effective in the mayor's chair that he was given the post for an eleven-year period between 1945 and 1955 inclusive. Under all of these mayors, Dauphin's municipal affairs were under excellent care.

By 1948, concerted efforts were being made to bring the public library to a level which would allow it to take advantage of tax support under the terms of the Manitoba Library Act. Until that time, both the adult and the junior libraries had been housed in the town hall, had irregular hours and depended on voluntary goodwill and memberships for support. Mrs. Leitch Stewart and Mrs. H.J. Everall in the adult library were very active in their encouragement of library facilities. In the civic elections, in the fall of 1948, the people of Dauphin supported a referendum which allowed the town to levy a one-mill tax on property, to be set aside for library purposes. As a consequence, the library board resigned to make way for a new board, set up according to the provisions of the library act. The adult and junior libraries turned over their assets to the new board which consisted of Dave McLean as president, Madge McFadden as secretary, Mr. Adam Little as treasurer and Ruth Goodhand. By August of 1949 a new home for the combined library was secured in the Legion Hall (formerly the Great War Veterans' Association Hall). The library remained in that location until the Lions' Club, in 1958, presented them with a new library building on Main Street North.

In spite of some delays in the completion of municipal projects, the townspeople were intent on making a significant gesture of commemoration for those who had given their lives in World War II. This resolve remained strong throughout the many discussions and debates which ensued as to the nature of the memorial — a park, a statue, a building or something else? In the end, and without knowing precisely how the idea got started, support was apparent for a community centre. There were facilities which needed upgrading, there were requirements for new activities and there was a community need to express its gratitude and to honour the war dead. Out of this came the Dauphin Memorial Community Centre, an organization born in 1946. The town and rural councils, the Dauphin Agricultural Society and many local groups and organizations, set up a central planning committee in 1946, of which Tommy Warnock was the chairman and Bill Strang the vice-chairman. By March of 1947, all of the local organizations had pledged full support.

A fund drive was started in early June. For months, the slogan, "Make Remembrance A Reality — Give With Your Heart" reminded people of the need and the purpose for giving. Some materials became available as the airports were dismantled. Hangars were purchased and the move to the new location in the southeast section of the town began. The willingness of the Agricultural Society to relocate from the old grounds, was a vital part of the success of the venture.

There must have been at least a twinge of doubt in some minds as the Society gave up the land on which George McCrae planted potatoes in 1883. The inclusion of the Agricultural Society's needs in the venture made it possible to obtain increased funding from the federal government. It also made possible the savings inherent in using buildings for multiple purposes. In May, 1947, property had been purchased in what was the old "ball park", south of the tracks and stockyards, east of Main Street. The town had passed an appropriation bylaw which gave the committee the legal basis for obtaining more land, if needed.

While all of this was going on, the spring run-off into the Vermilion river and the spring rains brought the water to heights which had not been known in the records, to that time. The powerhouse, that early flood-warning system, was almost put out of commission by the rising waters. The skating rink alongside, albeit built in a depression, had water to the top of its doors and was, literally, half-submerged. Dauphin was said to be 40% surrounded by water. Aerial views of the flooding, showed farms and roads completely covered by water. Throughout the summer, rains continued. By September, the meteorological bureau, which had first opened in Dauphin in February of that year, reported that 12.34 inches of rain had fallen in the district in the previous four months. This was believed to be a record rainfall for the area.

Needless to say, the summer floods and the rains put a crimp in the fund-raising drive of the Dauphin Memorial Community Centre but the stubborn persistence of its supporters kept the project going. The first block of Second Avenue Southeast became Memorial Boulevard and the cenotaph, which stood in front of the Canadian National station, honouring the dead of World War I, was moved to Memorial Boulevard, where it guards the entrance to the Community Centre grounds. The names of those killed in World War II were added to the Honour List between the words, "There Is No Wealth But Life — These Gave Their All". The cenotaph was re-dedicated on a cold, bleak November 11, 1947. The tablets bearing the names of the dead of World War II were unveiled by J.N. McFadden. Sixty-seven wreaths were laid by local organizations and individuals.

Until the end of 1950, the planning committee carried on the necessary work in the centre but when formal agreements between the town, rural council and the Agricultural Society were ratified in 1951, a new board was named. Bill Cruise as chairman, Scotty Robertson as vice-chairman, Margaret Marsh as secretary and Ed Johnasen as treasurer, together with their directors, gave yeoman service to the cause and were followed by others, in later years, whose work assured the success of the venture. The foundation was solidly laid in the early post-war years.

The end of the war brought changes that affected the business centre of the town. Early in 1946, Harry Breslaw bought the Malcolm Block and in January, 1948, he moved his People's Store from Burrows Avenue to his new premises in the Malcolm block. This move was made possible when John Gardner, who had, in that year of 1947, completed thirty years in business in Dauphin, formed a partnership with his son, Bob, and the partnership bought the Lepper building on the southwest corner of Main Street and Third Avenue Northwest, which had housed the Pollyanna Café and bakery. John Gardner & Son opened in their new premises in December of 1947. The game of musical chairs did not end there, however. Andy Newton, who had operated a butcher shop out of Archie Bennett's old stand on the east side of Main Street North, moved into the premises vacated by Harry Breslaw where he added a frozen-food locker plant to his butcher shop. Dr. Adam Little left the Dauphin Medical Clinic to establish his office in a portion of Gardner's new store with an entrance on Third Avenue Northwest. In 1950, Dr. Little took Dr. Marvin Brandt into partnershp. They purchased property from Mrs. Harrington and, on part of it, built a new medical office, housing themselves and Dr. Scotty Robertson and his dental office. Little's Business College moved into the lower floor of that building.

The changes along Main Street continued. F.W. Bumstead opened a new store on the east side of Main Street for plumbing and heating sales and services, in August, 1946. His son, George, who had returned from a prisoner-of-war camp in Germany, joined in a partnership with his father. Jack Ball bought the Rexall drug store from the Robson family in June of 1946. The Western Bakery, owned by Max Lanin and Ted Drabik, moved from their premises on Third Avenue Northeast, across from Eaton's and west of White's store, to a building on Burrows Avenue being vacated by Robert Hawkins Company. Mr. Hawkins was building new office accommodation on the north side of Burrows Avenue, near Allard & Dicks, into which he moved in October, 1948. Meanwhile, Bill McCormick, who had operated a stationery shop next to the post office for forty-five years, sold out to Mrs. Bertha Easterbrook who, in turn, sold out to Jack Blinkhorn in 1949. He and his family left shortly afterwards for Arizona and the business was taken over by Dr. Gordon Ritchie as Brett's. That store later moved to the east side of Main Street North.

Peter Cowtun, in business in the south end of Dauphin, on Vermilion Street, since the early twenties, also sold out and retired to Winnipeg in 1946. The butcher business started by Captain Scrase and his son, Bert, in 1926, which developed into one of Dauphin's best and busiest butcheries, sold out to Peter Hyndiuk and Herb Keats. H.D. Brewer closed the Avoca Dairy after ten years of operation. Gillis & Warren opened a Dauphin branch in 1948. Two new businesses that came to Dauphin in the early post-war period were Dennison Motors in 1946 and the Dent brothers' farm implement shop in the old Clark garage on Main Street South in 1948. W.J. Ward, now displaced as an M.P., was promoting a whale-processing factory, to be known as Adanac Fish Products Ltd., at Churchill, Manitoba.

Graham & Son opened a tinsmithing business in November of 1948 and The Singer Sewing Machine Company returned to Dauphin, after many years of absence, to open a shop in the space recently vacated by Sam Solomon in the Stelck block. Sam Solomon spent thirty-one years in business in Dauphin, during which time he established records for continuous service on the town council.

The T. Eaton Company bought the Ramsay-Wright building. Reichert's auto body shop on Burrows Avenue East, which had operated out of an old blacksmith shop, moved to their own new building on the southwest corner of Burrows Avenue and First Street East, in December, 1947. The Manitoba Telephone System announced plans for an enlarged automatic switchboard for Dauphin in 1947. The Dauphin Theatre announced that admissions to the theatre performances would increase from forty cents per person to forty-five cents per person.

There were several retirements and resignations of particular note in the period following the war. R.P. Eastman, who had come to Dauphin in 1926, retired from the managership of the Bank of Nova Scotia. No other banker in Dauphin had spent so much of his career in one place. Generally, like ministers, they moved every four years or so. He and Mrs. Eastman made very important contributions to the life of the community. They were very active in the church, in music and in the theatre. C.B. Steen, who had come to Dauphin in 1910, to the partnership of Hafenbrak & Steen, retired in 1946 from the partnershp of Steen & Patrick. He was succeeded by Wallace Ludgate, who joined in the partnership of Patrick & Ludgate. C.B. Steen's name was always listed among the early Dauphin tradesmen who insisted on quality workmanship. J.N. McFadden resigned from the presidency of the Board of Trade due to ill health.

The Dauphin Agricultural Society, having discontinued its annual exhibition and fair during the war years, announced its intention to reinstitute the event in 1946. The rural electrification program was in full swing during 1948 and Dauphin learned that there was a very good chance for a feeder airline through Dauphin connecting Winnipeg, The Pas and Flin Flon. In fact, the first plane came to Dauphin on June 2, 1947. Town council was, at that time, considering the installation of parking meters for Dauphin's main streets.

On south Main Street Prentice's barn was being dismantled. It had been built by William Whitmore, who had built the Manor House, behind which there was already a livery stable run by a Mr. McLean. The operation of this stable was disapproved of by Wililam Whitmore so he decided to build another livery stable across Main Street from the Manor House. It was managed initially, and for a short time, by Bob Hunt, who was succeeded by John McKinstry and his sons, Ed and Bird. The McKinstrys developed very large auctions of horses, often one hundred in one day, and were very successful. Ed and Bird McKinstry stayed on after their father had left Dauphin for the United States. Their names were amongst the best known to the farmers and settlers of those early days. Later owners of that livery stable included Bruce Lay, a veterinarian; H. Harkness; Archie and Ed Chute and then A.E. Prentice, who used it as a livery stable, an automobile garage and, later, a taxi stand.

The loss of the training airports proved a boon to the town, in many ways. A great deal of material and many buildings were made available at good prices. The town was offered the south airport for a dollar a year. The #7 Bombing & Gunnery School was used by 1200 air cadets, as a training site, in July of 1946. The south airport was a convenient location for the meteorological service which established in Dauphin after the war, and as a location for the new passenger air service. The majority of the buildings had been sold to an eastern Canadian housing firm in November of 1946. The demolition of the buildings was done, principally, by local labour, earning 63 cents an hour.

The Wartime Prices and Trades Board actually moved out of Dauphin in April, 1947. The space occupied by them reverted to a dining room for the King's Hotel. The country went back to daylight saving time in the summer of 1947, having been on double daylight saving time during the war. The matter of daylight saving time brought about some of the most emotional debates heard on any subject, unless it was the level of water on Lake Dauphin, a subject which arose again in December, 1947, following the very rainy summer and fall of that year.

Amongst the new buildings of the later forties must be included the Industrial Hall of the Dauphin Memorial Community Centre, which was started in the spring of 1948; the new warehouse and office building of the Western Grocers at Main Street and First Avenue Southwest, on the railway right-of-way; and the construction of Memorial Boulevard itself. Some of these projects were delayed by a cement shortage which resulted from a greatly increased demand, following the war. St. Paul's Home, built from barracks obtained from #10 Service Flying Training School, and officially opened in September of 1949 by the Sisters Servants of Mary Immaculate, was another important addition to Dauphin's facilities. The Bank of Montreal was renovated in 1947 so that it had considerably more room by taking over the space occupied by McGirr & Katz. That law office moved to the Second Avenue

THE RECONSTRUCTION 235

entrance of the Clarke block.

Agreements had been reached between the provincial government and the hospital board for property on which to build the new health unit and diagnostic services building. When it opened, the health unit, which had been temporarily housed in old buildings next to Bryce's bakery, moved to the new building on the hospital grounds. The federal Department of Indian Affairs moved into the vacated space until something more suitable could be found.

The late forties were active times in the medical life of Dauphin. At the close of the war, Dr. Michael Potoski practised in an office on the 2nd floor of the "Jaddock" building, originally the Franklin Block, on the west side of Main Street between Front Street and Burrows Avenue. Dr. R.E. Dicks, Dr. Frank Malcolm and Dr. Adam Little practised in the Dauphin Medical Clinic, on the second floor of the Burrows Block. In 1946 Dr. Malcolm left Dauphin for Swan River, after having practised in Dauphin for fifteen years. His place was taken by Dr. Gordon Ritchie, a Dauphin boy who returned to practise in 1947. Within a year Dr. Joseph Kagan joined Dr. Potoski but stayed only a short time, as did Dr. John Woods, who was in Dauphin from 1950 to 1954. In 1950, Dr. Adam Little left the Dauphin Medical Clinic, to enter a solo practice in an office in the rear of John Gardner & Son's store. Within a short time he took Dr. Marvin Brandt into partnership when they moved into a new set of offices on Third Avenue Northwest, where Johnston & Johnston's law office is situated now. Dr. Adam Little left Dauphin in December of 1952, to pursue postgraduate studies in New York. His place was taken by his brother, Dr. Harry Little, who remained in Dauphin until 1955, after which he pursued further studies in Pennsylvania.

The diagnostic unit began its life in the basement of the Dauphin General Hospital. Miss Mary McPherson (Mrs. Don Persson) and Irma Kitson were the first laboratory technicians, Dr. Harold Morrison was the visiting radiologist and George Grant was the radiology technician. The health unit was headed by Dr. Ross Creighton. Mr. Puls was the sanitary engineer. It was September, 1948, when the staff of both units moved into the new health unit building.

Plans for a national health system had been discussed in Dauphin since February of 1947. In November of that year, the Honourable Paul Martin, the federal Minister of Health, included Dauphin in his itinerary to promote the idea. Compulsory pre-marital blood testing for syphilis began on October 1, 1946. Compulsory pasteurization of milk was forced, after an enabling bylaw had been passed in that year.

The Dauphin General Hospital annual report for 1945 showed a total admission count of 3313 with 439 births and 90 deaths. The per diem cost in 1945 was $2.91. In the spring of 1946, sixteen nurses graduated. At about this time the Manitoba Medical Services organization began to sell policies in the rural areas of Manitoba. Until that time, many people were slow in paying their medical bills. Most doctors collected less than 50% of their fees, even though the fees charged were low. Pre-natal care and delivery was $25 in Dauphin until about 1949 when the fee was increased to $35. Office calls were two dollars, house calls were three dollars in the daytime and five dollars at night.

As a mark of respect and thanks, the Dauphin General Hospital board made Dr. H.N. Macneill the honourary president of the board. This honour was to mark the continuous service to the hospital over the entire period of the hospital's existence. Dr. Macneill had been previously honoured by the University of Manitoba, which granted him an honourary L.L.D. as a mark of respect for his contributions to education and health care in the province. Dr. Macneill was to die about a year later.

In 1946, Dr. Vernon Watson returned to Dauphin to resume the practice of dentistry left vacant by the death of Dr. H.E. Bewell in 1945. The Women's Hospital Aid, which had suspended operations in 1940 for the duration of the war, was reorganized in 1946 with Della McLernon as president and Helen Little as secretary. Mae McKee and Edith Paul succeeded Della McLernon for a period of two years each while Helen Little continued as secretary until leaving Dauphin in late 1952.

In legal circles, Stewart McLean arrived to join Mr. McGirr in the practice of law. This came about after the untimely death of Alex Katz in January, 1947, bringing to a close a productive career in criminal law. In August of the same year, Judge Frank Simpson died, leaving a vacancy on the bench which was filled by

Judge William Arsenych in 1948. C.S.A. Rogers completed twenty-five years as crown prosecutor, in 1948.

The debate about a large school administrative area was settled by referendum in April, 1946 in which the voters supported the idea by a two-to-one margin. The board elected to administer the new school area took office in January, 1947 with Michael Szewczyk as chairman. Members of the first board were Cecil Durston, Lou Kennedy, Basil Lazaruk, Sherman Hunt and Wilbur Fee. Ed Johansen became secretary-treasurer by appointment, a position he was to hold for many years. During the spring, a new school, the Henderson school, was started in the north end of town. The school was constructed, largely, from material salvaged from a hangar and a barrack block from the south airport. It was opened in the early months of 1948 and honoured the former principal of the Whitmore school, W.J. Henderson. The Mackenzie school underwent major alterations to make from it a composite high school, offering some trade, agricultural, home economics and business training, as well as an academic education. Meanwhile the board agreed upon a salary schedule for teachers which ranged from $1600 to $2400 per annum. There would be a $100 raise annually, if the teacher was satisfactory and if he or she took a refresher course during the summer months. There also would be a $100 premium paid to married teachers.

For the first time since Johnny Lawrence left the Dauphin Country Club for the Wasagaming Golf Club, a professional golfer took over duties at the Dauphin club. He was Doug Robertson. Following his appointment, golfing interest increased perceptibly. The new Dauphin Memorial Community Centre encouraged many local organizations to hold their fund-raising activities on the Memorial Centre site. The Rotary Club took advantage of the new location to hold some very successful carnivals. The Lions' Club did the same for their Bingo nights, to raise money for the future library. Before those successes, however, the Lions' club bombed out in the sponsorship of a Water Follies. It took some time to recoup from that loss. The Horticultural Society began to use the premises for their annual show.

During the war, Dauphin hockey fans saw limited hockey apart from some very entertaining games played by armed services teams; these often contained professional hockey players who were stationed in military units in Manitoba. It was obvious after the war, however, that Dauphin hockey required a new organization. Some beginning was made in this respect in the later forties but, as often happens, an unexpected occurrence provided the stimulus required to move ahead with greater speed. In this case, the occurrence was the burning and destruction of the hockey rink on Front Street West in July of 1951. This allowed the Community Centre to finance a new hockey rink on their site. This move stimulated the growth of the Dauphin Kings organization, which provided great hockey entertainment until Dauphin made an entry into Junior hockey in the mid-fifties. The Dauphin Kings, champions of the Big Six League on several occasions, brought back memories of the Intermediate teams of the twenties and thirties, although the players were, in many cases, imports to Dauphin. In that respect they could not be compared with the former teams, all of whose players were residents of Dauphin. Still, Pete Pisnook, George Tamblyn, Trigger, Stymie and Johnny Love, Bill Murray, Jim Mosienko, Paul Platz, Paul Allard, Jack Haddrell, Reg Kachanowski and others, provided many evenings of good hockey.

On the political scene, the post-war government of Mackenzie King worked on the transition from a busy, wartime industrialized economy to an economy directed towards peacetime industry and trade and a change of direction towards more and more social legislation. In addition to the organization and the expenditure necessary for a national hospital and health plan, there seemed to be an assurance of universal old age pensions, without resort to means tests to qualify. In April, 1949, an election was called for the summertime of that year and in June, the Liberals won a landslide victory under their new leader, Louis St. Laurent. In that election, W.J. Ward regained the seat for the Liberals in Dauphin. In December of 1949, J.L. Bowman was named a Privy Councillor. He had fought for the Conservative cause since his arrival in Dauphin in 1909. He had run as federal Conservative candidate in every election, from his nomination in May of 1915 to the election of 1945 — with the exception of the election of 1917, when he supported the idea of a wartime coalition government under Mr. Borden. On that occasion he had voluntarily withdrawn his candidacy in favour of the sitting member, Robert Cruise. He had served as Speaker of the House of Commons during the 1930-35 government of R.B. Bennett. On the provincial scene, E.N. McGirr won the seat for the Conservatives of Dauphin in the fall of 1949 and was to serve for one term.

The passing years and the stresses of the war years had more than the usual toll on the lives of many in the Dauphin area. By the end of the war, sixty-two years had passed since Tom Whitmore organized that first trip to Dauphin and sixty years had passed since the major influx of settlers began in 1886-87. Amongst those pioneers whose lives ended in the early post-war years were Harry Macneill in 1948. He had come across the Strathclair Trail in 1891. Mrs. W.H. Bigham, also deceased in 1948, had come to the Dauphin area in 1887 and, with her husband, had pioneered the area when only four other families lived in the district. Her husband, W.H. Bigham, who had come a year earlier, died in 1952. Isaiah Drinkwater, who had arrived in Dauphin in 1890, died in 1949. T.A. Nicholson, who had come as a child in 1888, died in 1949. Dr. E.E. Bottomley, one of the earliest of Dauphin's doctors, who had come in 1897, and who gave his home to serve as the first hospital, died in Smithers, B.C. in 1948. Early townspeople who were lost in the same period included A.H.F. Stelck who had helped to bring one of the earliest and finest hardware firms to Dauphin in 1897. He died fifty years later, in 1947. Archie Bennett died in 1948. He had been a butcher to the people of Dauphin for many years. He also served them as a town councillor and as their mayor in 1933. Major J.W. Skinner, who died in 1948, came to Dauphin when the railroad established the roundhouse. He served as a town councillor in the early twenties and as mayor in 1927 and 1928. Judge Frank Simpson, who made a major contribution to Dauphin's legal fraternity and to the political life of the community, died in 1947, forty years after having arrived in Dauphin. William McMurray, "Mr. Music" in Dauphin from its early days in 1908, until his death forty years later, in 1948, had a great influence as a band leader and a teacher. A great deal of this talent was passed on to his sons and his daughters. Dr. A.E. Gofton, who had come to Dauphin in 1904, died in 1949. He had served as a veterinarian and as a livery stable operator through most of Dauphin's early years. W.S. Marsh, who died in 1949, came to Dauphin in 1905 to operate a fruit and confectionery shop until 1923, when he became the town assessor. In 1925, he left that work to become editor of the *Dauphin Herald*. Others in the list of the deceased were Garth Johnston, a veteran of the Northwest Rebellion of 1885 and of World War I; John Delmage, who taught in Dauphin exactly half his life and who was affectionately known to his students as "Jiggers", both of whom died in 1946. Alex Katz's death, in 1947, brought to an end a brilliant career in the law. In the same year, the town was saddened by the untimely death of Jack Ball, a well-known and well-loved Dauphin citizen and pharmacist.

Notes on Chapter 10

Books, Reports, Ephemera:

Dauphin: Gateway to the North. Souvenir Historical Booklet. Dauphin Chamber of Commerce, 1958.

The Town of Dauphin. Brochure prepared of the Golden Jubilee & Reunion, July 1948.

Newspapers:

The Dauphin Herald & Press, 1946 to 1952.

POSTSCRIPT

By the end of the winter of 1952-53, seventy hot summers and seventy cold winters had come and gone since the visit of Ed and Jack Nagle to the Whitmore homestead in Gladstone.

When John Edwards spent his first winter in the area, he found himself in an empty land of forest and interspersed grasslands and muskegs with, here and there, rich bluffs of wild fruit and berry trees, some areas of shrub growth containing the ever-productive wild raspberries, strawberries and currants. Roads, of course, were non-existent. A few Indian trails could be found, especially along the high sand ridges and through the forests, where native fur trappers harvested the prized furs for the eastern market. Rivers and streams ran full most of the year; the spring torrents were moderated by the verdant growth in the surrounding mountains and along the river courses.

Gradually, the face of the landscape changed as pioneer hands hewed the forest trees and cleared the land for cultivation. In the early years this occurred sporadically as settlers moved into the country in small numbers. The pace of settlement increased as news of the abundant crops spread to other areas, particularly to the areas south of the Riding Mountain where farmers had suffered several years of drought in the mid-to-late 1880s. Settlers also came from Ontario and Quebec. By the end of 1895, some three hundred families or bachelor homesteaders were on the land in the Dauphin area.

Life was still simple and centred around two villages. Although the pioneers were independent by nature and fiercely self-reliant in many ways, they needed one another in the strenuous and hazardous business of survival in a harsh climate. Their response to these hard realities was to develop an interdependence which provided for co-operative efforts in many of their undertakings and a willingness to assist and succour one another in times of trouble. Out of this response grew a sense of community and a mutual respect for and interest in their neighbours' welfare. They were well known to one another, as were their children and grandchildren. It was decidedly a society formed around the family unit and, in particular around the farm family unit and those families had a strong community attachment.

The advent of the railway in 1896 brought great changes. The movement of people into the area increased rapidly, not only into the new town, but also, onto the farms where, it was felt, the ability to ship grain to new markets made the prospects of farming much more attractive. Again, as new farms were established and land cleared, warnings were issued to caution farmers about conserving some of the treed land to prevent losing topsoil in flood times and having torrential run-offs, especially during the spring melt. Tom Whitmore was one of the early pioneers who cautioned about the removal of too many stands of trees. It appears that only scant attention was paid to these warnings then and later. Many farmers continued to think that a larger crop would come from a larger clearing and that the benefits would accrue in direct proportion to the amount of clearing. Only too late did some realize the error of these ideas and in many cases the full effects were not seen until the drought of the 1930s.

In the urban area, the great change was the move from two villages into one town on the new railway siding. The early town fathers built well. They were undeterred in borrowing money for useful, necessary and long-term facilities. They were, however, careful husbandmen in respect of the tax money taken for civic purposes. The reputation of the town of Dauphin as a civic enterprise, was high and solidly entrenched for many years. As the farms prospered, so the town prospered and as the town prospered the farmers were provided with a larger and more sophisticated marketing centre, a good educational centre, a judicial centre and a medical centre of growing importance. The happy progress of the community had been marred only by the occurrence of the Great War of 1914-18, when some eighty-two of Dauphin's young men lost their lives in conflict while hundreds of others dedicated four years of their lives willingly to help the cause.

After the war the life of the town changed little. Essentially small farms, on lonely roads, lit at night by oil or gas lamps, were the homes of the great majority of farmers. Some of the camaraderie of the early days was disappearing as the numbers of people increased. Within the school districts, however, one could still find much of the sense of community which had characterized the early pioneer settlement. The post-war celebration of the 1920s was a happy and relatively contented time for most in Dauphin. Not too much attention was paid initially to what seemed a local problem between Japan and China and what was going on in Europe as Germany struggled to recover from the devastation of World War I. Even if there had been some interest in these matters, the interest was dulled by the impact of the economic downturn after October of 1929, and the occurrence of a worldwide drought which went on, in Western Canada, until the second half of the 1930s.

Followed as it was by World War II, the two events proved a turning point in the history of mankind. The atrocities of the war, the advent of nuclear power, the discovery of penicillin and the development of a pill to prevent conception, together with an apparent drift away from religious institutions during and after the Depression, brought about a major change in the ethical and moral outlook of individuals and communities. The general affluence which came into being during and after World War II brought a transformation toward a more materialistic society and one which seems to demand instant gratification for its every desire. The old ways of the pioneers gave way to the new economic and social philosophies, most of them yet unproven, of modern economists and sociologists. The theories of psychiatry, the least supportable of the medical specialities, began to permeate our educational systems, our judicial and penal systems and our very relationships with family and friends. Whatever may be said for these various philosophies, the impact of their influence is being seen in a completely changed society and these changes have taken on an increased intensity since the post-war years of the forties and fifties.

Dauphin has undoubtedly shared in these changes. A resident of the twenties and thirties would find much changed in the town of the eighties and, without doubt, changes will continue to take place.

It is hoped that this history will be recorded while those who helped shape it are still alive and able and willing to tell their story. Much has been accomplished in this way by the formation of the Fort Dauphin Museum, an enterprise which needs and deserves everyone's support.

INDEX

Adamson, Rev. W.W., 104
Alf, Roy, 221
Alguire, Dora, 222
Alguire, Jane, 122
Alguire, W.J., 206
Allin, James, 33
Alton, A., 33
Andruchowich, Father, 181
Argue, Robert, 82, 174
Armstrong, Merle, 203
Arnett, W.H., 73
Arsenych, Judge William, 156, 237

Baird, Frank, 155
Ball, J.A., 93, 117, 174
Ball, Jack, 148, 231, 239
Ball, James, 147-151, 192
Ball, W.N., 169-170, 200
Barager, R.D., 170
Barker, Billy, 29, 122-124
Barker, G.W.J., 122-124, 137
Barker, George, 29, 33, 64, 65, 78, 85, 94, 122
Barker, Joseph, 114, 115, 154, 155
Barret, Judge Gregory, 135
Barret, Rev. H.P., 131, 181
Bastchak, P., 57
Bates, C.D., 174
Batty, Edward, 32, 89, 119, 174, 207
Bawden, E.J., 102, 199
Bay, Eli, 117, 137, 173, 188, 207
Bay, Max, 195
Bayliss, W.R., 36
Beauchamp, P.J, 29, 34, 68, 100, 222
Beetham, Stanley, 176
Bell, Dr. W.I., 134, 158, 202, 207
Bend, Bobby, 189
Bennet, Archie, 125, 163, 231, 239
Best, John, 13
Bethel, Rev. T.E., 131
Bewell, Dr. H.E., 99, 223, 236
Bigham, J.H., 29, 67, 76, 120
Bigham, Minnie, 82
Bigham, R., 29
Birss, Alexander, 34, 222
Bishop, Dr., 154
Bjornsson, Mindy, 152, 191
Black, Charles, 206
Blackadar, W., 81, 183

Blackmore, Frank, 24, 25
Blackmore, James, 28, 85
Bladon, Stanley, 191
Blair, William, 141
Blinkhorn, Jack, 232
Blondeau, Maurice, 14
Bonnycastle, Judge A.L., 135, 143
Borden, Robert, 131
Bossons, J.W., 129
Bottomley, Dr. E.E., 68, 81, 82, 96, 134, 158 160 , 220, 239
Boughen, Arthur, 84, 141, 182
Bowen, Rev. J.C., 106, 199
Bowman, Helen, 221, 222
Bowman, J. L., 101, 103, 131, 134, 135, 154, 155, 161, 162, 193, 197, 198, 204, 211, 219, 238
Boyd, John & Mrs., 206
Boyd, S., 137
Bracken, John, 164
Brailsford, Rev. W., 131, 199
Brandt, Dr. Marvin, 203, 231, 235
Brereton, Miss, 98, 132
Breslaw, Harry, 231
Brewer, A.A., 174, 207
Brickman, S., 155
Bridgett, Rev. H.E., 131, 199
Brierley, Walter, 178
Broadfoot, Miss, 160
Broughton, Rev., 181
Brown, R., 154, 193
Brown, E., 193
Brown, R.C., 81, 84, 86
Brown, R.H., 182
Brown, Samuel, 135, 139
Bruce, David, 36
Bryce, John, 36, 75, 118, 177, 207
Buchannon, Jason, 29
Buchannon, William, 29, 33, 59, 130, 132, 206, 223
Buckwold, A., 117, 155, 192
Buckwold, Jacob, 76, 177, 181, 195, 223
Buie, A.B, 138
Bullmore, W.L., 228
Bumstead, Frank, 115, 122, 194, 217, 231
Bumstead, George, 231
Burke, W., 37

INDEX 245

Burns, Rev. D.K., 199
Burrows, T.A., 19, 71, 72, 79, 108, 164, 169, 178
Buzza, J., 85

Cadman, Ethel, 113, 201, 220
Caldwell, Dorothy, 200
Caldwell, Thomas, 117
Caldwell, Wilfred, 168, 176
Cameron, Sir Douglas, 130
Cameron, G., 79, 100
Cameron, Malcolm, 85
Cameron, Dr. S., 69, 82, 96
Campbell, Glenlyon, 11, 26, 124-126
Campbell, J.A., 32, 69, 101, 109, 110, 130, 134
Campbell, Robert, 11, 26
Caners, Leonard, 170, 204
Cardiff, Henry, 183
Cardiff, Mark, 67, 84, 115, 142, 156, 207
Cardiff, Robert, 37, 84
Cardiff, Wilf, 155
Carmichael, J., 29
Carmichael, Miss, 101
Carrol, W., 22
Cathers, J., 33, 37
Chapman, "Chappie", 207
Chase, Darwin, 78, 218
Chase, Frank, 78
Cherwinsky P., 57
Chipman, Percy, 72
Chipman, Sam, 36
Christie, Lily, 171
Churchill, Gordon M., 152, 155, 170, 191, 197, 200, 201, 210
Church, Rev., 181
Chute, Archie, 154, 234
Clark, Thomas J., 178
Clay, Mary, 170, 173
Cockerton, Robert B., 80
Code, S., 79, 81
Code, Willis, 129
Coombs, A., 33, 155
Corman, S., 76
Cornell, Dr., 158
Cornwall, George, 182
Cotter, Miss, 161
Cousins, A.E., 131, 181, 199
Cowtun, Bill, 152, 189, 191
Cowtun, Peter, 232

Coxworth, S., 86
Craig, "Butch", 152
Craig, D., 114, 213, 222
Craig, D. Jr., 189
Craig, Gavin, 114, 222
Creighton, Dr. Ross, 235
Crerar, T.C., 163
Crosby, A.C., 113
Crowe, Beth, 170
Crowe, J.J., 154, 222
Crowe, Jack, 155
Cruise, Robert, 109, 125, 131, 162, 206, 239
Cruise, W., 154, 195, 231
Culbertson, Dr. R.B., 97, 98, 132

Daniel, John, 70, 85, 206
Davie, Pinky, 221
Dawson, S.J., 17-19
Delmage, John, 151, 239
Delmage, Marion, 192
Delmage, Sadie, 151, 155, 192
De Mattos, Dr., 131
Dickie, John, 24
Dicks, Dr. R.E., 159, 161, 193, 202, 220, 235
Dicks, Ray, 222
Dickson, Duncan, 32, 216
Dixon, F.J., 162-163
Dmytriw, Father Nestor, 57
Donati, G., 18
Dorundiak, I., 55
Doupe, A.N., 174
Dowler, G., 219
Drabik, Ted, 232
Drinkwater, W.J., 120
Duffy, Father, 105
Duncan, Rev. Phillip, 180
Dunstan, S., 193
Durston, Albert, 222
Durston, John, 26
Durston, W.
Dyck, J., 156

Eagle, Alex, 77, 154, 174
Eagle, J.R., 77, 139
Easterbrook, Bertha, 232
Easterbrook, W., 211
Edwards, C.H., 101
Edwards, John, 24, 85, 184, 240
Elyniak, Wasyl, 51

Esplen, Henry, 137, 223
Everall, Mr. & Mrs. H.J., 173, 203, 229
Everall, Ron, 226

Fagen, Grace, 215
Fagen, R., 167, 171
Fallis, A.B., 113
Farrel, A.F., 138, 196
Farrel, "Dinky", 195
Farrel, R., 36
Fawcett, J.B., 37, 104, 111
Fee, Frank, 37
Fee, W., 36
Feldman, A.A., 138
Ferguson, R.G., 73, 85, 164
Finklestein, Bessie, 76
Finklestein, T., 76
Fisher, John A., 183
Fleming, Rev. David, 104, 180
Fox, E.F., 75, 176
Foyer, Miss, 132
French, Arthur, 183
Fulkerson, E., 84
Fulton, Hugh, 32
Fulton, J., 14

Gadzosa, M., 57
Gardner, James, 183
Gardner, John, 139-140, 143, 155, 188, 193, 217, 231
Gardner, R.S., 221, 231
Geekie, Stewart, 37, 79
Geiler, Felix, 178
Gelling, J., 84
Geryluk, Jan, 57
Gibson, Robert, 28, 85
Gilles, A., 30, 85
Gilles, Mary, 30, 120
Gilles, Peter, 30, 85
Gilmour, Rev. R.H., 104, 106
Gofton, Dr. A.E., 137, 239
Goodhand, Bruce, 100
Goodhand, Cameron, 164
Goodhand, Ruth, 229
Goodhand, Thomas, 161
Gorby, Mr. & Mrs. Thomas, 32, 143, 183
Gorby, W., 206
Goulding, Rev. A.W., 105
Grant, J., 192
Greig, Alice, 215

Griffin, Nelson, 115
Gunne, Miss Beatrice, 78, 93, 111, 113
Gunne, Dr. J.R., 29, 33, 68, 72, 82, 84, 96, 100, 110, 134, 160, 206
Gunne, Robert, 29, 33

Hafenbrak, Isaac, 115
Halde, Father Joseph, 105
Hall, G.H., 125
Hall, W. & Mrs., 38, 183
Hamilton, Daniel, 118, 132, 141, 174, 207
Hamilton, Earl, 155
Hanna, D.B., 59
Hanna, J.B., 72
Harding, Mr., 142
Harrington, Gerald, 193
Harrington, Dr. W.J., 69, 82, 96, 130, 132, 134, 139, 154, 160, 162, 193, 222
Harrington, Mrs. W.J., 231
Harvey, Frank, 141
Harvey, J.G., 66, 69, 73, 80, 101, 110
Hassard, John, 32, 206
Haw, Rev., 130, 180
Hawkins, Robert, 114, 136, 140, 198, 219, 232
Heaslip, Dr., 132, 154
Heaslip, O.E., 101, 130, 148, 193, 195
Hedderley, J.E., 72, 79, 81, 207
Hedderley, T., 36
Henderson, A.J., 37
Henderson, W.J., 223, 237
Henry, Alexander, 14
Herchmer, F.K., 84
Herrick, E.C., 122
Hewitt, E., 37
Hextal, Bryan, 189
Hicks, Christine, 113
Hill, F.C., 159
Hjalmarson, H.J., 195
Holloway, Father W., 180
Hong, Charlie, 138
Hopper, Rev., 104
Hopwood, H.R., 174
Hosegood, J.F., 64, 67
Hoy, Archie, 80, 115, 207
Hoy, Charles, 80, 85, 115
Hoy, Earnest, 115, 143
Hryhorchuk, Nick, 195
Hueston, W., 36
Hughes, Harry, 85

INDEX 247

Hunt, A.J., 115
Hunt, Robert, 65, 66, 73, 81, 89, 233
Hunt, Vina, 171
Huska, P., 57
Hyde, Miss, 98, 132

Iredale, Albert E., 82, 114, 218
Iredale, Jane, 82, 120
Iredale, Thomas, 72, 83, 85
Irwin, George, 67, 77, 81, 125

Jackson, M.G., 67, 69
Jardine, G., 32
Jeffrey, Rev. C.N.P., 105
Johnasen, E., 231, 237
Johnson, E.W., 73
Johnson, Garth, 122, 125, 239
Johnston, Isaac, 155, 228
Johnston, J.W., 119
Johnston, Jonny, 204
Johnston, Miss, 132
Johnston, Pauline, 85
Jonasson, J.T, 170
Jones, Bill, 84
Jordan, Thomas, 117, 120
Jullian, Rev., 181
Justice, Adam, 158
Justice, Agatha, 158, 159
Justice, David, 125, 218

Kagan, Dr. Joseph, 235
Katz, Alex, 135, 197, 221, 236, 239
Kelley, Father, 105
Kennedy, Louis, 237
Kerr, Andy, 221
Kerr, Jim, 37
Kettles, Miss, 161
King, Dr. Frank, 202
King, George, 72, 81, 86, 139, 183
King, W.D., 73, 139, 207
Kitney, D., 174
Klym, T., 191, 221
Klym, W., 191
Knowles, Beulah, 206
Krakiwski, Father, 181
Ksionzyk, Basil, 56, 64
Kydd, A.E., 84, 111

La Fleur, Louis, 117
Lafontaine, Al, 206
Laidlaw, Miss, 132

Lauzon, Father, 105
Law, F., 84
Law, W., 84
Lawrence, Johnny, 154, 192, 237
Lay, Bruce, 234
Lee, Mathew, 34, 143
Lee, Wing, 80
Lepper, Harold, 125, 174
Lewis, Rev. W.A., 104
Lilly, Robert,, 75, 93, 113, 117, 136, 203
Lineham, Dr. D.M., 96, 98
Little, Dr. Adam, 203, 220, 229, 231, 235
Little, Dr. Harry, 235
Little, Helen, 236
Little, Thomas, 129, 155, 171, 173, 198
Lochead, Rev. A., 173, 180, 199
Love, George, 152, 191
Love, Herman, 114
Love, Sam, 191
Love, Thomas, 114, 221
Love, V., 84, 221
Lozinski, I., 57
Lynch, George, 83, 84
Lyons, Rev. H.M., 180
Lys, H.E., 223
Lysecki, Jake, 170

Macniell, Harry, 32, 81, 94, 99, 102, 103, 107, 140, 173, 200, 202, 236, 239
Macniell, Jack, 32, 83, 84
Macniell, Peter, 32, 84, 199
Macoun, John, 8
Maguire, Inspector, 78
Malcolm, Andrew, 36, 70, 143, 206
Malcolm, Mrs. Andrew, 36, 120
Malcolm, Dr. Frank, 178, 202, 220, 235
Malcolm, R.J., 29, 72, 95, 167
Malcolm, T.T., 69, 100, 119, 130, 134, 142, 161 178, 207
Malcom, Winnifred, 82
Marsh, Bill, 139
Marsh, Helen, 139, 192
Marsh, Jim, 139
Marsh, W.S., 114, 139, 176, 211, 239
Masterman, Mr., 156
Matheson, Archbishop, 104, 131
Maughan, J.A., 64, 69
May, John, 125
Maynard, A., 36

Mayo, E.J. "Teddy", 137
McAllister, Hugh, 153
McAllister, R., 152
McArthur, Mrs. Mary, 183
McCall, R.M., 129
McClean J.R., 32
McCormick, W.R., 138, 232
McCorvie, Archie, 38, 84
McCorvie, Harry, 38, 84
McCrae, George, 230
McCreary, Commissioner, 61
McDonald, Charles, 25, 34, 206
McDonald, D.D., 114, 167, 222
McDonald, Duncan, 25, 34, 83
McDonald, Mary, 183
McDonald, Neill, 25, 34, 85, 222
McDonald, W., 79
McFadden, J.N., 134, 139, 167, 171, 202, 211, 215, 219, 221, 230, 233
McFadden, Mrs. Madge, 173, 229
McGirr, E.N., 134, 198, 236, 239
McIntosh, David, 28, 30, 33, 67, 72, 76, 82, 85, 154
McIntosh, William, 28, 78, 84, 85, 120, 154
McIntyre, A.H., 68
McIntyre, J.B., 79, 107
McKee, Dr. A.D., 134, 202
McKee, John, 141
McKerchar, Mrs. A., 37, 120
McKillop, D., 30, 85
McKillop, James, 183
McKinnon, John A., 69, 78
McLaren, John, 24
McLauchlin, C.W., 32
McLaughlin, James, 38, 84
McLaughlin, Janet, 38
McLean, Charles, 33, 67
McLean, Thomas, 73, 77
McLeod, R.C., 37
McMartin, Edward, 206
McMaster, Duncan "Mickey", 152, 191
McMaster, Jim, 155
McMurray, W., 94, 168, 239
McNiel, Angus, 85
McPhail, D.L., 159, 202
McPherson, A.J. "Sandy", 33, 37, 76
McPherson, Mary, 235
McPherson, Robert, 174
McQuay, W.J., 132

McRae, George, 24-25
McWilliams, Miss E., 78, 93, 111
Mecklenberg, Dr., 97
Meighen, Arthur, 162-63
Meredith, Miss, 213
Merrell, Florence, 112
Middleton, Bruce, 211
Middleton, Donald, 213
Middleton, Douglas, 211
Middleton, Mrs. F.C., 203
Middleton, Rev. F.C., 211
Miles, H., 114, 155
Miller, R., 84
Miller, W., 36, 39
Miller, Winnifred, 161
Mitchel, E., 115
Monkman, James, 17
Montgomery, Mrs. I., 118, 173
Moody, Dr. A.W., 68
Moore, A.S., 170, 201, 219
Moore, Fred F., 73
Moore, H.H., 122
Moore, Ronald, 198, 218
Morris, Miss, 161
Morrison, Frank, 65
Morrison, W.H. "Ikey", 100
Morton, W.L., 18
Mouat, J.N., 59, 79
Munson, A.E., 100, 102
Munson, Neville, 122, 135
Murphy, W.G., 117
Murray, W., 66, 102, 238

Nagle Brothers, 21-22, 240
Nantais, Norman, 152, 191
Neville, Rev. T.
Nex, Frederick, 57, 73
Nicholson, Alton, 222
Nicholson, H.P., 66, 114, 206
Nicholson, J.B., 64, 67
Nicholson, John, 37
Nicholson, W.B., 79
Nimetz, L., 57
Nizalowsky, I., 57

Odger, Thomas, 73
Ogilvie, W., 19
Olenchuk, Father, 181
Oleskow, Joseph, 51
Oleskow, Vladimir, 55
Oliphant, Harry, 174

Oliphant, Jimmy, 114, 154
Oscar, M.J., 159
O'Grady, B.S., 134

Padfield, James, 32
Palmer, George, 162, 167
Park, Hasley M., 75, 114, 176
Parker, James, 13
Parsons, Thomas, 29, 85
Pascoe, Drs. Les & Ethel, 202
Pasichnyk, Father, 181
Paulitski, J., 57
Payne, Albert, 33
Peacock, Drs. K. & E., 220
Peebles, Gary, 178, 192
Peebles, Grace, 215, 222
Perchaluk, Petro, 57
Percy, Walter, 174
Perry, Samuel, 29
Persson, Mrs. Don, 235
Phillips, Stanley, 178
Picken, Sarah, 81, 132
Playford, Chauncey, 32
Playford, James, 32
Playford, Thomas, 32, 206
Pollon, Mrs. Thomas, 183
Pollon, Thomas, 29, 77, 78, 85, 154, 184
Porter, Bill, 221
Porter, Jake, 38, 206
Potoski, John, 161
Potoski, Dr. Michael, 57, 161, 220, 235
Potoski, Paul & Katherina, 57, 161
Potoski, Peter, 161
Poucher, W.B., 115
Prentice, A.E., 137, 234
Purdy, H.C., 140
Pyllipiw, Ivan, 51

Race, F., 115, 207
Ramsay,, 140, 161, 174
Ramsden, Jack, 103, 199, 228
Reid, A.E., 201
Rennolds, J., 84
Reznoski, A., 117, 174, 176, 207
Ringstrom, Emma, 176, 195
Rintoul, William, 102
Ritchie, Rev. D., 181
Ritchie, Dr. G., 232, 235
Robertson, Dr. C.S., 202, 231
Robson, Harold, 170

Robson, W.E., 161, 167-68
Robson, Wilfred, 100, 130, 154, 193, 207
Rogers, C.S.A., 156, 237
Rogers, Dr. W.G., 98, 132, 134, 160, 193, 202
Roscoe, C.N., 159
Ross, Chester, 36, 67, 85
Ross, Gilbert, 26
Ross, Noel, 36, 64, 67, 85
Ross, Dr. W., 98, 132
Ross, William, 77
Rowat, A.P., 138
Ryan, Bertram, 103
Ryan, Judge J., 69

Sanderson, E., 108
Saunderson, Hugh, 170
Scott, Rev. R., 104
Scrase, Captain, 177, 232
Scrase, Hebert, 177, 232
Scrase, Thomas, 137, 152, 155, 191
Secord, Thomas, 206
Shand, James, 29
Shaw, James, 32, 69, 79, 206
Shaw, Thomas, 32, 69, 79, 81, 206
Sherwood, A.J., 137, 158
Shipley, W.T., 72
Silverwood, Isaac, 183
Simpson, Frank E., 134, 135, 137, 155, 221, 236, 239
Sinclair, Daniel, 36
Sinclair, J., 37
Sinclair, Mrs. J., 206
Sing, Toy, 178
Sinnot, Msgr. A.A., 180
Skinner, Major J.W., 167, 174, 239
Skinner, W.F., 159
Slocum, S.A., 73
Slobodzian, Jay, 222
Slobodzian, Mary, 222
Slobodzian, Metro, 152
Slobodzian, Peter, 191
Smith, Rev. A.E., 104, 163
Smith, "Clue", 167
Smith, F., 37
Smith, H.V., 156, 167
Smith, R.C., 156
Smith, R.G., 86, 118
Smith-Jackson, W., 113, 142, 169
Solomon, S., 140, 232

Spence, Rev. R.E., 131
Spenceley, Mr., 142
Spillet, Charlotte, 36, 183
Spillet, Isaac, 36, 222
Spillet, Merrit, 36, 137, 138, 206
Staranchuk, H., 57
Steckley, Lydia, 113
Steen, R.I., 174, 193
Stelck, A.H.F., 76, 114, 239
Stevenson, R.M., 107, 174
Stewart, C., 138
Stewart, Dr. D.A., 160
Stewart, Isobel, 170
Stothart, Miss, 160
Strang, Gavin, 29, 184, 206
Strang, Isabelle, 113
Strang, William, 154, 229
Street, Miss, 160
Sumpter, H.W., 167
Sumpton, George, 117
Sumpton, John, 80
Sutherland, A.W., 101
Sutherland, David, 66, 76, 114, 154, 177
Swewczyk, Michael, 217, 237
Symons, J., 178

Tate, Syd, 84
Teeple, Charles, 100
Tefler, Rev. Douglas, 199
Thorne, Mrs. Bella, 107
Tomison, W., 14
Trimble, N.G., 133, 134, 154, 160, 161
Tripp, Dr. A.J., 159, 160
Tritschler, G., 156, 161
Trotter, Dr. Harold, 158
Tucker, George, 84
Tucker, Joeseph, 37
Tupper, Sir Charles, 55
Turner, C.F., 76, 80, 86
Turner, W.C., 80, 93, 117, 136, 138

Voychesin, Steve Sr., 140

Wait, James, 75, 86, 114, 207
Waite, Jack, 33
Wakefield, Rev. H.G., 83, 105
Walker, E.H., 170
Walker, Dr. G.C.J., 69, 93, 99, 129, 158, 202, 223
Walker, James, 67

Wallace, W.H., 114, 207
Wallwin, E.J., 139, 140, 154
Walser, William, 105
Walton, John, 86
Ward, Annie, 83
Ward, W.J., 83, 162-3, 193, 218, 232, 237
Waryniuk, T., 156
Waters, Wallace, 137
Watson, J., 156, 183
Watson, R., 112, 154, 193
Watson, Dr. Vernon, 206, 228
Watt, Roy, 173
Weir, Dr. Wilbur, 158
Weir, William, 174
Whaley, Bonar, 211
Whatson, W., 36
White, W.G., 117, 137, 193
Whitmore, Bessie, 183
Whitmore, Emma, 81, 173, 183
Whitmore, H.B., 27, 34, 65, 85, 183, 206, 240
Whitmore, Tom, 21, 23-24, 34, 69, 77, 82, 85, 86, 239, 240
Whitmore, William, 34, 65, 77, 83, 120, 233
Wickes, W.J., 37, 217
Wicklund, Joseph, 170, 173
Widmeyer, E., 80, 223
Wiley, Dr. A.S., 131
Wilkes, A.E., 69, 81, 102
Williams, M., 155
Wilson, S.T., 24, 27
Wishart, R.J., 29, 120
Wood, Paul, 29, 33, 59
Woods, D.S., 113
Wright, Fred, 101, 161, 164, 174
Wright, Gertie, 177, 222
Wright, Warren, 174

Yasinchuk, W., 57

Zarowny, Caroline, 57
Zworon, Michael, 192

PERSONS ENTITLED TO VOTE AT MUNICIPAL ELECTIONS.

No.	No on Roll	NAME.	OCCUPATION.	LOT OR DESIGNATION OF LAND.	HOW HELD.	POSTOFFICE.	RES. OR N R
103	240	McKenzie, Murdock	Butcher	Lot 6 block 12	O	Dauphin	R
104	241	McLay, Kenneth	Carpenter	Lot 10 Block E	O	"	R
105	242	McLay, Allan	Carpenter	Lot 10 Block E	T	"	R
106	243	McLean, Jas. H	Liveryman	Lot 8 Block 23	O	"	R
107	244	McKinnon, John	Bailiff	Lot 18 Block 23	O	"	R
108	247	McKinnon, Jas.	Farmer	Lot 5 Block 9	O	"	R
109	250	McKinnon, D. C	Hotl keeper	Lot 20 Block 23	O	"	R
110	251	McPherson, A. J	Merchant	Lot 14 Block 9	O	"	R
112	252	McSherry, Mrs. D	Lady	Lot 2 Block 22	O	"	R
112	255	McGee, Charles	Gentleman	Lot 20 Block 22	O	Ottawa	N R
113	257	McCombs, Wm. J	Pump mkr	Lot 19 Block 26	O	Dauphin	R
114	258	McKenzie, —	Contractor	Lots 5,12, 14, Block C	O	Toronto	N R
115	226	McLean, S. A	Policeman	Lot 11 Block 23	T	Dauphin	R
116	421	McLean, Thomas	Laborer	Lot 20 Block 24	T	"	R
117	300	Newton, Fred. J	Farmer	Lot 3 Block 9	O	Dauphin	N R
118	304	Nicholson, W. B	Farmer	Lot 11 Block 6	O	"	R
119	307	Nicholson, Jas. B	Merchant	Lot 5 Block 12	O	"	N R
120	309	Nicholson, H. P	Agent	Lot 14 Block 10	O	"	R
121	323	Odger, Thomas	Printer	Lot 8 Block 27	O	Dauphin	R
122	333	Paul, George	Carpenter	Lot 7 Block 6	O	Dauphin	R
123	208	Pearson, H. J	Grain merch	Right of way	O	"	N R
124	334	Perry, C. A	Merchant	Lots 19, 20, Block 11	O	"	R
125	335	Philip, Wm	Merchant	Lots 7, 8, Block C	O	"	R
126	338	Playford, Jas. E	Farmer	Lot 16 Block 7	O	"	R
127	339	Playford, Thomas	Farmer	Lot 7 Block 8	O	"	R
128	340	Poucher, W. B	Contractor	Lot 1 Block 24	O	"	R
129	341	Poucher, C. M	Lady	Lot 1 Block 24	O	"	R
130	342	Pugsley, John E	Carpenter	Lot 19, 20, Block 12	O	"	R
131	343	Playford, James	Farmer	Lot 14 Block 7	O	"	R
132	350	Race, Fred	Barber	Lots 14, 15 Block 5	O	Dauphin	R
133	353	Rankin, Mack	Liveryman	Lot 17 Block 23	O	"	R
134	854	Renno, S. A	Farmer	On N W ¼ 10, 25, 19	O	"	R
135	855	Rintoul, Wm	Merchant	Lot 15 Block 9	T	"	R
136	361	Shaw, Thomas	Lumber mer	Lot 11 Block 24	O	Dauphin	R
137	362	Shaw, James	Lumber mer	Lot 18 Block 24	O	"	R
138	364	Stewart, Peter	Laborer	Lot 8, 9, Block 23	O	"	R
139	365	Stacey, Wm	Teamster	Lot 5, 7, Block 23	O	"	R
140	366	Steenson, Wm	Constable	Lot 12 Block 9	O	"	R
141	367	Steenson, Will. J	Billiard r kp	Lot 12 Block 9	T	"	R
142	369	Stevens, W. R	Carpenter	Lot 13 Block A	O	"	R
143	371	Smith, A. E	Clergyman	Lot 11 Block A	T	"	R
144	372	Smith, Robert	H. maker	Lot 12 Block A	O	"	R
145	374	Smith, R. W	Farmer	Lot 8 Block 10	O	"	N R
146	375	Sumpton, John H	Hotel kpr	Lot 16 Block 10	O	"	R
147	75A	Sumpton, George F	Hotel kpr	Lot 16 Block 10	T	"	R
148	87	Sutherland, David	Merchant	All south of lane B	O	"	R
149	378	Stelck, Arthur	Merchant	Lot 4 Block 12	O	"	R
150	410	Sparling, R. C	Agent	Lot 4 Block 9	T	"	R
151	14	Scarlet, H. S	Agent	Lot 1 Block 23	T	"	R
152	425	Silverstien, Simon	Merchant	Lot 13 block 9	T	"	R
153	386	Trilibard, E. S	Photographr	Lot 8 Block 7	O	Dauphin	R
154	387	Turner, C. F	Policeman	Lot 9 Block 11	O	"	R
155	388	Turner, W. C	Merchant	Lot 9 Block 10	O	"	R